THE COMMANDER OF HAWKINS HILL

THE COMMANDER OF HAWKINS HILL

a memoir

J. BARRIE FARRINGTON

Copyright © 2019 by J. Barrie Farrington. All rights reserved. Printed in the United States of America. No part of this book may be used or reproduced in any manner whatsoever without written permission except in the case of brief quotations included in critical articles and reviews. For information, address Permissions@Citrinepublishing.com. The views expressed in this work are solely those of the author and do not necessarily reflect the views of the the publisher.

Library of Congress Cataloging-in-Publication Data

Farrington, J. Barrie
The Commander of Hawkins Hill: A Memoir

p. cm.
Paperback ISBN: 978-1-947708-01-3
Hardcover ISBN: 978-1-947708-41-9
Ebook ISBN: 978-1-947708-06-8
Library of Congress Control Number: 2017963513

10 9 8 7 6 5 4 3 2 1
First Edition, September 2019

CITRINE PUBLISHING

Murphy, North Carolina, U.S.A.
(828) 585-7030
Publisher@CitrinePublishing.com
www.CitrinePublishing.com

This book is dedicated to my mother, Pearl Melinda Farrington, who gave her daily life to the service of God and to her children.

I know that her deep and abiding love and her personal sacrifices provided us, her children, with a strong foundation on which we constructed our bright, success-driven futures.

TABLE OF CONTENTS

Foreword by Former Prime Minister Hubert Ingraham		*ix*
Prologue		*xiii*
Chapter 1	In the Beginning	19
Chapter 2	The Kindness of Strangers	23
Chapter 3	A Mother's Sage Advice	27
Chapter 4	Questions of the Soul	31
Chapter 5	A Typical Day	33
Chapter 6	The War Years	39
Chapter 7	A Game for All Seasons	45
Chapter 8	The Forbidden View	53
Chapter 9	The Scrums	59
Chapter 10	The Uncertain Road to Higher Education	65
Chapter 11	The Government High School	73
Chapter 12	Behold the Lamb	77
Chapter 13	Nassau Yacht Haven	83
Chapter 14	Lee Rose	87
Chapter 15	My First Home	93
Chapter 16	Politics	99
Chapter 17	Road Traffic Authority	105
Chapter 18	Sporting Activities	109
Chapter 19	More Politics, 1962-1967	119
Chapter 20	Even More Politics	129

Chapter 21	The Fall	137
Chapter 22	A Fresh Direction, Personal and Political	143
Chapter 23	Josephine Elizabeth Merlin Mackenzie	151
Chapter 24	Ira Willis Farrington	161
Chapter 25	Resorts International and Paradise Island	167
Chapter 26	Bahamas Sportswear Manufacturing Limited	191
Chapter 27	The Casino: A New Economic Model	197
Chapter 28	A Change of Government Impacts Paradise Island	207
Chapter 29	Industrial Relations and the BHEA	217
Chapter 30	Rebirth of Paradise Island: A New Tourism Beginning	247
Chapter 31	Nation Building: Labour and Capital	259
Chapter 32	Resorts International Bahamas Limited	271
Chapter 33	The Shah of Iran in Exile on Paradise Island	285
Chapter 34	Building Blocks for Paradise Island's Future	295
Chapter 35	Life After Divorce from Jo	301
Chapter 36	Bahamas Independence and the Company's Expansion	305
Chapter 37	Merv Griffin	319
Chapter 38	Henry Kissinger	327
Chapter 39	Nelson Mandela	331
Chapter 40	National Insurance Board and the B.E.C.	335
Chapter 41	Bahamasair	349
Chapter 42	The Kerzner Years	367
Chapter 43	Important Helpers Along the Way	403
Chapter 44	Stowe, Vermont	407
Chapter 45	Pearl Melinda Farrington	411
Chapter 46	Susan	415
Chapter 47	New Year's Eve	419
Chapter 48	Health, Fitness and Quality of Life	421
Chapter 49	My Life in Tennis	427
Chapter 50	Special People	433
Chapter 51	Travel	439
Chapter 52	Final Day on the Job	447
Chapter 53	I Always Did My Best	451
Chapter 54	Concluding Thoughts	453
Special Memories		455
Epilogue		467

FOREWORD

The Commander of Hawkins Hill, a recounting of the life and times of J. Barrie Farrington, is a welcomed addition to the literature of The Bahamas. Barrie's autobiography is an important record of that period of Bahamian history during which we transformed from a sleepy village with limited scope for economic and social advancement to a period of empowerment for those willing to apply their natural talents and hard work to the task of nation building.

His reminiscing about his early life on Hawkins Hill, his education and his early involvement with sport paint a bucolic existence many Bahamians of his generation remember fondly. It similarly demonstrates how individuals with limited resources overcame their circumstances to become icons of our business and civil community.

Barrie recounts his journey into business tracing his elevation from assistant to accountant to becoming a giant figure among hoteliers; along the way he became also an entrepreneur and manufacturer and importantly, a consummate civic-minded citizen.

Early he dabbled in politics and served in the Senate in the later part of the 1960s. He was well positioned, representing the establishment while being knowledgeable about the aims of the emerging political majority.

In business and as a representative of employers he played an instrumental role in the evolution of labour relations in the country. The special relationship that he developed and maintains with leaders of the Trade Union Movement in The Bahamas makes for interesting and informative reading.

Over the years Barrie served as Chairman or a member of numerous Government Boards and Committees, including, most notably the Bahamas Electricity Corporation and Bahamasair. His memory and the record of his public service fully justifies his sometimes expressed view that at public enterprises he had become a full-time but unpaid employee.

Barrie's natural athleticism and especially his love of tennis has remained a lifelong characteristic and accounts without a doubt for his youthful defiance of the laws on aging.

This dedicated family man's recounting of his relationship with his children and with his dear wife, Susan, stands as an example to be emulated not only in personal relationships but in dedication to a lifelong pursuit of healthy and fit living.

Hubert A. Ingraham
Former Prime Minister of The Bahamas
April 2018

A midday reflection on safari on the Serengeti Plain in Tanzania, Africa, in 2012

Howard "Butch" Kerzner
My "Young Winston"
A brilliant young man, gone too soon

PROLOGUE

Discovering the meaningful lessons of life is a slow, reflective process. Not one that you are likely to unearth in youth but more likely after you have walked through times of light as well as the dark days. Yet with understanding we awaken to the goodness of human beings.

It was the first of November in the year 2009, a cool morning when the sun was about to peek above the horizon and to raise the curtain on a very dark night. The leaves on the trees were still covered with dew and awaiting the warmth of the sun.

The early dawn has, for as long as I can remember, evoked a great sense of spirituality—the darkness being penetrated by the different shafts of orange, gold and yellow—announcing a new day and the presence of Him who guides and protects us.

My morning ritual has been the same for several decades. I sit in my rocking chair on the second storey of my home in the quiet neighbourhood of San Souci and sip on a hot cup of Iron Goddess green tea. To make it all perfect, I start my classical music, which gently emanates from the Bose speaker in front of me.

At the same time the birds are awaking and the chirping coming from the trees in the garden—flourishing with mango, poinciana, spice and soursop—produces a medley of songs acclaiming nature's wonder.

Time passes, the music plays on and soon enough my cup is empty. It is time to move on. I, without fail, stand, look to the rising sun, and taking several chest-expanding deep breaths of the morning air, once more remind myself that God has given us a new day.

That day was to be different as I decided to work from home rather than going to my office at Atlantis.

Susan, my wife, was still asleep so I ventured into our bedroom and then into the bathroom to shower and at last put on fresh clothing for the day.

Surprisingly she did not stir. I was able to quietly open and close the door and started down the stairs.

Some of Susan's watercolour paintings line our wall. The paintings are of such breathtaking quality that I never tire of looking at them. She is an extraordinarily talented artist.

As I reached the bottom of the stairs, my mind turned to the main reason for remaining at home. The thought of what I was about to do caused my heart to skip a few beats.

My destination was my writing desk in my library. The very moment I made the first step in that direction, Pula, Susan's American Bobtail overweight cat, ran ahead repeating meows. Pula knew what he wanted and so did I.

He dashed to the double door that opens to the terrace, pool deck and gardens and then looked back with unfeigned impatience. He wanted to be outside to inspect every nook and cranny, at the same time expecting to capture an unsuspecting lizard. With Pula out the door and into the garden, I turned my attention to preparing my mind for the writing I was about to begin.

After my opening a few windows, a soft breeze transported the fragrance of the early morning inside, where I again entered my place of peace and tranquility. The final stage was to start the playing of a CD of classical music—Bach Oboe Concerto in B flat. Listening to classical music might give the impression of pretension, but I enjoy listening. The state of mind evoked is quietly and wonderfully influenced.

I love writing with a fountain pen and for what was immediately before me, I chose one of my favourites, a Mont Blanc 149 Meisterstück. I possess a relatively decent collection of mostly antique fountain pens with a good number being manufactured by Mont Blanc. I believe that my fascination with fountain pens dates back to school days at Government High, where we were required to write with fountain pens. To this day, I receive great satisfaction in using a fountain pen for letter writing.

At this moment my world was in perfect alignment. Poised in my comfortable, black leather upholstered chair, with my white blotter pad, richly framed with beautifully varied insets, I turned on the lamp located on the left corner of my desk. A calming light bathed the writing surface. With my Mont Blanc in my right hand, I adjusted the sheet of linen paper in front of me and with a deep breath, I began to write.

Dear Butch,

The grief caused by permanent separation despite the passage of time, for me, gives reason for frequent visits of times shared, and the vision of a better life for many less privileged people.

You are gone, but I remember.

Even though there was a generational gap and a difference in cultural backgrounds, there was an instant and positive connection when we first met—a kind of unspoken prediction that we would be sharing a future.

What we could not predict was the brevity of that future together. Your dad had a vision of creating a resort destination on Paradise Island that would be without parallel in the entire world. We had the good fortune of being able to participate in the transformation of Paradise Island, and to witness the considerable and positive impact upon Bahamians and the economy of our country.

During our years together our bond grew, and there emerged another element of the relationship that moved us to engaging in activities that brought unspoken happiness—we began the journey of reaching out into our Bahamian communities to improve the quality of life of Bahamians and to influence the direction to be taken by Bahamian children.

It is unnecessary to recount the good works done, but it was during these times that I captured the true essence of you as a person—sensitive, kind, interested, caring, concerned, and appreciative of the best in people. Of course, there were disappointments, but they never caused you to waver in your purpose to keep moving forward. In fact, in times of disappointment you would say, humorously, "no good deed goes unpunished." You wanted to use your position and access to resources to make a difference in The Bahamas; what a remarkable and wonderful delivery of an undefined purpose in life!

For me, the most touching moment of our experience together was the time when you were speaking to the children and faculty at St. Anne's School in Fox Hill. You admitted that making the transition to living in The Bahamas was not easy, but after being a part of the country for over 11 years you could now say "I love The Bahamas and I want my family to live in The Bahamas."

It has been three years since you were taken away from us, but your legacy lives on. I am committed to assisting in making the purpose of your life an infinite and integral part of Bahamian life.

Trying to say "goodbye" is never easy, and for me, with you, it is impossible.

As I finished the letter it seemed like a million memories were coursing through my mind. I raised my head slowly and at that moment tilted my head a little to the left to look at the framed photo of Butch that I keep on my desk. My mind drifted to a special place shared by him and me.

Butch lost his life tragically on the 11 October 2006. Vanessa, his wife, was deeply moved to find a meaningful way to create an imprint of his life that could survive the passage of time. My letter to Butch was written at Ness's request for this purpose.

THE COMMANDER OF HAWKINS HILL

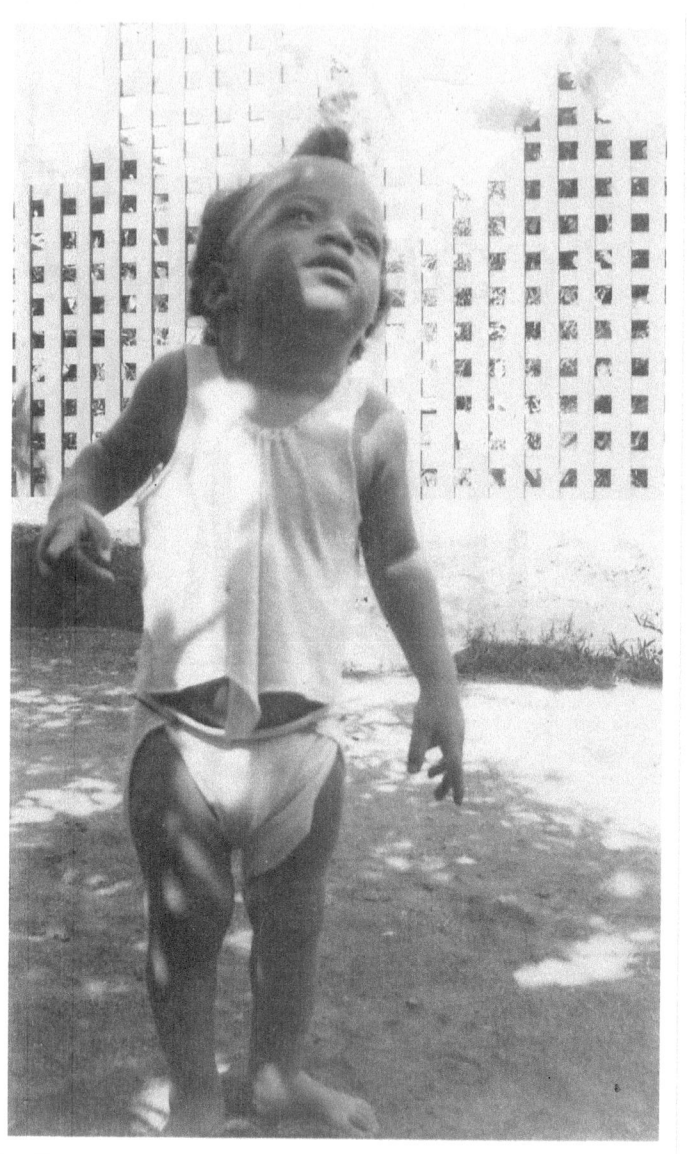

J. Barrie at eighteen months

CHAPTER 1

IN THE BEGINNING

From the north window of the family two storey house on top of Hawkins Hill, I could see Hog Island on the other side of Nassau Harbour. Hawkins Hill, usually referred to as Mount Airy, is located in the northeast section of Nassau—a short walk away from the harbour.

In 1939, following the purchase of a lot from Willie Weeks for 65 pounds, my father, Ira, began construction of the family home. The work was done with the help of several semi-skilled labourers and was painfully slow, but my father persevered and was able to move the family into the unfinished house. I was born in 1936 and was about three years of age at that time.

Born at the turn of the century in 1901, my father was the product of a hard-working middle-class family. He was a hard, rigid man given to volatility and yet Victorian in many ways. He possessed a strong entrepreneurial spirit but found success permanently elusive. In October 1926, my father married my mother, Pearl Melinda Dean. Marriage in this era especially was considered to be permanent; vows of faithfulness were inviolate.

My mother was a devout Anglican, the religion that sustained her throughout her life. Church was her pillar of strength. Although her education was limited, she was smart and possessed a strong mind and extraordinary willpower.

Beyond a doubt, she made home a refuge of love and care for me and my three siblings, Earle, Ramon and Fay.

My family lived in a close-knit neighbourhood that covered all of Hawkins Hill, top to bottom. All families here, irrespective of station in life, shared common values, principles and beliefs—the Kellys, Morees, Prosas, Seymours, Aranhas, Havens, Elliots, Lightbourns, Dameses, Pearces, Dillettes and Halls.

I had two very special friends, Maurice Prosa and Sidney Kelly, who lived next door. Within this community the theme of oneness was incredibly strong.

At age seven, I was prone to waking in the early hours of the morning not because I wanted to get out of bed but because I continued to be haunted by a scary occurrence when I was just three years of age. My recollection of this event is unbelievably clear, even to this day.

My father decided to take me to his tomato farm located somewhere on Soldier Road. The mode of transport was his bicycle fitted with a baby carrier over the back wheel. I was put into the carrier and off we went. As one can imagine I was happy and excited as my dad coasted down Hawkins Hill toward Shirley Street and then all the way to the farm.

At the farm, my father had set up a tent with a canvas sheet that rested directly on the ground. The tent had been pitched at the front side facing the road with the field extending far to the back. My father placed me on the floor and proceeded to walk into the farm. Left alone, I was attacked by fear as there was only quietness all around except for the chirping of birds nearby. With each passing moment the beating of my heart grew faster and with each quick breath, panic set in. I was alone, vastly alone. I began to whimper, which soon escalated to sobs. There was no repressing the fear and soon I was crying and screaming uncontrollably.

My father, upon hearing my wailing, had little choice but to return to the tent. There was no consoling me; the only rational choice was to take me back home. Knowing my father's nature, it was easy to believe that he was annoyed with me for disrupting the peace.

This was the first conscious memory of my life. Could this maybe have been the beginning of the difficult and complex relationship with my father? Was it a precursor of things to come?

What a beginning!

*My mom Pearl Melinda and me,
a special outing on Eastern Parade*

CHAPTER 2

THE KINDNESS OF STRANGERS

Inevitably at various stages of your life, there are events that can be recalled and then there are those about which you are told.

My brothers Earle and Ramon, who were older than me, attended Eastern Senior School on East Shirley Street just above Mackey Street, currently the Shirley Street Post Office. I was five years of age and quite fascinated with my brothers going to Eastern Senior. According to my mother, I was in a way most curious about Eastern Senior, a curiosity she failed to understand. Then one day, as told to me by my mother, I went missing. Her inquiries in the neighbourhood produced negative response—no one had seen me.

My father, who was working for Sir Harry Oakes whom he in later years described as a rough, tough, no-nonsense kind of man, could not be contacted. Actually, there was no telephone available at which he could be reached. Of course, during the World War II years, telephone services were at a premium.

As the minutes passed and there was still no sign of me, my mother's panic and nervousness reached a level of frenzied disbelief.

It is now easy to understand the sickening feeling of helplessness that swept over her—her youngest son had disappeared without a trace. And then a miracle happened. Along came a Bahamian gentleman down Fairwind Street with me in tow. The relief was so extreme for my mother that she burst into tears.

As I clung to my mother who was awash in her tears, the gentleman consoled her. "Mrs. Farrington, don't cry. The Lord has brought your son, Barrie, back to you safely. I know that you must have been very scared for your son's safety."

My mother was so relieved but still trembling as she replied, "I am so grateful to you for saving Barrie and for being such a kind and considerate person. I will pray for the Lord to always bless you."

They shook hands and the man left. Moments later, my mother put her hands to her head and acknowledged with horror that she had not asked his name. This occasion was on her mind for a long time.

The question was, how did that all come about.

It seemed, according to my mom, I decided to go to Eastern Senior school to join my older brothers. Somewhere in our home, I had found an old school bag complete with a handle on top, and so equipped and probably improperly dressed, I began the trek down Hawkins Hill, school bag virtually dragging on the road.

I was not interrupted on my journey until I was in the vicinity of St. Matthew's church. The good man who took me home thought it strange that such a young child would be walking alone on Shirley Street. According to the story given to my mom, when questioned as to where I was going, I responded that I was on the way to Eastern Senior school. He soon realized that I had left home without permission and was at risk.

After a while, based on the limited information I could give, he understood that my name was Barrie and that my parents lived on Hawkins Hill.

My mother was effusively grateful to the stranger for returning her wayward and youngest son home.

For many years this story was repeated and generally accompanied with much laughter. However, as the years passed I reflected on this story, especially in the context of unfortunate and seemingly unrestrained move away by many Bahamians from civility, respect, dignity, and caring for your neighbour. The act of kindness and concern was embedded in the Bahamian way of life. Strangers were willing to lend a helping hand if there were a need, to offer sympathy in times of sorrow, and to give food in times of hunger.

I never got to know the name of the gentleman who saved me. I never got to thank him. Maybe to him it would not have been expected; however, in return, it was and still is important to me and my family to hold on to the fundamental values of being a good neighbour, always.

Mom's moment of contentment near to her flower garden

CHAPTER 3

A MOTHER'S SAGE ADVICE

My mother lived her life with strict observance of the Christian principles embedded in the Ten Commandments. Her church and what it represented was the foundation upon which she relied to serve her neighbours, fellow church members, and the sick and suffering with unfaltering willingness and purity of heart.

My grandmother, Caroline Dean, my mother's mother who I never knew, died on 3 July 1916 at the early age of thirty-five years. My mother was ten years old. And since my grandfather, Joseph Dean, was unable to adequately care for my mother, it was decided that she should go to live with her Aunt Ethel and Uncle Martinas Bethel who lived on Virginia Street. It was while she was living with them that she attended St. Mary's Church and thus began her never-ending service and commitment to God and the Anglican church.

By the time my mother married my father, her Christian beliefs had been established. After their marriage, mom and dad could not live with Aunt Ethel, whom we called Auntie and

Uncle Martinas, because there was insufficient room in the house. As planned, they moved into the Farrington family home on the northeast corner of Dowdeswell and Armstrong Streets. With the move into the Eastern District, my mother started attending St. Matthew's Anglican Church. As to be expected, a family was started with Earle being the firstborn.

As we children grew older, my mother made us a part of her religious ways. Attendance at St. Matthew's Church was a must.

My mother was not fanatical about religion but she wanted her children to live in accordance with the teachings of the Bible.

As I grew older, I could recall her many sage advices and I still can.

"Barrie, always do what is right."

"Love your neighbor."

"If it doesn't belong to you, don't take it." (In other words, do not steal.)

"Always tell the truth." (This is not easy when you know that you will get the belt for wrong doing).

"Help others in need."

For me, the one piece of advice she gave that sustained me through my adult years was: "Barrie, always do the best you can." This indeed was Pearl at her very best.

Our home was divided when it came to religion. My father was not at all inclined to commit but this did not cause a rift in the family. On the other hand, had there been unity in religion maybe some of the stormy periods could have been avoided.

My dad never went to Sunday Mass and only set foot in church for baptisms, weddings and funerals. And in all cases, very reluctantly, he always argued that the temple of God was in his heart.

*Pearl Melinda beside her flower garden
at our Hawkins Hill home*

J. Barrie's determined look for the future at nine years old

CHAPTER 4

QUESTIONS OF THE SOUL

Very early in my life, I was intrigued with death and the aftermath of death. I have no recollection of when my grandfather Joseph Dean died and of his funeral. The same was true of my father's mother, my grandmother, Rosamond Alice Farrington née Dupuch. She was the sister of Leon Elias Dupuch, who founded *The Tribune* newspaper.

I did not know my grandfather, Clarence Thorpe Farrington, as he passed away before I was born. But I learned that he was a large man standing about 6'7" tall and possessing a very gentle but strong personality. He worked for John Alfred, a Portuguese businessman who took up residence in Nassau and who owned waterfront properties, one part of which was a dock named after him—John Alfred Wharf.

After Grandma Rosa died, my Uncle Willie and Aunt Nezzie, whose name actually was Inez, moved into the Lakeview Avenue Homestead.

Uncle Willie was an evangelist and was large in stature and strong. When he came to visit us on Hawkins Hill, and we were still living on the second storey of our unfinished home, he would lift me high above his head. That was always a thrill.

He would say to me, "How is John Barrie today?" He always called me John Barrie. Then one day he died. I do not know if he had a serious illness, but I was quite saddened that he was gone. After he was embalmed, he was put in a casket that was placed in the front room of the Lakeview home.

Oddly enough, I found myself alone in the front room with Uncle Willie in the casket. I remember the setting very vividly. I was quite young—maybe seven or eight years old—an impressionable age, and barely tall enough to look into the casket from the side. I knew he was dead but I wanted to know how he felt. With my heart beating wildly and hands perspiring, I reached into the casket to touch Uncle Willie on his face. It was cold and hard and, of course, scary. I did not know what to expect but I could almost hear him asking, "Are you satisfied, John Barrie?"

Where was his soul? Did he go to be with his father? They were questions of an inquisitive young mind.

Nobody likes going to funerals and to this day I avoid funerals, even when possibly out of respect or friendship I should attend. I believed my experience with Uncle Willie in some way had a lasting effect upon me.

CHAPTER 5

A TYPICAL DAY

In the early days of living on Hawkins Hill, my mother socialized fairly frequently with other young mothers with young children being the common denominator. I gleaned from photographs in our family album that my mother took me to the Eastern Parade and Malcolm's Park where she would meet Millicent Minns, Ivy Kamelar and Rona Dorsett. Here in this tranquil place, the young mothers would talk about everything from family matters, their spiritual lives, cost of living, special holidays, and life in general.

"How is Bert doing at *The Tribune*?" my mother would ask Millicent. Bert was a nephew of Leon Elias Dupuch, founder of *The Tribune*.

"He is doing fine but the work is difficult and at times he doesn't cope well," Millicent would reply.

As you can imagine life was not easy in the early 1940s. Remember there was no transportation so Millicent walked from the family residence on the corner of Mackey Street/Shirley Street, Ivy walked from Bay Street just east of Armstrong Street, and my mother walked from the top of Hawkins Hill—all with children in tow.

When I was seven or eight years of age, my friend Maurice Prosa would accompany us under the ever watchful eyes of my mother and Millicent. Maurice and I would wade in the shallow water off from the small beach and of course during season, we picked and ate sea grapes.

There were other families who also came to the Eastern Parade and Malcolm's Park, a gathering place for socializing.

At the west end of Malcolm's Park was the Pan American Airways Seaplane Terminal and Ramp. Watching the seaplanes land in the harbour and taxi up the ramp was magical. Passengers would disembark and be whisked away in cars. I do not believe that there were immigration and customs clearing requirements in those early years.

The ramp was inviting but moss-covered and slippery. Our bravado overruled good sense and we would run down the ramp and slide on the mossy surface into the water. We did not understand how dangerous this was until one day my feet slipped from under me and I fell backward, slamming my head on the concrete ramp. I thought that my time had come. I was dazed and my head hurt terribly.

Maurice was scared to death. He thought that I was headed to the other side, but luckily my recovery was rapid. Maurice said to me, "I don't want to slide down this ramp ever again." With my ego in tatters I weakly replied, "Not again will I go on this ramp."

My mother and friends with children, unaware of the near tragedy, continued to meet on the Eastern Parade and Malcolm's Park to talk and breathe in the fresh air. It was a place of freedom from the day-to-day humdrum of housekeeping and cooking.

In those days, mothers were the keepers and nurturers of children, the lovers of husbands and the caretakers of the family home. In the course of the day or week, the tasks were numerous and repetitive, but in them necessary creativity flourished

I shall describe a typical day in the Farrington home.

Because our house lacked all conveniences such as flush toilet, an electric iron, a refrigerator, or a telephone, each day although simple in context—was complex in different ways. It was in this daily management of meager resources that my mother excelled as a strong-willed, understated leader.

Even in this situation we did not feel deprived because in the main, other than the Kellys next door, we all shared the same privations of life.

Although not original, I identified with the story of this interview of a successful comedian in the U.S.A. who had grown up in a neighbourhood that lacked many of the basic needs of living.

The reporter asked "Dick, you grew up the hard way, living virtually from hand to mouth. How did it feel growing up poor?"

Dick's response was unexpected. "It did not matter because I never knew that we were poor."

Most weekdays were the same with highs and lows.

As an eight-year-old, there is the beginning of understanding and awareness. My father with his austere ways was a reflection of the Victorian-like rules imposed upon him as he grew from childhood to maturity. I do not know if he really reflected upon events beyond his bachelor days, but one characteristic shone through glaringly and it was his dream of becoming a successful entrepreneur, a vision that further limited his outreach to his family. But in the face of many adversities in a limited economy, he was a good provider for the family.

For my mother, the end of the day was the most satisfying because she could give thanks to the Lord for seeing her and children safely through the day. Every night all the children knelt at the bedside and repeated the Lord's Prayer and asked God to love mom and dad.

I don't remember exactly how old I was in this instance, but my mom would sit in the wicker rocking chair, which was about twelve feet from the north window, and rock me until I was quite sleepy. Obviously, I outgrew this practice but because it was so comforting I probably would have continued until I started high school. When we awoke we also said our prayers. When you are that young, you cannot understand the spiritual underpinning of such a physical act.

Early morning was a beehive of activity—breakfast consisting of Kellogg's Corn Flakes, toast, maybe some cheese, and a cup of hot cocoa. Not fancy, but wholesome. Occasionally, there would be boiled eggs. For a short while, we raised chickens but it all came to an end because we did not know how to raise chickens, added to which fowl snakes and raccoons assisted in depleting the stock. Not to mention, only a four-and-a-half-foot wall separated us from the bush of the Collins Estate.

By this time, Earle and Ramon were attending Government High School. Fortunately for Earle, he had a benefactor in Iris Bethel, Aunt Ethel's daughter; otherwise he would not have gone to that school because dad did not have the money to pay the ten-pound annual fee. Iris worked for Public Works, which was located next to the Government High school in Nassau Court. A way was found to pay school fees for Ramon, who also attended the Government High. Our sister, Fay, attended St. John's College.

The uniform for Government High was blue shirt and white long pants. For St. John's College, it was green and gray. Mom had to wash all of the clothes by hand using a wooden scrub board. The place of washing was adjoining the outside toilet. Washed clothes were hung on the clothesline for drying. Rainy days were brutal. Wet clothes had to be draped over furniture and the upstairs banister.

The ironing of clothes was another brutal piece of the process. My mother had to use a goose iron, which required you to place smoldering charcoal frequently into the chamber. This produced significant heat for the shiny steel surface which enabled, with care, scorch-free ironing of clothes, particularly white ones.

Another type of ironing required the use of four or five irons, without chambers. It was necessary to place them on smoldering charcoal and then use them one at a time when the ironing surface was sufficiently hot. Mom used both approaches as she saw fit.

Even at a very early age, I felt an appreciation of the way my mother so smoothly switched from one iron to another. Also, at specific intervals she rearranged the sequence of irons on the hot coals so that she could maintain a certain rhythm of movement.

This method of ironing was used for many years and though it was tiring I never once heard her complain. My mom was product of an age that when there was work to be done you rolled up your sleeves and did it. And in today's context this approach is still essential while striving for success.

With dear friends at a young age
L to R: Terry Johnson, Donald Johnson, John Knowles, and me

Barrie at seven years of age striking a grownup pose

CHAPTER 6

THE WAR YEARS

Living on Hawkins Hill in the 1940s was not very exciting but in the rest of the world, particularly in Europe and the Pacific Ocean, World War II was raging. The direct effect, of course, was the limited availability of goods and foodstuffs for local consumption.

The Bahamas being a British Colony, the Government through its citizens wanted to show tangible support for Great Britain and its allies via the sale of War Stamps. I remembered my mother having a folder with empty stamp outlines imprinted on the inside. Each time she bought a stamp, she would apply a little water to the adhesive and place it on empty spot in the folder. Once all the empty spots were filled with "Help the War Efforts" stamps, you submitted it to the Colonial Secretary's office and then got a new folder. And the process would start again. Bahamians generally were supportive of the mother country.

News about the war was constantly updated on ZNS, The Bahamas' national broadcasting station, and in *The Tribune* and *The Nassau Guardian*.

In my youth while all this news was swirling around endlessly in our midst, there was little I could understand but I was still curious about what was happening as were Maurice, Sidney, Maurice's brother Rudy, and my brothers and sister.

Although I was timid about getting into a conversation with my father about the war I said, "Dad, the news about the war makes everything sound so scary. Why are they fighting? Are we going to lose this war?"

I did not know what to expect in response, mainly because my father never really showed an interest in what we were doing or feeling. Surprisingly, my father took the time to explain as simply as possible what was going on.

"The Germans, under Adolph Hitler, want to conquer and rule the world. Japan and Italy have joined forces with Germany, and while in earlier years Germany had many victories, the tide was beginning to go the other way." He added, "Barrie, no one can explain why Hitler started the war, but the loss of life has been very great. We must have faith that Germany, Japan and Italy will lose the war in the end."

I was pensive and with my childlike optimism felt relieved by the comforting words of my dad.

Even in the midst of this great turmoil around the world, the Farrington family had to go on living each day with limited resources and with a belief of a better day tomorrow.

Except for Saturdays and Sundays, each day was positively occupied with early arising from the night's sleep, except for dad who slept late because he stayed up late reading and drinking tea at the kitchen table. The first chore in the morning, which was rotated among the boys, was to empty the contents of the latrine, the pail dad used during the night for urination into outside toilet. No one complained about doing this only because we learned early in life that where success is to be sustained, each team member must contribute to the effort. Mind you, as to be expected, there was some siblings' resistance between Earle and Ramon.

Earle, in exercising his elder brother position, would attempt to change place with Ramon for latrine duty.

"Ramon, why don't you take the pail out and empty it and I will make up your bed."

Ramon's response would be one of simple negotiation.

"I will do the trip to the outside toilet if you make up my bed for the week."

Obviously a standoff happened but all returned to normal pretty quickly.

Once mom gave us our modest breakfast, she would then finish making bologna sandwiches for Earle and Ramon to eat during lunchtime at school. Fay and I did not get lunch because we could eat at home as we both got out of school at midday—me from the Hawkins Hill Seventh Day Adventist School and Fay from the Jayne Camplejohn School on Deveaux Street. Once we were off to school then mom went into high gear washing dishes.

Our home had only one source of potable water. A water line was installed on the exterior wall of the house together with a waste pipe that ended under the southern windows on the second storey. A proper faucet was attached to the water line. A white enameled pan was situated in a wooden frame supported by wooden stilts. Near to this multipurpose bin was a table with a cracked marble slab used for food preparation. On this table were two white enamel pans six to eight inches deep—the larger one was used for washing dishes and the smaller one for rinsing them. For drying the dishes, they were set in a more multi-compartment-like drain, which sat atop the dishwashing pan. This was not very efficient but it was functional.

While my mother washed dishes during the day, the washing of dishes in the afternoon following the midday meal, and evening after supper fell to the children. Because I was the youngest and lacked essential skills, I was given exemption. My good fortune was that I was able to retain that status until I married. My mom spoiled me because I was the youngest and favourite.

Once general cleaning was finished, mom had to place her attention on preparing the dinner—the midday meal. To add to this planning, she also had to plan ahead for the next days' nourishment. At least twice a week something special would happen.

At about 9:30 to 10:00 a.m., the whole neighbourhood was called to action. "Fish Man. Fish Man. Come get your fresh fish."

Of course, it is Leonard the Fish Man pushing his new fish cart to the top of Hawkins Hill.

Leonard was a large man with a barrel chest and broad shoulders. He wore khaki pants with a light-green shirt and shoes, but I don't remember the colour. He also wore a straw hat that gave him protection from the blazing sun. I could only witness this event when not in school.

Leonard's cart was special. It functioned like a wheelbarrow but the body was of wood painted green. The interior was caulked and waterproofed, and inside Leonard placed his live fish. To keep insects and flies out of the interior, a screened square was inserted exactly into space cut out on the top.

My mother, Alice Knowles, Olive Kelly, Mrs. Moree and others would gather around Leonard's cart to select and negotiate prices for the fish. He would have goggle eye, grey snapper, grunts, and the occasional hog fish. As fish were selected and paid for he would bundle them by taking a strip of thatch, push it through the gill and mouth of each fish, and tie a knot for security.

Leonard also resided on Hawkins Hill and knew all the neighbours by name, therefore coming together on fish day was like a social event.

My mother would take her fish back to the house and at a special table in the back garden would prepare the fish for cooking—cutting away fins, gutting the fish, scraping off scales, and finally since they were to be fried, making incisions in the sides of the fish, seasoning them with rock salt and lime juice, and letting them marinate.

The fish were fried, including the head. To accompany the fish, mom would cook the world's best peas and rice, adding salt pork and thyme to give it flavour. We never got tired of eating fried fish on the appointed days during the week.

The big meal of the day for all of us was the mid-day meal that was generally eaten between noon and 2:00 p.m.

At the end of the day, with a simple supper, a hearty sumptuous mid-day meal finished and school homework behind us, we would settle in the family area, the only one. The centre piece of our evening was listening to the melody and soothing sounds of *Evening Symphony*.

The RCA Victor radio was the only source of our entertainment in our household. It was a model that arrived on Noah's

Ark, but it had character. The cabinet was about three-and-a-half feet in height and two feet, four inches in width. The dial was magnificent with a knob that was connected to a long needle-like indicator which could take you to ZNS for classical music. In later years, the termites took up residence—a sad day to say the least.

On our special nights, we would turn off all lights and with a match, light the ends of short pieces of cord. The effect was glowing embers that we twirled slowly and in different patterns. The effect for us was pretty magical.

For our parents, these evenings were quiet times for reflection on that day and unfortunately the worries of tomorrow and beyond.

My father worked most days away from home, even as he continued the construction of the family home. Money was lacking and work was progressing slowly. With six of us living in one area, it is easy to understand that on occasions there was certain edginess in attitude.

In fact, one day Ramon was teasing Earle while he was having supper, much to Earle's dislike. Ramon continued with the teasing and Earle warned him, "Ramon, please stop your nonsense or I will get angry."

Ramon persisted and Earle, with a blow of his right hand while in a sitting position, hit Ramon flush on the jaw. Ramon, in total shock, lost his balance and stumbled hard into the wall under the east window and sat down. I thought that maybe a fight would ensue but no threat was made in the end.

Earle always possessed a most gentle and thoughtful demeanor. This one explosion illustrated that for virtually everybody there is an emotional limit.

The Farrington family had interesting twists and turns that in many ways created special and lasting traits within each sibling's character.

During the war years, the British had a presence in The Bahamas but mostly concentrated in New Providence. The Royal Air Force was based at Windsor Field and as to be expected the crew spent time making friends in the community—such a friendship serendipitously happened with our family.

John Pugh attended mass at St. Matthew's church and as our family was at St. Matthew's quite frequently, a casual acquaintance occurred. Finally he was invited to our house for Sunday dinner and this began a friendship that lasted for many years.

John was a devoted Anglican and it did not take long for him to tell us that he was determined to become a priest following the war.

I remember John very well even though I was just eight years old. He was of slight build and very gentle, which I interpreted as meaning that he never got angry about anything.

As time passed and John's visits became more frequent, the family's affection for him grew significantly.

And then something wonderful happened. Mom encouraged John to practice giving sermons to our family whenever he visited. This he did willingly. Imagine, having a private "congregation."

John was committed to helping young boys find their way through healthy and Christian activities. He started a boys' youth club, The Blue Bats. Even though I was very young, I was allowed to attend activity sessions with my brothers Earle and Ramon in St. Matthew's schoolroom located immediately across from the church. It was a great experience.

After John left the Bahamas following the end of World War II, my mother decided to continue with the club. However, she made two big changes: she opened attendance to boys and girls and changed the name to the Peter Pan Club.

John Pugh, as an ordained priest, returned to the Bahamas and in due course became the priest in charge at St. Anne's church in Fox Hill. He did much good work including the significant improvement to the education system.

His sister Rita came from England and joined in his good work at St. Anne's.

John knew from his early experience with The Blue Bats club that young boys were in many ways neglected by society. He devoted much attention to this deficiency and during his many years of serving God at St. Anne's, he adopted more than twenty Bahamian young men and guided them successfully to adulthood and independence.

CHAPTER 7

A GAME FOR ALL SEASONS

Growing up on Hawkins Hill required using your own young and untrained wisdom to create engaging activities for entertainment. I cannot help but think about those wonderful tales of Tom Sawyer and Huckleberry Finn we read about while attending school.

How many people ever played "kick the can"? Whoever made up such a game? Who can be given credit—no one person, but here is how the game was played. Of course we needed a can, which turned out to be an empty Milkmaid condensed milk can. There would be about eight of us from the neighbourhood and the game was played after dark. The can was placed on the ground under the one street light in Fairwind Street and one of us would volunteer to be the "can keeper." The keeper would close his eyes for a count of 10, given out aloud, during which time we would scatter in the dark areas around the Farrington and Kelly homes. The "can keeper" would have to venture from the "can" in search of hidden players. The idea was for any one of the players to locate the keeper and to run and kick the can.

If the keeper caught one of us before we could run and kick the can, that game was over.

The shout of "I kicked the can," accompanied with much laughter, was joyous. If someone was caught (tagged) by the "can keeper," he became the keeper.

At eight to ten years of age, going into the dark was scary so in a way for us it was a small test of bravery.

One night we did have an incident that made us sad. Rudy Prosa, in hiding, decided to climb into the "mami sapote" tree just outside of the kitchen doorstep of the Kelly's home. He made it into the tree okay but when he tried to get down, the limb broke, he fell and broke his wrist. Our friend had to be bundled off to hospital in Sidney's dad's truck. Luckily he recovered without too much suffering and as to be expected received a lot of sympathetic attention from all of us. Rudy was especially happy with the attention from my sister Fay and Sidney's sister, Rosalie. We worried that his parents would prevent us from playing "kick the can" but no, the game continued.

We never knew when to stop playing. If our parents had ignored us we would have played all night but my mother, at around 8:45 p.m., earlier in winter, would come to the upstairs eastern window and make the call—"Barrie, it is time to come in. It is bed time. And the rest of the boys should go home as well."

"One more game mom. Please! Please!" I would plead.

Olive, Sidney's mom, would then chime in, "Sidney, that is enough for the night. You have played enough."

With hung-dog looks we would say our good night and head home. Maurice would add, "We will play again tomorrow. Night-night."

That thought cheered us up.

The absence of the expensive toys or games meant little to our group because we possessed a natural capacity for playing games that made boredom a stranger.

For us young boys—Sidney, Maurice, Rudy, Valdo, Jarvis, Eric, Basil—a season for each game evolved. And yet we were not unique as the games and seasons seem to be played in other communities in Nassau. There was something supernatural about the way each season started at the same time each year.

There were four distinct seasons—kite flying, spinning tops and by extension "pegging" of tops, shooting marbles, and roller skating. When feeling creative, we would take time to construct box carts and scooters.

There were two elements about our activities that probably were an indication of young men heading to puberty and the need to express ourselves more aggressively—the first being the deep need to win. In our games losing had consequences and the second was that girls were absent from our games—except for kick the can, which made "showing off" unnecessary.

Shooting marbles had all the ingredients linked to win/lose outcomes. Each player had a set number of marbles that would be put into the game, all of which were placed in a circle drawn into an agreed place in the unpaved lane.

To start the game a lead off player had to be selected. The process was simple. A line was drawn in the dirt about eight feet from the circle of marbles and each player from an upright position would roll his "tar" toward the marked line. The player who got his marble closest to the mark started the game by rolling his "tar" at a controlled speed towards the ring where all "game" marbles were placed. The intent was to knock a marble out of the ring in his first roll. If that didn't happen, the other players followed suit in the order of closest to the "line."

Once all the players had rolled their "tars," the lead player then attempted to knock as many marbles out of the ring. The "tar" was placed in the shooting hand between the thumb and the middle and index fingers. And then through a "flicking" motion the "tar" was propelled towards the ring. Surprisingly the speed, accuracy and power generated were amazing. The player who knocked any marbles out of the ring kept those marbles. And so the sequence of play continued until the ring was cleared. At the end of play, the marbles won were kept and the losers had a chance to recover when the next game was played the next day. A player's "tar," which was his most-prized marble, was at risk if by chance during play it remained in the ring during the game. There were many times when a "tar" was knocked out of the ring and lost to the owner.

Over the season marbles were won and lost. In some cases

marbles were traded between players only because of the beauty of the embedded design which made possession desirable.

I had a very small weekly allowance so my mom was never too pleased when I purchased marbles from the Stop N Shop on Bay Street. At the end of the season, which lasted six to eight weeks, marbles were secured and put into a special place until the next season.

Another game with marbles was "knucks." This activity was designed to test courage and pain endurance. Only two players at a time played but occasionally spectators were allowed. Since we played on an unpaved roadway, we were able to lay out the pitch—three holes were dug three feet apart—about four inches in diameter and three inches deep. To start the game the first player from a line drawn in the road and about three feet from the first hole would attempt to "shoot" his marble along the ground in an attempt to get it into the first "cup." Once accomplished, the marble was taken out of the cup and placed at a spot about five inches outside of the cup from which a player can shoot for the second hole. This sequence was followed until successfully sinking a marble in each hole. A score was kept of how many shots were taken to complete the course. The second player went through the same steps. At the end, the player with the lowest score got the opportunity to inflict a little pain. The loser had to place his hand in the cup with fingers extended and with "knuckles" facing the winner. The loser held his position as the winner, from a distance of fifteen inches, shot a marble with as much speed as possible at the knuckles. The winner was allowed three shots. A marble travelling at such a speed which hit the knuckles caused pain. This was the game of "knucks."

Then came kite season. Our group was skilled in making kites with thin strips from wooden roofing shingles, tied together with No.10 thread complete with a curved arch at the top of the frame.

The frame of the kite was connected by thread, which gave the kite its shape. Tissue paper purchased from the Stop N Shop was cut to fit the frame. Since we did not have access to regular glue we made our own: a paste comprising flour and water was applied. This homemade glue was most effective.

To ensure good aerodynamics, we applied a "tail" made of pieces of cloth, the length of which depended on the size of the kite.

To be able to hoist the kite evenly, the thread was affixed triangularly to the face of the kite and knotted centrally. The reel of No. 10 thread would be connected here.

And once our beauties were completed, off we went to the open lot which belonged to Ronald Fountain so that we could launch our kites. This lot we used is now home to The Bahamas Immigration offices.

On top of Hawkins Hill, there was always a breeze but it still required teamwork in getting the kites into the sky.

It was quite a sight to see five or six kites flying at one time reaching for the clouds. Sometimes we would let the line out through a hole made in the bottom of any empty can. And what did this do for us? Well, we could place our ear to the open end of the can and hear the kite "singing"—beautiful but eerily at the same time.

Disaster would strike every once in a while much to our very considerable dismay.

No. 10 thread, although generally strong and reliable, would "pop" and the kite would go sailing to the west into the Collins Estate, which was separated from Hawkins Hill by a high concrete wall.

We all knew that our kites were made with great care, pride and cost. The loss of a creation could not be passively accepted.

Finding our way into the Estate, which was like going into a jungle, was not too difficult because the wall that separated the Farrington home from the bush was only about three-and-a-half feet tall. So we would hop the wall and ramble through the bush in the general direction of where the kite went down.

We knew through rumour that the Collins family had guard dogs roaming the estate, as they owned a huge orchard of fruit-bearing trees that was always tempting to dishonest people. With the thought of guard dogs on the loose, we proceeded with as much courage as we could muster. Fortunately we never encountered any dogs but unfortunately we never found any of our escaped kites.

And so for each kite season, we joyously and creatively made our kites to fly from the top of Hawkins Hill.

Roller skating season required the acquisition of skates without stealing. I was fortunate to receive a pair of skates from Santa Claus. We all clung on to the myth for as long as possible as it was the only way you might get something special. Except for the Kellys, there was no extra money for "play" things.

In addition to merely skating for the fun of it we would play hockey with very simple rules. A crushed milk can was the "puck" and hockey "sticks" about three feet in length and two inches in diameter were stripped trees out of the Collins Estate bushes. Goal posts were drawn on the asphalt using "chalky" limestone. Depending upon how many showed up, there would be three or four boys on each team. Play was intense as winning was important. The by-product was that we reached a pretty high skill level. There were some casualties but other than a bruise on the shin or arm, no one suffered serious injury. Learning how to skate backwards was fun and challenging.

Building a box cart required a team effort. Wheels were taken from broken skates. Ordinarily, the size of any skate could be adjusted by a special device in the middle of the skates and in this way any foot size could be accommodated. The rear wheels were fixed to the rear crossbar, which was stationary. The front bar with affixed eye hooks had a centre pinion that made it possible to turn left or right (with limitations) with heavy lines attached to either side of the bar to which the wheels were attached. The driver of the cart could, by using the joined lines, change direction of the cart.

Except for one occasion, rides on Hawkins Hill were limited to the smallest slope.

We would take turns riding in the cart. Then one day we decided to go down the steepest part of Hawkins Hill and because I was the only one with tennis shoes, I was to be the brakes. All went wrong and we crashed into a wall. Fortunately we survived but I could not remember what happened. I had suffered a concussion.

I was indeed fortunate that I fully recovered. I wanted to know exactly what happened to me so I revisited the events. I was told by Maurice that I picked myself up off the road after colliding with wall and walked back up the hill. Mrs. Knowles Prosa, Maurice's mom, who just happened to be on the corner of Fairwind Street, noticed that my arm was bruised and bleeding. She took me into her house and cleaned the wound. Coincidentally, my father with aid of a helper was cutting down two trees growing in Fairwind Street. When I left Mrs. Prosa, I apparently walked by my father without acknowledging him and proceeded home which was nearby. I obviously went directly upstairs and to bed as this was my location when I awoke a couple of hours later.

And as if by some mysterious signal, cart season would be over.

From time to time there were rainy days. What did we do?

We were never at a loss. There were no TVs in any house so we played Chinese checkers, a game using marbles and dice and requiring patience. As we grew a little older we added "whist," an interesting card game. There was another weird card game we called "noses." The "loser" in this game had to undergo the discomfort and indignity of having his nose spanked with six to eight cards by the winner. There was no ducking, you had to grin and bear it.

The lessons learned from these early years experience were for sure character building. We learned how to win through effort, and that to lose was not the end of life. There was always a tomorrow. And maybe most of all we learned how to be self-reliant and creative. I remain baffled to this day how the seasons for our various games changed in our "village of Nassau" without a calendar.

Barrie practicing his home-run swing. A fabricated pose as the ball was tied to the bat. Jack Moree was the helpful catcher. At the Kelly home on Lake View Avenue

CHAPTER 8

THE FORBIDDEN VIEW

Unsurprisingly, while growing up with no regard for age in years, the imagination of doing things of adventure seemed to come forth. And so it was with me.

Looking out of the upstairs windows, I could see different parts of Nassau—from the west window I could see the water tower, which I later found out was located at the top and west of the Queen's Staircase or the 66 Steps. To this day, I wonder if anyone really counted them.

To assist with water pressure for the cruise liners and businesses located in the downtown area and low lying places, water was pumped into the tank at the top of the water tower and in a mysterious way, gravity of course, was distributed.

Also in the area, at the top of the Queen's Staircase, was the asylum for the insane. The asylum was referred to as the "crazy hill." As you can guess, in ignorance, the "crazy hill" was the subject of many absurd and tasteless jokes.

At some stage I found out that Uncle Clarence, my dad's brother, was a patient there. On occasions when Uncle Clarence's condition improved, he was released to his family. I remembered meeting him only once. He came to see my dad at our house on Hawkins Hill. I had no idea of his history but he was soft-spoken and seemed very shy. He had come to help my dad do some painting.

That night at supper, dad was talking about that day with Uncle Clarence. He said that Uncle Clarence was wearing black gloves and when he asked, "Clarence, why are you wearing gloves on such a hot day?" Uncle Clarence replied, "Ira, I am wearing them because my hands have been cut off." No one laughed. I never saw Uncle Clarence again but did hear stories about him that were not good.

The water tower was an imposing structure standing on a hill that was slightly higher than the top of Hawkins Hill. For safety reasons, there was a large searchlight positioned on the top of the tower. The light was turned on at night and revolved in circles constantly at a fairly slow speed. It was intended to warn low flying planes of the tower and was also a beacon of sorts for vessels sailing in the vicinity of Nassau.

The area at the top of the Sixty-Six Steps is also known as Fort Fincastle. Along with other forts constructed in Nassau, this fort formed a part of the defence of the island.

From the window in my dad's bedroom, I could look into the interior of Nassau. I could see all the way to Oakes Field and view planes landing and taking off.

The south view from our kitchen window was not too stimulating and there my interest was limited. Looking into Sears Addition all I could see were homes and to the southwest, the undeveloped land belonging to the Collins Estate.

The view from the eastern window was special because I could see the steeple of St. Matthew's Church where we attended Sunday masses and special religious celebrations.

The north window gave the look at Hog Island and the harbour. At the western tip of Hog Island, on a rugged, unprotected piece of honeycombed rock, a lighthouse was constructed to mark the entrance to Nassau Harbour.

My mom told me about her Uncle Jack, who was the lighthouse keeper. Apparently Uncle Jack was a seafaring man who sailed back and forth across the harbour to service the lighthouse every day. He liked his rum, and Saturday was his special day for having more than a few drinks. Then one weekend Uncle Jack disappeared. His boat was found but he never was. The belief was that he accidentally fell overboard and drowned and was swept out into the ocean.

Having spent many hours looking out of the windows, I wanted to see more. The only way I could was to get on to the roof of our house. But how was I going to get on the roof? Of course there was no way that either my mom or dad would consent to my doing so. The thought of doing it scared me and yet there was the compelling need to have the experience.

It was a Friday afternoon in January with a cool wind blowing in from the northwest. My dad was at work at Hobby Horse Hall and my mom was out visiting friends. So here it was: I all alone and adventure beckoning to me.

First of all, getting out of the east window was going to be difficult because I would have to stand on a chair, hoist myself to the window sill, remain balanced while reaching around the side of the dormer window, and then gradually make my way up the side while holding on to the overhang. Had I slipped I would have fallen onto the porch roof at the next level and if unable to stop my fall at that stage, I would have ended up on the ground either in mom's flower garden or next to it on the not-so-soft lawn.

I proceeded slowly and carefully with a pounding heart and then came a terrible thought that increased my anxiety. Should either Mr. or Mrs. Kelly witness my escapade, I could be assured that a report would be made to my mom and dad.

A report to my dad meant being beaten with his leather belt. But I was too far advanced to stop and, besides, I did not want to stop.

Making my way to the apex of the roof took forever; at least it felt that way. I sat there for a few minutes and then, gathering my wits, I slowly stood upright. It was wonderfully scary and exciting.

I could see all of Nassau. The excitement was coursing through every vein and nerve in my body. It was a discovery equal to Christopher Columbus' landing at San Salvador in

1492. I couldn't believe I had done it. And then I had to get down; everything was in the reverse. At last I backed in over the sill of the dormer facing to the east and felt my feet on the chair. I felt a huge relief. And my heartbeat started to slow down.

I made a number of trips onto the roof throughout the months, and while perched there surveying all the places near and far, my thoughts focused on what I wanted to do in the future. I had this inner spirit talking to me about reaching far beyond the horizons that I was looking at. And yet at that time the family circumstances were such that reaching beyond the apparent unscalable barriers weighed heavily upon me. A young boy living in the midst of a poor, dysfunctional family—what in reality was to be my future, my destiny, obviously, only time would tell.

Farrington home as it looks today—the dormer out of which JBF ventured on to the roof is still in evidence

The original rugby team, circa 1953

*L to R: Coach Donald Butler, Johnny Lunn, Charles Pearce,
"T" Russell, Hartley Albury, JB, Cecil Cooke, Coach Robert Albury
Middle row: Vincent D'Aguilar, Sydney French, Harold Stuart, Jude
Kemp, Basil Butler, Bert Malone
Front Row: Ralph Hall, Mario Parotti, Bobby Parotti,
Rene Albury, unknown, Charles Moss
In front with ball: Coach Albury's son*

CHAPTER 9

THE SCRUMS

With The Bahamas being a British Colony for so many years, it is easy to understand that the sports played internationally were influenced by the significant pressure of British personnel. Cricket, soccer and rugby became central to our sporting structure. This was true with virtually all colonies in the Caribbean.

The Bahamas has always been known for its beautiful weather year-round. This allowed the scheduling of sports that avoided the overlapping of one with the other, as is the case with countries in northern climes.

Earle and Ramon played rugby, but being too young to play on a team I would attend practices and when the "big boys" were finished I could take the rugby ball and pretend I was in a game. Many times I did this when it was quite dark and only the street lights made it possible to see the ball.

I fell in love with rugby and it was my passion for many years.

The rugby pitch known as the Eastern Parade was located, strangely enough, between Dowdeswell and Bay Streets, which were paved. On the south side of the road were the residences of Gurth Duncombe, John Thompson and Sir Kenneth Solomon overlooking the pitch and at the western end, the home of Fane Solomon. On the north side between the pitch and Bay Street was a long line of almond trees.

Rugby season started in January and lasted for about three months.

For those who saw me play the game, they described me as "the bull" who was fearless during every match. No quarter given and no quarter asked for.

Rugby was once described as a "game designed for gentlemen but played by ruffians."

Matches were played on Saturday afternoons with many spectators in attendance. To control crowds and traffic, Dowdeswell Street was closed off to traffic from Armstrong Street eastward.

In January the weather was generally cool and the wind gentle. Preparation for the game was crucial both physically and emotionally. I was always supercharged while waiting for the game to start.

As a rule and without making it obvious, I would stand off to the side for a few moments to gather my thoughts and to visualize how the game would be played. It is funny how you recall some of the thoughts in those moments.

This moment is unbelievable—the warmth of the sun, the gentle cool breeze, the smell of the freshly mowed grass, the white lines defining the pitch, and an incredible sense of invincibility. The goose bumps that made me tingle all over for that split second were all consuming. In fact, I could envisage the emotion and excitement of a Roman Gladiator about to enter the arena in which he would imminently engage in mortal combat.

Before the game started, there was time to chat about nothing in particular but with special emphasis on girls and girlfriends. Since most of us were still bachelors, there was a definite increase in the words of bravado.

Peter, our inside three-quarter player, who generally showed little emotion, kept saying, "I can't wait for the game to get started. We owe the Sea Scouts a beating."

Bobby agreed and added, "We must play as if there is no tomorrow. Let's leave it all out on the field."

He turned to me and asked, "Barrie are you ready?"

I smiled but there was little warmth reflected in my eyes as I replied, "I am beyond ready. Victory will be ours today. Remember, there is no such thing as a good loser."

This was such an important game for us, which explained a little of the edginess in the attitude of our team members.

The referee, a no-nonsense guy, signaled that the game was to begin, blew his whistle and waved both captains to the centre. There were some last-minute reminders of how he would referee the game.

The linesmen who patrolled the sidelines were in the ready to mark the point at which the ball would go outside of the pitch. The toss of coin was next, to decide which team kicked off and which would receive the ball.

At 4:00 p.m., the referee blew his whistle and the game began.

From the very outset the game was played with great skill and yet the tackling was harsh. The loose Scrums were brutal and the "glory boys" in the three quarter line showed off their speed and agility.

I played in the forwards and in the set Scrums I was a "prop." Eight players from each side formed the Scrums. Every ounce of strength was exerted by each team member in concert in trying to push the opponents off the ball.

The game raged back and forth and at half-time the score was even. After the fifteen-minute break, we changed field position. I had an unfortunate incident in the second half which made me lower my intensity. One of the opposing three-quarter players was running toward the fifty-yard line and I came in from his left side and tackled him pretty hard.

Unable to get up, he looked at me from the ground and said, "Barrie, you just broke my collarbone." Of course I was shaken by this. I wanted to impose a punishing tackle but certainly did not want to cause injury.

I was downcast for a few moments but soon returned to the job at hand.

The crowd, about 500 to 600 people, was excited and screaming for the team they favoured. With just two minutes left, we were behind by two points and defeat was looking into our very souls.

But then, behold, a penalty was called against our opponents and we were awarded a penalty kick.

Since I was the kicker with the stronger leg, I was handed the ball to try for a field goal. My heart was beating wildly, my throat was dry, and it was to be a very long kick, a dropkick. The spectators were shouting excitedly because this was the end.

The penalty mark was just outside the 50-yard line and maybe 10 yards from the southern sideline near to Dowdeswell Street. As I prepared to kick, there was a sudden hush in the crowd; not even a cough was heard. I noted the mark, stepped back about one yard, stepped forward dropping the ball toward the turf and as it touched the ground, I swung my right leg mightily. I did not lift my head until the ball was well on its way.

A slight breeze at my back, I watched without breathing as the ball shot through the air towards the two goal posts. It seemed like an eternity. The ball sailed through the goal posts with only inches to spare. We won by one point.

There was a great roar of appreciation. My teammates hoisted me onto their shoulders for about five minutes. The euphoria was palpable.

I wished the moment to last forever but I had to remember that it was all the hard team work that placed us in the position to win. And then reality set in. During our short team meeting before we dispersed, I said, "Guys, it was a great win, but remember practice is on Monday and we have another match next Saturday that we must win. And bear in mind, 'one swallow does not make a spring.'"

And so it was like a soldier returning from battle—sweat-stained white shorts streaked with brown dirt and the green from the crab grass of the pitch—white socks no longer white.

The sun was about thirty minutes from setting and the blue sky streaked with slow-moving white clouds was absolutely beautiful.

Four members of the winning rugby team:
Jerome Darville [back row]
Barrie, Peter Isaacs, and Roger Pyfrom [kneeling L to R]

Barrie at fifteen on back porch of family home on Hawkins Hill

CHAPTER 10

THE UNCERTAIN ROAD TO HIGHER EDUCATION

Despite the relatively poor condition that governed our daily lives, my parents were determined that the four children would be given the opportunity to obtain a decent education. It should be said that in those early years and before, all parents from every walk of life wanted a good education for their children.

On reflection, it was decidedly a time in our history when the country as a whole, including the government, was committed to ensuring that "no child be left behind."

Colonialism had severe drawbacks but with education there was strict adherence to prepare children for the future. This was so serious that the education department had a complement of full-time truancy officers. They patrolled the streets and if during their patrolling, either on foot or bicycle, a young person was discovered not attending school when obviously he should have been, a report was written and parents were dutifully advised. I suspect in each home there was a price to pay for truancy.

At thirteen years of age, I had a sense of an undefined future. But here I was reminiscing about being a young child who'd been saved by a stranger near St. Matthew's Church and returned to my frantic mom. It seemed that I was destined to follow in the footsteps of my older brothers in the pursuit of an education. When Earle and Ramon attended Eastern Senior and I was five years old, my curiosity made me attempt the impossible and that was to go to Eastern Senior school to find them. Fortunately, no ill befell me but the die was cast.

Imagine my surprise and joy when I was told by my parents that I would be attending Eastern Senior school.

"Barrie, the Headmaster of Eastern Senior has advised that our application for you to attend Eastern Senior has been approved."

I was really at a loss for words but mumbled, "I am so glad for this chance" and then I added almost in a whisper "I promise that I won't let you down."

I knew even then that our living circumstances were indeed hard and though Eastern Senior was a public school, more family sacrifices would have to be made.

Deep inside, I was afraid only because I did not know what to expect in a new environment. None of my school chums from the Seventh Day Adventist school on Hawkins Hill would be attending.

The Kelly family was Methodist therefore Rosalie and Sidney went to Queen's College primary and middle schools. In those early days, Queen's College was located on Charlotte Street and was private. Actually, it is private still. There was no envy on my part of Sidney going to a private school. In fact, I did not make the distinction between public and private schools. An education was to be obtained at all schools.

The quality of teaching at Eastern Senior was at a very high standard. I was not an outstanding student but I worked hard. In the years at Eastern Senior, my father offered only once to review my homework with me.

I remember the two of us sitting at the dining table in the tiny kitchen. For general lighting there was a bare fixture in the ceiling and a forty-watt bulb with an off white shade that hung low over the table—a green Formica top trimmed with a chrome strip.

And so we began.

The mathematical homework was perplexing to me but I guess with deeper study on my own I probably could have arrived at the right answers. I can remember the text book from which we were working. With each passing minute, as I was not quick enough to chart the way correctly to the answers, my father began to get irritated. He had a great mind for numbers and could not understand my inability get an answer rapidly. Finally, the dam of irritation broke and his uncontrollable temper emerged.

"Barrie, for God's sake, can't you understand how to make this simple calculation."

"I am trying," I stammered.

With each exchange his language became more abusive.

The Lord smiled on me and at the end of a grueling and unpleasant hour or so we called it a night.

The solace of bed was heaven-sent. My mother could not intervene as to have done so would have worsened the situation.

We never met again to review my homework. This was just fine with me. I believed on the other hand that this encounter strengthened me and inspired me to work harder to excel.

Days at Eastern Senior were filled with learning all the subjects that would be in the curriculum of a high school if you were lucky enough to get into high school. However, outside the tedium of general schoolwork there were certain events that remain indelibly imprinted in my mind.

The playground at the back of the school was as primitive as one could be—rectangular in shape with an oval track not clearly marked in the centre and with some space for a little soccer practice and other sports. It was located some distance from the main school building. Boys played on the east side and girls on the west.

The grounds were almost totally lacking of grass and in the main there was mostly dirt with small pebbles, which made playing soccer awkward for me. The girls generally did rope skipping and the more athletic of them would do some running. There were never any real competitive events just general athletic activities during school break for lunch.

In addition to the academic studies, a part of overall development toward self-sufficiency was to travel to the Southern

Senior public school every Thursday for vocational and technical training.

Since I did not have a bicycle or access to transportation, I walked from Hawkins Hill to Southern Senior, which was located in the same place it still stands, the junction of Wulff Road and Collins Avenue.

They tried to teach us carpentry. On reflection, I would guess that I was their most notable failure. The boys were skilled with measuring pieces of wood and then sawing them into a "T" joint.

"Hey, Barrie, you should pray and hope you ain't ever going to build a house when you get out of school unless it is going to be for a blind man."

My acid reply: "I don't plan on building anything because you guys will do it for me."

Lunch at Southern Senior was memorable for the wrong reason. I had maybe a potted meat sandwich for lunch and an orange soda. And, how can I forget, a coconut tart. Sally B, we called her, made a tart that, although tasty, was so heavy it felt like lead in your stomach. I always felt full after one of those tarts—but perhaps a not-so-healthy means of satisfying a growing body.

We were fortunate to have all good teachers at Eastern Senior but there was one teacher in particular who caused my heart and the hearts of many other young boys to flutter pretty wildly. Corinne Gibson, all of nineteen years, taught us English. She was the prettiest woman who even walked the face of the earth. The highlight of each school day, except Thursday, was to be taught by Ms. Gibson.

"Barrie."

"Yes, Ms. Gibson."

"Will you help me move this desk to the window?"

"Yes ma'am."

The other boys would look at me with daggers in their eyes, or was it just pure envy.

I would like to believe that I was her favourite but I am sure that was pure fantasy?

Even before my class graduated from Eastern Senior, Ms. Gibson married Hubert Fountain. They lived in the Fountain family homestead, which was just east of the Model Bakery on

Dowdeswell Street, a two-storey green building made mostly of concrete. It didn't matter because she was still the prettiest girl around, and with the warmest smile you could ever imagine.

Could she have possibly known that she had totally captured my young and immature heart? I wondered. In the law of nature and human behavior, women are intuitively equipped to perceive when men, however young, are attracted to them: a noticeable swoon is probably the answer.

Donald W. Davis, the principal, exacted total obedience from the entire student body. Yes! He was feared but on the other hand he was one "helluva" teacher. He took such satisfaction in being able to push willing students to academic heights beyond what the students felt they could achieve.

There are those of us who on talking about getting an education in Nassau will say with undisguised pride that we attended "The Government High School" (GHS) but Eastern Senior was the academic womb in which the embryo of intellect was nurtured and developed. I am proud to say that I attended Eastern Senior school.

Donald W. Davis, as principal and teacher, was an unrelenting disciplinarian—the ruler, widely known within the school, as "the rule—no exceptions." His constant companion was a long, skinny, tan-coloured cane. If you broke the rules the cane was applied with sufficient force, but not cruelly, as an instant reminder of the price for infraction.

I was not worried about Mr. Davis's disciplinarian tendencies because I knew from my time at the Seventh Day Adventist school that no bad act goes unpunished. On more than one occasion, I ended up on the wrong end of Miss Lawrence's leather strap. Added to which my father did not tolerate misbehaviour in the Farrington household and used his leather belt liberally.

I might have been a slow learner with respect to behaviour but learned I did, definitively.

Graduation from Eastern Senior was a nonevent for me. And even if there had been some formal occasion, my parents would not have attended. For some reason they never witnessed any of the siblings being recognized at a graduation ceremony at any school and oddly enough, we never felt deprived.

On that final day, two events occurred that stuck with me. With purpose I fearlessly searched for Mrs. Corinne Gibson-Fountain to say goodbye. We met in her classroom, with other students milling about.

"Ms. Gibson," I said.

I still liked to think of her as being single.

"I am on my way. Thank you for guiding me through the years. I am heading to Government High in January."

My eyes sparkled with mischief as I shook hands with her but there was nothing to be added even though I was thirteen years of age.

"Farrington, I expect great things from you at GHS. Remember, it is all up to you to get high marks."

This she said with a warm smile playing gently in her face. I knew then I would always remember her.

And then there was the solemn, mature (at least I thought so) handshake with Donald W. Davis. He stared straight into my eyes unblinking and gave me fatherly advice.

"Farrington, you have a willingness to learn, use the chance at Government High to be the best. You are very fortunate to have been awarded a scholarship. Use it wisely and good luck."

Surprisingly, words stuck in my throat because it became an emotional moment. Entrance to GHS was not automatic—a highly competitive entrance examination had to be taken and only high achievers were accepted.

"Mr. Davis, thank you for encouraging me I just hope that I get through okay and that I can make my mom and dad proud of me. And by the way, I am so glad I avoided the fury of your cane. The Lord was on my side."

Mr. Davis laughed, one of the few times he did in the years I attended Eastern Senior. I took that special memory with me.

Our school systems were very much anglicized. Students were never called by their Christian names and thus it was "Farrington this, and Farrington that." Earle and Ramon attended Government High school at the same time, so it was Farrington I and Farrington II.

The scholarship for Government High school was heaven-sent. In order to be accepted at that school, every applicant had to sit an entrance examination. Earle and Ramon did well in the examinations and were accepted but they were required to pay school fees. Without a scholarship I might not have been able to go there because my parents would have been hard-pressed to find the money to send me.

No one can explain destiny but in my opinion there is a force that governs our universe and those who inhabit it, and there is an undeniable path that we follow notwithstanding all the forces that swirl around us. In some mysterious way, we become what we are destined to be.

With clenched right fist, J. Barrie projects a look of confidence

CHAPTER 11

THE GOVERNMENT HIGH SCHOOL

With the memory of Eastern Senior behind me, I felt more confident in myself and looked forward with unfettered excitement to begin my time at Government High School (GHS).

The class of 1949 was the twenty-fifth class of GHS and I was one of the twenty-seven students enrolled in that January term. In keeping with customs during the student assembly, a roll call of new students was made. Can you imagine having your name called and being recognized? We stood one at a time when our names were called:

Donald Archer	John Barrie Farrington
Everette Cartwright	Wellington Drexel Gomez
Luther Donaldson	And so on.
Bertram Evans	

There I stood in my new school uniform—royal blue shirt, white pants and polished black shoes—bursting with pride. At this point I could not begin to imagine fully what the year ahead held for me, but I knew the significance of my being at GHS.

There was, however, that voice in my head that gently reminded me of my promise to my parents to succeed.

Imagine being at GHS. This was the ultimate.

GHS opened in 1925 as the first state-supported secondary school in The Bahamas. It was located in Nassau Court next to the public works department. In order to accommodate the entire student body that had grown through the years, the Good Samaritan Building was leased and several classes were housed there.

Even though government supported, attendance for the majority of students was not free; tuition was ten pounds per year. Fortunately, a few scholarships were awarded annually. My good fortune was that I received a scholarship, a blessing for my parents.

The GHS, because of its goal-stretching curriculum, produced many very smart scholars. The achievement bar for students was never compromised by the faculty. Hugh Sands, Head Boy, was intellectually gifted and always acknowledged during his successful business career that "one could only gain entry into GHS on meritocracy." Hugh later on in his career became Head Master of GHS and subsequently Managing Director of the Barclays Bank group in the Bahamas.

As I stood on the threshold of the next stage of my life, it seemed like yesterday that my parents had received my acceptance letter. The short letter was written by hand and without flourish.

Although very simple and straightforward, the just over fifty-word letter carried with it such tremendous potential and turned out to be one of the most important letters in my life. It read:

> Eastern Senior School
> East Shirley Street
> 9 December 1948
>
> Dear Mr. Farrington,
> I beg to inform you that your son Barry has been awarded a New Providence Scholarship for a period of four years. I wish to congratulate you on your son's achievement.
> Details in regards to the signing of documents for admittance in January 1949 to The Government High School will be sent to you shortly.
>
> Respectfully Yours,
> D.W. Davis

Dr. A. Deans Peggs was the headmaster of GHS. He is best remembered for the eleven words he uttered on each occasion when he was about to impose disciplinary action—"Good gracious, boy! Have you taken leave of your senses?"

Dr. Peggs, during his tenure, wrote a short history of The Bahamas. A few of the senior students, including me, were recruited to assist with the review just to be sure there were no obvious errors and that pages were properly numbered. We felt quite privileged to assist in this relatively minor way.

In summer months, Dr. Peggs' school attire was special—white shirt, white shorts, white long stockings, and white shoes—much like what would be a sailor in the English Navy. We never considered it an oddity.

I was definitely not valedictorian material but I thoroughly enjoyed school.

Because I did not have a bicycle in the early years, I walked from Hawkins Hill to GHS and back home every day. I never thought of it as being deprived but merely a reality of life.

The staff of GHS was a mixture of foreign and Bahamian teachers. Mr. C.V. Bethel was a tough, no-nonsense teacher, but approachable. He taught us geography and Spanish. For some reason, I decided to test his humour. One morning before class was called to order I approached him at his desk.

"Mr. Bethel, I have a moral question that I wish to present to you."

He replied, "Okay, Farrington, what is it?"

I proceeded, "Should you blame or penalize a person for something they did not do?"

Mr. Bethel did not hesitate for a moment before replying, "Of course not, Farrington."

I then added, "Well, Mr. Bethel, I did not do my geography homework last night."

He looked at me with a wry smile, a hint of humour in his eyes and said, "Farrington, get back to your desk."

Mrs. Anatol Rodgers taught English and Latin. She set very high standards for our class and did not tolerate slackness by any student. And yet, I always had this feeling that she cared deeply about us and our success.

As we moved up to a different Form each year, it was not unusual for us to have different teachers. In my final year, our Latin teacher was Marjorie Davis. Despite all best efforts, there was nothing in my mind that could make Latin stimulating but this did not matter. Latin was one of the subjects to be included in our Cambridge Matriculation Exams. I studied exceedingly hard. I virtually memorized every line of Virgil Aeneid and yes, I still came up short.

However, overall, I did get a Grade II result.

Barbara Hawkins, a Canadian, was our science teacher and accomplished much in teaching us. Joan Darville sat immediately in front of me. We were friends socially as well because we belonged to the Peter Pan Youth Club created by mom.

Mrs. Hawkins was also a dancer and by some unusual coincidence she taught Joan and me how to tap dance. About a year on, Joan and I performed a tap dance routine in a Peter Pan concert which was held in St. Matthew's schoolroom.

Graduation exercises were not memorable mostly because I did not have any of my family in attendance. There was no real sense of disappointment because I realized that destiny awaited me.

We know the past. We live in the present, but the mystery of the future allows us to dream of what we want it to be. And dream I did.

CHAPTER 12

BEHOLD THE LAMB

Having finally finished my schooling at Government High the previous year, I now enjoyed the freedom that came with being a working man. My employer was Herbert Deal, a public accountant who took me under his wing and provided me with some early guidance in the "numbers" world.

My mother was responsible for me going in this particular direction.

Following my graduation, she said to me, "Barrie, now that you are finished school, what kind of job are you going to apply for?"

I had no idea what I wanted to pursue so my impulsive response was "Gee, Mom, I really don't know" and she said, "Why don't you become an accountant?" to which I responded, "That seems like a good idea." At seventeen years of age, what else do you say?

A week after starting my job, I received my first cheque for £7, a princely sum that I wisely put to use. I also gave my mom a big surprise, an event about which she spoke fondly and frequently for many years to come.

It was early one Friday in mid-January 1954 when I walked east from Herbert Deal's office at the west end of Bay Street.

In my pocket was the envelope that contained my first week's wages. I was brimming with excitement as I passed shops on the south side of Bay Street—City Pharmacy, Fine's Department Store, The Nassau Shop, G.R. Sweeting—all the familiar places I had taken note of while strolling down Bay Street with mom and Millicent Minns on many Saturday evenings.

And then I arrived at my destination, the Royal Bank of Canada, Bay and Victoria branch. I entered the bank feeling pretty satisfied with myself. I was about to open my first bank account.

I deposited all of my money except 2 pounds that I would need for one of the most important events in my life, ever. Bert Pritchard was the bank's manager but I did not need him.

I crossed to the north side and continued to my next destination—Smith's Butcher Shop located next to Maura Lumber Company.

I was poised to execute a transaction with Mr. Smith, the owner, which I can recall today with uncanny clarity. The butcher shop had so much character and in many ways was an extension of Mr. Smith's strong character and sensitive nature.

Upon entering the store from the sidewalk through the single screen door, you were greeted by the smell of a variety of meats including pork chop, bologna, salami and ground beef, some refrigerated and some just freshly butchered, but all carefully and nicely displayed.

What was most striking for me was the layer of sawdust on the floor. I wondered why it was there but never asked the obvious question.

The day turned out quite sunny, making the relatively dark interior of the shop come to life.

Mr. Smith walked toward the counter with a pronounced limp that caused him to shuffle his feet unevenly. As he stood before me I said, "Good afternoon, Mr. Smith."

"Good afternoon, Barrie. How are you? And how are your mom and dad?"

The inquiry was sincere because it was customary to ask about the family when meeting each other. It was definitely a continuing confirmation of the closeness and mutual respect people had for each other in the broader community.

"We are all fine, Mr. Smith. Thank you for asking."

In our community news travelled quickly, an early "grapevine" without any malicious or gossipy content, therefore it was no surprise when he said, "So, Barrie, I understand that you are now working."

"Yes, I am," I responded proudly. "I am working for Mr. Herbert A. Deal, Public Accountant, whose office is on the floor above General Equipment, owned by his brother Freddy Deal."

Mr. Smith added, "This sounds like a good opportunity for you. Accounting?" he mused aloud, "I thought that you might have pursued a career in rugby." But there was a twinkle in his eyes.

"Well to tell you the truth, this idea came from Mom, sir."

"And now, Barrie, what can I do for you today?"

This was my big moment.

"I am here to make a very special purchase for my mom."

Mr. Smith seemed a bit perplexed as he looked at me over the rim of his glasses, and after a brief pause continued, "Okay, Barrie, what I can get you for your mom, who by the way I respect greatly?"

"Well, I got my first week's wages today and I opened an account at the Royal Bank of Canada but I kept some money to make this purchase."

At that very moment an unbelievable happy emotion swept over me. I opened my mouth to speak and at the same time I felt the tears come to my eyes that caused me to look away from Mr. Smith.

I recovered fairly quickly and looking Mr. Smith directly in the eyes, I said, "For a long time I have been dreaming of buying a leg of lamb for my mom. We have never had a leg of lamb for a meal because it was too expensive."

In my mind, I added, *I promised myself that once I started working and from the wages of my first week at work, I would buy a leg of lamb for my dear mother.*

Mr. Smith then said, "Barrie, today we will make your dream come true."

He brought out a leg of lamb that must have weighed 4 to 5 pounds.

"Will this do, Barrie?"

"Yes! It will. Please wrap it for me."

Mr. Smith wrapped the leg of lamb in a double sheet of white paper and secured it with a few pieces of sticky tan tape. I paid for it with a happy heart.

"Goodbye, Mr. Smith, and thanks."

"The best is yet to come," he replied.

I remembered the journey from Smith's Butcher Shop, east along Bay Street, south on Armstrong Street and across Shirley Street passing the homes of Ida Pearce, Edwin Elliott, Louis Dames, the Havens, Seymours, Robinsons, and finally arriving at our home on top of Hawkins Hill with the leg of lamb in my hand and a song in my heart.

I entered the front door and found my mother at the sewing machine. I presented her with the leg of lamb. As she unwrapped the package and saw the leg of lamb, tears began streaming down her face, and needless to say I too was overcome with emotion. No words were spoken. There was no need for words. The quiet look of unrestrained love we exchanged said it all.

As we had a used refrigerator, my mom could keep the leg of lamb fresh until she decided on how and when she would cook it.

There are those moments and events in every life that are permanently stored in the attic of memories which can be recalled for soul recovery. And so it is with the leg of lamb—a constant available reminder of parental love.

Looking to the future with a sense of purpose and confidence

West Dock for fishing boats for charter at Nassau Yacht Haven

CHAPTER 13

NASSAU YACHT HAVEN

At eighteen years of age and having gained employment with Herbert Deal, Public Accountant, I was feeling buoyantly confident about my future. In addition to being paid a weekly salary, I also made extra money working at Hobby Horse Hall in the parimutuel on race days. Herbert Deal's company was in charge of all financial matters connected with the management of the race track.

The season for horse racing commenced in January and covered thirteen weeks with race days being Tuesdays and Fridays. Once the season was finished, Herbert Deal and Garth Kemp, Herbert's business partner, were required to complete and report on all financial matters to the owner Dr. Raymond Sawyer who, coincidentally, was a member of parliament.

During the post-season cleanup of business matters, I was required to assist but my inexperience was so pronounced that my involvement was minimal. But it was a time of learning.

My base rate of pay was seven pounds per week, which was not a princely sum but it was a good initiation into the business world. The extra money earned while working on race days came to an end, but I was assured that I would continue to have a position with Hobby Horse Hall for subsequent seasons.

And then May 1954 the unexpected happened. Herbert called me into his office with Garth Kemp to advise that his company could no longer continue my employment. However, he added that he had been able to secure for me a position at the Nassau Yacht Haven at a higher rate of pay.

My reaction was subdued but at least I was not being abandoned.

And so it was on the 14th June 1954 I joined the Nassau Yacht Haven in the small accounting office as an operator of the Burroughs Sensimatic Accounting machine. It did not take long for me to become skilled in the operating of this machine.

The change of jobs turned out to be the most fortuitous event of my life.

New Management of Pilot House Club, 1968

Front row [L to R]: Barrie, Konrad Zeilman and Bernard Perron
Middle row: Thomas Roberts, Florence Pritchard and Susan Pinder
Back row: Sylvia Roberts, Edward Kemp, Paula Rice and Eddy Bethel

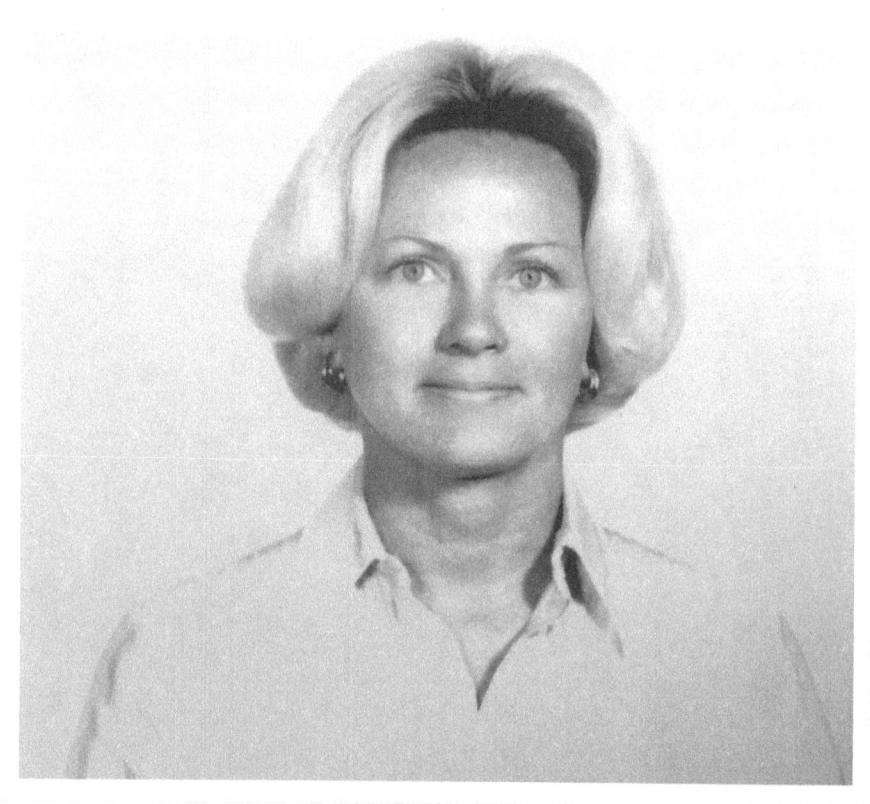

Lee Rose

CHAPTER 14

LEE ROSE

During the four years since joining Nassau Yacht Haven, I've had the experience of growing into manhood and sowing wild oats, then coming to the realization that life had to take on a more serious and responsive structure. It was as this crossroads where I saw myself and knew that I had to establish a more stable foundation for my life.

At twenty-one years of age, I felt spiritually hollow and in this state I recognized the need for some kind of stabilizing force. Once during that time, I was spectating at a girls' basketball game at the court located in the grounds of St. Francis Xavier Church off West Hill Street. The question for me is "Why was I there to begin with?" It was while I was at this crossroad that I, from afar, was attracted to Lee Rose Hall and was smitten by her vibrancy on the basketball court. I was hooked.

Lee Rose at sixteen years of age was faced with surviving in a somewhat hostile world on her own because of an irreparable disagreement with her father, Roderick Hall. She had no choice but to leave the family home at Coral Harbour.

Lee Rose could have gone down the wrong path but she was a good athlete, fortunate to have been recruited by Betty Cole to play on her girls' basketball team, the Dizzy Dames. Lee Rose was outstanding.

She was living with a distant relative in a home on Armstrong Street, a situation that was not good for her. Betty, being aware of the circumstances arranged for Lee Rose to move in with her family on Sears Road. Betty's father, the Honourable A.K. Cole, treated Lee Rose as if she were a daughter.

The Dizzy Dames played some of their matches at the court at St. Francis Xavier Church on West Hill Street. For some reason, I attended some of the practice sessions of the team. It was at one of these practices that I saw her in motion and was immediately captivated by this young, very pretty, athletic girl who seemed to possess a sense of purpose. I didn't know her age but I knew that the attraction was like being struck by a lightning bolt. When we were introduced, there was an immediate connection which, as time passed, became stronger and stronger.

Here I was in August 1957 making a quiet commitment to make her happy forever. Our romance was intense. We had eyes only for each other. We talked with each other at length and learned a lot about each other, which heightened our belief in our destiny of being together forever.

In a way, it was a background of unhappiness that bound us together. We realized that we were both products of a dysfunctional family life.

When we decided to marry, it seemed like a very natural outcome. However, because she was sixteen, her father had to give his consent in writing.

Lee Rose knew that any encounter with her dad was likely to be unpleasant. So, together we drove to the house on Coral Harbour Road and with considerable trepidation walked through the front door. Roderick, upon seeing his daughter shouted at her, "What the hell are you doing here? Get out. Get out of here right now!" Lee Rose did not risk being defiant so she withdrew to wait for me in the car.

With that introduction, I was scared beyond belief but knew that I had to stand my ground.

"Mr. Hall, with respect, I have come to ask your consent to marry Lee Rose."

He looked at me a long time. It felt like an eternity. I tried not to fidget and above all I wanted to appear respectful even though beneath the surface, deep anger and resentment were replacing my fear almost like a bush fire out of control.

Finally, with a deep sigh, he said, "You look like an intelligent young man. I give you my consent for you to marry Lee Rose."

Do you believe in fairly tales or in the destiny of two persons being brought together for better or worse irrespective of circumstances?

And so Lee Rose and I, with hands clasped together, stood looking deeply into each other's eyes. We believed that we were about to start our special voyage to a distant shore of love and happiness where the chains of unhappiness would be loosened and cast aside.

We had fun together and felt invincible against the dark forces that had occupied our lives for so long.

We decided to marry on December 13, 1957, which was a Friday. Since we were not superstitious, there was no hesitation in setting the date, and besides our marriage would get off to a good start with the joy of spending our first Christmas together. We did not expect Santa to come to us but attending church on Christmas Eve was, to us, a confirmation of our being made over.

The wedding was at St. Matthew's Anglican Church and Father Lambert, the priest in charge, performed the ceremony. It was a small affair. Lee Rose's mother and father did not attend. This was expected.

I have a recollection of our standing together looking into the faces of family and friends in attendance, and Lee's eyes glistening with tears. I knew that mingled in the tears of happiness were tears of sadness because she knew at last that the relationship with her parents was gone forever.

I whispered, "My dearest Lee, the future belongs to us and the past is the past."

She nodded and held on to me more tightly.

I also recall standing before Father Lambert and saying our vows of marriage with unhesitating conviction and commitment.

Jerry Lewless, my best friend, was the best man and Mag Darville was bridesmaid.

The reception was held at the home of the Honourable A.K. Cole on Sears Road. He kindly paid for the reception in keeping with custom. He was a "father" to Lee while she lived there and Betty was a sister.

Robert H. "Bobby" Symonette proposed the toast to me and in his humourous style wished us happiness, good health and—as a quote from a constituent from Steventon, Exuma—"I wish you life until glass rottens." In the back of my mind all I could think was *"Oh boy! That is indeed a long life."*

Friday the 13th was such a big day in our young lives. Maybe we should have given more thought to it.

We lived with my parents for a while. We were young and somewhat inexperienced. We knew so little about birth control but we were happy and in love. And behold, Lee became pregnant quickly. Her pregnancy was not too difficult and she continued to work at a travel agency located on Bay Street well into the eight month. Delivery was without complication and Dr. Andrew Esfakis was the attending physician throughout her pregnancy. Our first son, John Barrie Jr., was born on 26 September 1958.

We were managing our lives fairly well with the help of my mother. And then Lee told me that she was pregnant once more. It was, in a way, unexpected but we had to deal with it.

Robert Bruce was born on 17 August 1959.

Living with my parents was not ideal. I was determined that we have our own home before too much time had passed.

With our savings, we purchased a piece of land on Prince Charles Drive. Walter Key, husband of my Aunt Ernestine, was a builder, who upon her direction drew a house plan that was modest in design but would have been sufficient for our needs. I was able to arrange a mortgage through Kelly's Lumber Yard, owned by Trevor Kelly. My employer, Bobby Symonette, guaranteed the mortgage. Walter built our first house and by the time Bruce was eighteen months old, we moved into our home.

Lee, though not well educated, was smart and intelligent. Even with two children to care for, she continued to work;

therefore we engaged Patricia, a young woman, as housekeeper. She was very good with John and Bruce.

My drive to be successful was pushing me forward in a way that virtually became all-consuming. This blind ambition of mine was largely due to a deep-seated and unforgiving obsession to be totally different from my father. He had failed to deliver on his dreams and each failure was placed at the feet of someone other than himself. My mother bore the brunt of such failures.

*A modest start on Prince Charles Drive
with our sights set on a bright future*

*Standing in carport is Mom, Pearl Melinda, leaning on the car is
Lee Rose, standing on the lawn is Dad, Ira W.,
and on the tricycle is Robert Bruce*

CHAPTER 15

MY FIRST HOME

Happy in our new house, Lee Rose and I were fully engaged with trying to make it comfortable and yet tiny cracks of differences began to invade our relationship.

We struggled to maintain some semblance of financial stability. In addition to my primary job at the Nassau Yacht Haven, during the first four months of each year I worked at the Hobby Horse Hall, which was owned by Dr. Raymond Sawyer.

Race days were Tuesdays and Fridays. My initial job was in the parimutuel, which entailed making sure all the ticket dispensing machines were ready for ticket sales between races. This required changing codes and taking sample tickets for distribution to all cashiers at the "pay out" windows.

Three years after doing this job, I was promoted to chief cashier in the money room. Although there was more money to be made, it meant longer hours.

A typical race day started at the Royal Bank of Canada collecting the cash needed for the day. At the end of the day, cash receipts were collected and counted. The cash was transported under police protection to the Royal Bank of Canada. For security reasons, the money was under dual control—Garth Kemp and I were so assigned.

Without really thinking of consequences, I then would return to my office at Nassau Yacht Haven and work until midnight.

One night while working late, Marteca Hartley was walking by the office and saw me at my desk. Mrs. Hartley and her husband, Bronson Hartley, operated an underwater helmet diving business from the Yacht Haven. She came into the office and after a few social exchanges looked at me in a most serious manner.

"Barrie, I have noticed that you work late frequently. Let me tell you something that you should take to heart. I know that you have young children. If you continue to work the way you are doing, they will grow up and you will have missed the happiness of sharing their lives while they get older."

When the naked truth is given, however well-intentioned, it's not uncommon to react as I did that evening.

"Marteca, I understand what you are saying, but how am I to support my family if I don't work hard?"

"Barrie, only you can find the right path but you can avoid looking back with regret by changing now."

Her words of advice rattled around in my head for days and weeks. *How can I change from who I am and what I am doing?*

I remembered reading somewhere that "there are none as blind as those who refuse to see." So in the end what did I do? I continued on hoping for all to be okay. My ambition would contribute mightily to what was destined to be a bad outcome. And then a tragedy struck that almost took my beloved Lee Rose to the other side.

Five years into our marriage in 1961, Lee had a miscarriage. All seemed to be okay but she developed an infection that did not respond well to antibiotics. She had to be airlifted to Miami to the Mount Sinai Hospital. She was placed in the care of Dr. Anderson, who after a thorough examination did not mince his words when he told me, "Your wife is extremely ill and quite frankly I would not give two cents for her life at this moment."

I was devastated. *This could not be happening to my Lee Rose.*

I spent long hours every day at her bedside. Through my brother-in-law, Gordon Carey, arrangements were made for me to stay with a business associate in Miami. Sleep at nights was evasive and extremely difficult as I expected a phone call at any minute from the hospital giving me bad news. There is no way to describe the fear and sense of hopelessness that held me ruthlessly captive. Fortunately, no such phone call came.

And then one day, a most frightening and unexpected event happened. As done on previous days, I made my way to the hospital and went straight to Lee's room. The room was totally empty as if there had never been a patient there. My heart started beating wildly. I virtually stopped breathing. Dreaded fear gripped me mercilessly and then a nurse entered the room and seeing my extreme degree of agitation quickly told me, "Mr. Farrington, don't be upset but your wife was taken for a dialysis treatment."

"Nurse, you cannot begin to know how fearful I was. When I left last night there was no word about a treatment being given this morning?"

I felt tears welling up in my eyes and my body being sapped of all energy.

During the days that followed, Lee started to regain her strength even though her diet consisted of boiled white rice and apple sauce.

While I was with Lee, our sons, John and Bruce, were taken care of by my parents. Somewhat surprisingly my dad spent playful times with the boys far beyond any time with me. It gave me pause and a question, why not with me?

Lee's serious illness made me assess our relationship in a way that brought me agony of enormous proportions. We were brought together in marriage for better and or worse. Our love, which was real, seemed never to be sufficient to sustain us—for love requires emotional, spiritual, intellectual and physical growth all in harmony, and a model to follow, but for us there was no model.

How does love change to unhappiness and eventually to bitterness?

My quest to succeed created a type of blind ambition that drove me to work exceedingly hard almost night and day. But I found time for sports.

Our marriage was suffering in spite of all that was being done to make our life together more comfortable. I thought that what I was doing really mattered but Lee didn't see it that way. Lee was strong-willed and very smart but she was not the easiest person to communicate with because in many ways she was combating the incredibly bad parts of her own history.

And when Lee became seriously ill, with it came the realization that our life together was of the utmost importance.

Lee came through her death-defying ordeal with a strong purpose for the love of life. After being released from the hospital and returning to Nassau, she began the slow climb back to a healthy and vibrant life. We were happy together. The question was, *would it last?*

A short while before departing from the hospital, Dr. Anderson told us that Lee would in all likelihood not be able to have any more children. But then a miracle happened. Lee became pregnant, and after much gentle care and attention, Andrew Scott was born on 7 September 1963.

On a rational level, the birth of Scott should have been the glue that made our marriage undissolvable but this was not the outcome. As our relationship evolved, it was becoming evident that we were growing into different people. Where Lee wanted to spend every Sunday, all day on the beach, I chose to play tennis or baseball or worked on projects at home or at the office.

While all this was swirling around in our lives, I decided I wanted to be actively involved in politics. I felt that I could make a difference in the development of our country.

Lee could not comprehend my interest in politics, which became a serious and continuing source of mutual discontent.

Given the deterioration in our relationship and the accompanying unhappiness, we should have tried to find a way to reconcile our differences and begin again, but the bitterness worsened and life together was nearing to an end that carried unintended consequences.

Our severe disagreements resulted in Lee moving out and staying with her sister. I always persuaded her to come home with the sacred promise of doing better but, like an alcoholic I had relapses.

For John and Bruce, life at home was most unsettling and might have been emotionally scarring.

It was ironic that we were arriving at the crossroads of our lives and even though we could not discount the love that had made us one, it was becoming more and more evident that our stars of destiny were no longer aligned with harmony.

Despite it all, we would sit on the patio that overlooked the garden with special fruit trees for which we collectively dug large holes in the limestone rock for planting. It was a family effort all around.

Lee and I searched within our souls for common ground.

"Barrie, what are we to do? The love that joined us together has changed so much and there are no good answers."

"Lee, I wish that I could explain what has gone wrong. It just seems that we did not grow emotionally and intellectually in the same way as we did when the passion of our love overcame all. We should avoid destroying each other."

"My dear, you have worked hard and you are a good provider. But, now you are in the middle of a political situation that makes me uncomfortable. We have so little in common with people with whom you are associated. It is not the life that I want to be a part of."

It was funny sitting and talking with Lee like this. It was all so natural but at the same time confusing. Lee was a pretty woman, with sparkling blue eyes, a pert little nose and endearing smile when amused. But I believe that we understood that the end for us was not that far into the future.

And so we continued living within an emotional world that was pretty fragile. Admitting defeat was not to come easily. My political career in a way flourished, as did my participation in various sporting activities.

There are certain historical events that we identify with, situations which on their own would be forgotten instantly except for me there was one that remained. It was about 4:00 p.m. on 22 November 1963. Lee and I with the children were just arriving at the Fort Charlotte baseball diamond when on the car radio the assassination of President John F. Kennedy was announced. Scott was just a few months old and was in his carrier on the back seat of our Chevrolet Fleetwood, licence plate number 1120. This was a used car I purchased from Paul Aranha, with whom I shared many years of my youth and who at a very young age became an airplane pilot—and at a mature age and being ambitious, he started his own airline Trans Island Airways and achieved considerable success. We sat there stunned as was the rest of the world.

In 1962, I campaigned for Geoffrey Johnstone, the United Bahamian Party (UBP) candidate for the Montague Constituency, a very large area with the voting public widely distributed. It was during this campaign that I began to speak at public meetings. Partisan politics was taking on a very ugly appearance. My life was threatened more than once and my family was also subjected to abuse. Though we were not afraid, we were concerned about the future.

As to be expected, Lee became increasingly disillusioned with my political career, and in a way I could understand that. There were a couple of incidents that give an insight to the state of the people during these political campaigns that were beginning to amplify the division among the people of our country.

On one occasion, a political rally for Johnstone was held at Fort Montague. In fact, the Fort itself was quite close. It was night time and the flood lights and loud speakers had been set up strategically. I was to play a very minor role in the night's line-up.

I was called to speak and I don't know what made me pause to more purposely look at the setting and the audience. I felt a deep elation of humility as I stood there because in my mind's eye there emerged an image of me as a boy living on Hawkins Hill in very modest circumstances.

As I began to speak, quite suddenly a man from the audience jumped upon the stage, snatched the microphone from me and shouted, "You are a UBP gangster."

This was Granville Symonette.

The police removed him quickly. I regained my composure and continued my brief comments.

Granville was charged with disorderly conduct and being found guilty had to pay a fine of two pounds.

CHAPTER 16

POLITICS

Here I am at twenty-five years of age, deeply committed to Bahamian politics and acting fearlessly despite the undercurrent of deep-seated discontent that was gaining traction within the country.

In 1961, election campaigning was heating up. Public meetings were held and although boisterous, there were no encounters where harm came to any of the persons attending.

My first political speech happened almost by default. Geoffrey Johnstone was holding a meeting on Rose Street in Fox Hill and he was short of speakers, so he asked me to address the voters. The setup in my opinion was pretty primitive—a used speaker system powered by a car battery. The meeting, however, was well received and without incident other than some heckling. Following that, I became a fixture on the list of speakers for Geoff.

The most memorable and most frightening public meeting was held in the front yard of Ike McKenzie's home on the corner of Kemp Road and Parkgate Road. This night turned out to be a test of courage, willpower and character.

Anticipating there would be trouble, we took precautions. First we ensured that there was a strong police presence and in addition we arranged for a strong contingent of supporters from Five Pound Lot to be amongst the audience.

We were in a very exposed setting. We assembled on the grass just feet from Kemp Road itself. The microphone, amplifier and system speakers were powered by an electrical drop cord from Ike's home. And so the evening began.

I spoke third and while standing there under a single street light, stones and cans were being hurled over the roof of a small building, which was on my immediate right, into the area we occupied. As I spoke, I had to duck frequently in order to avoid being hit in the head or face. It was most uncomfortable and frightening. It was the first time since we had started campaigning that I felt unsafe. To compound this somewhat volatile situation, Mr. Arthur D. Hanna, a candidate for the Progressive Liberal Party (PLP), continued driving up and down the street, generally exhorting the crowd to be disruptive.

Finally the meeting came to an end and it was time to get out of there. Not expecting to be confronted with this kind of situation, I had travelled to the meeting on my Lambretta scooter. This decision was to be almost the cause of bodily harm to me or something worse.

Geoffrey Johnstone was obviously the centre of attention. I calculated that as he moved so would the crowd and it would be at that point I could escape on my scooter.

Geoff moved and so did the crowd. My chance came so I jumped on my scooter and headed for the opening that would take me to Village Road. But no such luck. A person in the crowd saw my move and immediately alerted the crowd accordingly. All of a sudden I was surrounded by a bunch of screaming men who seemed to be intoxicated. They lifted me and the scooter off the ground. Having no escape, I figured that there was not going to be a happy ending. Fortunately for me the police saw the problem and responded swiftly. They disengaged the crowd and cleared a way for me to leave. But, the danger was not quite over. Just as I was driving away, a huge stone was thrown at me and whistled by very close to my head.

I drove as fast as I could and did not look behind.

I made it home safely. Geoff and his brother Peter came to my house on Prince Charles Drive to confirm that I was okay.

Lee was less happy with me than normal because of this incident. We talked at length, which was insightful as it pertained to our life together, but in the end there was pure resignation to what seemed to be inevitable.

Lee and I actually sat holding hands because she realized that despite everything else my ordeal had left me shaken.

"Tell me exactly what happened, love?" she asked.

These words of endearment caused my heart to miss a beat and for a fleeting moment there flooded through my mind a recollection of happy times past.

"Quite frankly, I was very stupid to drive to the meeting on my scooter. It is now obvious that the political environment is beginning to rapidly change. I never thought that violence would seep into our society."

I recited the events of the evening.

"Well, Barrie, you were very lucky to escape without being hurt."

I could sense a certain sadness coming from her and a hint of tears was evident. In silence we sat there with private thoughts swirling around wildly. For me, I felt a deep sense of regret. Fate had set a course and there was no turning back.

Electioneering continued at an ever-increasing tempo and I remained faithful to my own pursuits. For Lee and me, there was the occasional moment of levity and family that lightened the emotional load.

We were holding a public meeting on Lincoln Boulevard but on this particular evening I was not speaking. I stood in the crowd, which in the main was well behaved. Peter Graham was speaking in support of Geoff. He said, "I can assure you that Geoffrey Johnstone is a man of integrity."

Standing next to me, two older women turned to me and one asked, "Who got this ting, integrity?" What could I say except the obvious? "He is a very good man."

The outcome of the General Elections in 1962 was not viewed with confidence by the leadership of the United Bahamian Party.

In fact, I gathered there was a pretty strong feeling that the Progressive Liberal Party would win. But then the unpredictable occurred.

Prior to 1962, women did not have the right to vote. Considered in the context of universal suffrage in other countries, this made The Bahamas an oddity. In 1961, however, the United Bahamian Party enacted legislation that gave women the right to vote and this turned out to be pivotal in the General Elections. The UBP's win at the polls was definitely attributed to the support of the women voters.

As to be expected, much speculation ensued as to the cause of the outcome. There was one common thread of thought that served to explain what had happened at the polls. The explanation most widely accepted was that women with families, who were generally responsible for keeping the family together, were not prepared at that stage to support political change for fear of a result that could upset economic stability. Of course, this thinking would evolve into a different mindset, which the Progressive Liberal Party used to great advantage the next time around.

On a personal level, 1962 represented another move forward with my political commitment to make a positive contribution to the country's development and wherever possible participate in effecting change in political philosophy and practice.

The euphoria of a political victory for Geoffrey Johnstone, 1962

L to R: Harold Eldon, Peter Johnstone, Jack Moree, Geoffrey Johnstone, J. Barrie, and an unknown

CHAPTER 17

ROAD TRAFFIC AUTHORITY

I was appointed chairman of the Road Traffic Authority though at twenty-six years of age I was unsure of my ability to capably carry out the responsibilities of this Authority.

Frank Ashmole, an Englishman, was at this time engaged by The Bahamas Government to be Controller of Road Traffic Department. He was a somewhat reserved gentleman who seemed to be constantly smoking a pipe but despite this idiosyncrasy he performed his job very competently and the advice given was always sound.

The first and most important step to take as chairman was to become totally familiar with content of the Road Traffic Act. I was determined to do the job to the best of my ability.

The Authority comprised five appointed members, one of whom was Donald Sands, a good friend and political ally. Donald was one of the most dedicated and transparently honest men that you could have by your side.

Donald once said to me, "Barrie, I believe in my country and I want to serve in any capacity to make it a better place for all."

As it happened, we were having lunch at the Pilot House Club when he made this statement. I thought for a brief moment and replied, "I feel strongly that in some way we, along with others of our age, sense the urgent need to effect improvement in the way our country is managed."

Donald smiled as he wiped his glasses and said, "It is a tall order but we must try."

For a reason I never quite understood, Donald was accompanied to lunch by his office associate, Sandy Isaacs. She was to make notes but I believe he merely wanted to make an impression.

The function of the Authority was prescribed by Statute. It was a legal requirement that we discharged our responsibility with complete transparency.

The Authority was requested to consider all licence applications for the taxicabs, public bus transportation, tour cars and requests for the varying of existing licences. With respect to applications for private or public omnibus service, applicants were required to provide information on routes to be served, frequency of service, and fares to be charged.

All applications had to be gazetted so that any person willing to object to an application would have sufficient time to lodge such an objection with the Authority. The Authority was obliged to hear all applications in an open forum, which was always done in magistrate's court. This kind of sitting afforded applicants to act on their own or through legal representation and this was the situation for objection as well.

It was within the power of the Road Traffic Authority to set dates for public hearings and relevant notices, which were published with sufficient time for applicants and objectors to finalize preparations for appearing before the Authority. And then the time came for our first Authority sitting in the magistrate's court on Bank Lane. Mr. Ashmole had carefully and patiently coached me and members on how the hearing should be conducted.

On the day of our very first meeting, my nervousness was palpable. I played over many scenarios as to how the hearing would go. I had prepared for the sitting with excruciating care and yet the tension mounted. And then the moment came. I took my seat, which under every other circumstance would be occupied by a magistrate. I looked into the court and felt glad that there were mostly lawyers in attendance who were representing applicants and others who had a vested interest in the outcomes of the hearing.

I took a deep breath and with as much confidence as I could muster brought the meeting to order.

"Good afternoon. I welcome you on behalf of the Road Traffic Authority to this our first official meeting of 1962. I hope that we will be able to deal with all matters in an efficient and productive manner."

And then the meeting began. There were no contentious issues on this occasion, which was a relief but that was not to be the case always. At the fourth meeting of the year, I was to experience the litmus test of my chairmanship. An application was before us and Mr. Arthur D. Hanna was representing the applicant. There were certain aspects of the presentation that were not strictly conforming to the Act and the attendant Regulations. The exchanges between us were pretty lively but not aggressively so. In the end, he wanted approval of his client's application despite the difficulty with interpretation of the law.

Mr. Hanna advanced his position. "Mr. Chairman, it is wrong to withhold approval of my client's application given that if he is unable to operate his business as he deems fit, he will suffer financially, which could have an impact on his ability to adequately support his family."

"Mr. Hanna," I replied, "the Authority will not reject the application but with all due respect we cannot approve this application without the benefit of legal advice from the Office of the Attorney General. To repeat the application of your client will remain alive but at this time is not approved."

Mr. Hanna looked at me somewhat quizzically bordering on distain but thank goodness some of his legal colleagues who were also in attendance for other applications murmured to him, "A.D., you know the chairman is right." And so that crisis passed. For the remainder of my term as chairman of the Road Traffic Authority, there were no noteworthy incidents of contrariness.

*Captain of The Bahamas Softball Team
participating in the World Softball Championships
in Mexico City, 1968*

CHAPTER 18

SPORTING ACTIVITIES

While serving as chairman at the Road Traffic Authority, I also served on the Bahamas Sports Commission under the chairmanship of Basil T. Kelly, Member of Parliament for the Crooked Island District. The Commission was established mainly because of the representations made by the younger Members of Parliament. There was a very strong demand for the construction of a comprehensive sports centre in Nassau. The government fully understood this need.

In the midst of all that was happening in my life, I was totally addicted to playing every sport in which I was reasonably competent irrespective of the lack of sporting facilities.

The Bahamas Baseball Association was formed on 28 August 1954. Subsequently the executive team comprised Hiram Lockhart, president, Reno Brown, secretary and Lester Mortimer, commissioner. Some of the teams that were accepted into the Association and the league were Winnie Ann Reds, St. Bernards, Penny Bank, Burns House (formerly the Ahepas) and I Need-A-Laundry.

We played on the Western Fort in the shadow of Fort Charlotte. Though the conditions were primitive, we were determined to make good with what we had. It was necessary to make special rules to allow for physical constraints. For instance, the distance down the right field to the ridge that sloped down toward Bay Street was about 250 feet. A ball hit on the fly over the right-field ridge was limited to a double.

The Association's leadership was creative, which added to the excitement and quality of play. One such initiative was determining what a home run was. There was no fence to delineate the outfield and no signage marking distances from home plate. The selection was pure genius and at the same time quaint.

Through discussions and negotiations between officers of the Bahamas Baseball Association, team managers and umpires, it was patently apparent that there was little choice but to apply "special" rules for balls that were hit beyond players in the outfield. It was therefore essential to be very creative as the topography did not lend itself to normal baseball regulations and dimensions. And thus the "special" applied rules were as follows:

Any ball hit on the fly to the left of the designated sea grape tree and landed beyond the boundary and onto the sloping ungraded patch of land was to be ruled a home run. Any ball hit into this designated area but rolled over the ridge was declared a triple. Another special rule had to be made for balls hit down the left field line and bounced off the face of the rocky outcrop. Runners were allowed to advance at their own risk.

Despite the physical handicaps of the baseball diamond, we produced some outstanding players, including Andre Rodgers, Tony Curry, Lionel Rodgers, Ed Armbrister and Edmund Moxey, to name a few.

The Burns House team had substantial visible support from ownership. Every game played was attended by Winnie Sands, wife of Sir Stafford Sands, and her daughter, Teddy. Their constant presence stimulated the team to perform to the best of our ability.

It was obvious that a proper baseball facility was required.

We also created a soccer league. All matches were played on the Western Fort as well but immediately east of the baseball field.

Although the soccer pitch was of regulation size according to international guidelines, the surface was appallingly bad and exceedingly hard. Notwithstanding, competition was tough between some of the top teams—Police, St. Georges, Sea Scouts and Westerns.

It was not unusual to play baseball in the morning and then change attire to play soccer in the afternoon. Peter Isaacs and I on any number of occasions made such a changeover. We both played baseball for Burns House.

While playing for the Sea Scouts one year we won the championship. We were presented with our floating trophy by the sponsor, the Honourable Herbert McKinney, owner of John S. George and Company.

I subsequently played for St. Georges, a team loaded with talented players such as Rinky Isaacs and Bob Isaacs. To those of us who played on the Western Fort, there was also recognition of the need for a proper soccer pitch.

The Western Fort was the centre for sporting activities of all kind. Although not a participant, I witnessed several multifaceted track and field events. The contestants were generally members of a sporting club such as St. Georges, St. Bernards and Police.

In particular, I remember one sun-drenched Friday afternoon when final events were scheduled. One such race was the 200-yard dash. For years Rinky Isaacs was the stellar and uncontested sprinter in The Bahamas. However, on this day Tommy Robinson was in the lineup. When the starting gun sounded, it was evident that it was a two-man race. Rinky tried to keep pace but Tommy ran beautifully and powerfully. In the end there was no contest. Tommy was the new king.

For me another event that was memorable not so much for power and grace, but for determination and steel-like nerves involved Charles "Geech" Moss, who was in a tightly contested pole-vault battle with someone who was unknown to me. Geech had one more try to cleanly get over the 10-foot bar. He prepared for this last attempt with a final deep breath and then began the approach with ever-increasing speed to the launching divot. Geech was 6'4" tall and powerfully built, and with the pole planted he elevated himself over the bar with only inches to spare. He was the champion. But the amazing thing to me was that he made this championship leap using a 10-foot "bamboo" pole—a far, far cry from today's modern synthetic poles.

In a woefully inadequate facility on the Western Fort, track and field championship Bahamian athletes were still able to perform at internationally recognized levels of accomplishment.

And thus the mandate for the Bahamas Sports Commission was to produce a complete plan with renderings for the establishment of a sports centre. It would encompass all the sports that needed modern facilities for the conduct of sporting events and for the development of young Bahamians desirous of participating in all such sporting activities.

It was decided early in the deliberations of the Bahamas Sports Commission, and with the approval of government, to establish a comprehensive sporting facility and to do so on the land known as Oakes Field Airport, subsequently named Queen Elizabeth II Sports Centre.

The Commission was diligent in its work and consulted with sporting bodies to ensure that the planning included all essential elements.

This process was the beginning of government's commitment to create a first-class centre for all major sports and simultaneously to ensure that there was efficient and productive administrative management. From my enthusiastic perspective, the creation of the Queen Elizabeth II Sports Centre would be recognizing the great opportunity for uniting people through sports.

Basil Kelly, as chairman, was clearly supportive of the work of the Commission and used his parliamentary office to clear the way for the processing of budgets to cover costs of essential work. It was gratifying to be a full participant in the planning of the Queen Elizabeth II Sports Centre and to witness the groundbreaking for a baseball field and of a track and field stadium. Other sports, including basketball, were on the drawing board.

Yet even without a proper baseball diamond, there was a move afoot to bring change in the management of the Bahamas Baseball Association. Somehow I was pulled into the controversy and persuaded to put my name forward to be Commissioner of Baseball. Oswald Brown was a strong supporter for my election.

A general meeting was called for the election of officers for the next year. The meeting was held at the Mothers Club on East Street opposite to Mortimers Candy Shop. Mortimers was famous for its peppermint candy, a reputation that has continued through the decades.

The content of the meeting at times was somewhat bitter but it was evident that everyone in that meeting had a sincere interest in pushing baseball upward to levels of accomplishment not previously achieved or anticipated.

And then the big moment arrived. Nominations were called for, and the voting process began. My election to Commissioner of Baseball, although surprising, caused me to reaffirm my commitment to make my term in office one in which, with the other officers, substantial success in furthering the sport would be achieved.

The team consisted of Lester Mortimer, Reno Brown, Hiram Lockhart and me. We decided to bring baseball aggressively to the forefront of Bahamian sports.

Lester Mortimer reminded us, "We have a great Bahamian player, Andre Rodgers, playing shortstop for the Chicago Cubs and we need to give him special recognition."

Reno said, "Wouldn't it be outstanding if we could find a way to make a presentation to Andre at Wrigley Field?"

And we all chimed in and put forward a number of suggestions, all of which were quite impressive.

While in this mood, we talked about a special award presentation budget for the Bahamas Baseball Association. Agreement was instant.

Hiram said, "To make the banquet truly spectacular, we should try to get a major league player to be our guest of honour."

We quietly reflected that this was growing into quite an impressive undertaking.

Coincidentally, an offshore bank, the Bank of Washington, sponsor and owner of the Washington Senators, a national league baseball team, was based in Nassau and at that time occupied the building located on the northeast corner of Bay and Victoria Streets. It was subsequently changed to the Myers House and now the Mosko Building.

I suggested we meet with the senior management of the Bank of Washington, Nassau Branch, to explore the prospect of one of the players coming to Nassau for our awards banquet. And by good fortune, we met and were well received but it would be necessary for us to meet and speak with the president of the bank in Washington.

Another bit of good fortune occurred when I approached a successful merchant and outlined what we were attempting to accomplish with the Bahamas Baseball Association. He was enthusiastically impressed with our programme and upon my advancing the proposition of his sponsorship of what we wanted to do, he agreed.

When I reported on the sponsorship approach and the success achieved, we could hardly contain our elation. Reno Brown was the most effusive. "This is wonderful. Just maybe we are on the brink of pushing our association toward a much better future. It will not be easy, but I am sure we can do it."

We all felt the same way.

There were details to be worked out, but in June of 1966, the plan was to travel to Chicago, stay at the Palmer Hotel on Michigan Avenue, and to place ourselves in the hands of Abel Famey, the Bahamas Tourist Board's representative. In fact, the representative was well connected in Chicago and made all the necessary arrangements for a most successful visit.

Our excitement was uncontrollable.

On the appointed day at the home plate of Wrigley Field, Hiram, Lester, Reno and I along with Vince Scully, the voice of the Cubs, acting as Master of Ceremonies, presented a special plaque to Andre Rodgers. Words cannot describe our pride and joy on this occasion.

Later that day, with Andre taking us in tow, we visited with Ernie Banks at his apartment. Could you believe that there we were with Ernie Banks, the greatest player in the Cubs' history?

The next day was extra-special for me, as it was arranged for me to do an interview on radio with the incomparable Jesse Owens. Imagine me sitting there talking with the man who made history in track and field by winning three gold medals in track during the 1936 Olympic Games in Berlin! Adolph Hitler was furious with this outcome. A black man winning so dramatically over Hitler's touted Aryan athletes. This was history changing.

Here was greatness sitting opposite to me and yet I detected a quiet strength, serenity and confidence in who he was as a person. Jessie inquired, "I am interested in The Bahamas. Tell me a little about your way of life."

With my being in tourism, my response was more promotional than emotional. "We have discovered that Americans want to travel in the winter especially, and in The Bahamas we offer the ultimate in a warm weather destination—sun, sand and sea coupled with great and friendly Bahamian customer service."

Trying to recall the full content of Mr. Owens' interview with me is not so easy, as this happened in 1966. However, we did exchange pleasantries at the conclusion.

"Barrie, having you on my show as a part of the Bahamas giving special recognition to Andre Rodgers has been a real pleasure. And, I wish you and your colleagues all the best in the future."

My response, although brief and respectful, gave me the opportunity to add a little humor. "Mr. Owens, it has been a great honor for me to be on your show." With a big smile I added, "You won three gold medals at the 1936 Olympics which was the year in which I was born. On behalf of my country, the Bahamas, I salute you and your greatness."

Hiram, Lester, Reno and I almost experienced disaster before leaving Chicago. After nightclub crawling until 2:00 a.m., we returned to the Palmer Hotel to find many hotel guests standing in the street. There had been a fire on the fourth floor that required guest evacuation. A few hours later, chilled to the bone we were allowed back into our rooms.

Our visit to Chicago was a huge success and then on to Washington, D.C.

Before we departed from Chicago, Andre in his own easygoing way said to us, "You guys are the greatest. You made me feel really, really proud to be a Bahamian and to represent my people at the level I do. I will never forget my day at Home Plate."

The Bank of Washington was an impressive institution. We were received warmly by the bank's president and colleagues. It was obvious that the president had been alerted to the purpose of our meeting and thus we were able to get to the bottom line very quickly.

The president was quite happy to tell us that arrangements would be made for Gil Hodges, manager of the Senators and former great first baseman for the then Brooklyn Dodgers, as well as George Selkirk, president of the Senator organization and former right fielder for New York Yankees, who had the nickname of "Twinkle Toes," to travel to Nassau for our Baseball Banquet.

We returned to Nassau shortly after the meeting quite content with what we'd accomplished.

While I was doing all these things that I seemed driven to do, the situation with Lee Rose was still on the decline. I seemed unable to change direction. Love was there between us but our past histories of upbringing compounded by severe unhappiness haunted us relentlessly. Our conversations became more and more acrid, our differences less and less resolvable.

"Barrie, what are we to do? I don't want to continue to live this way."

When she said this, I felt a sharp pain shoot through my heart.

"Why couldn't I change my life's course?" I asked to myself.

"Lee. I really don't know what we should do, but it is hard to think that we are on the brink of failure despite all we have been through."

Without resolution we continued with our daily living with dark emotional clouds hanging over us.

Would there be restoration for us in the end?

Home Plate at Wrigley Field
L to R: Lester Mortimer, Barrie, Andre Rogers, shortstop for Cubs,
and Vince Scully, the voice of the Cubs

Barrie breaking away from a loose rugby scrum

CHAPTER 19

MORE POLITICS

Once the excitement of the General Election had subsided somewhat, it was time to return to some degree of normalcy. It had been almost eight years since I worked with the public accountant Herbert Deal. During my short time at his firm, it was under his guiding hands that I acquired certain principles and practices that have remained constantly with me.

When I joined the Nassau Yacht Haven and Pilot House Club in 1954, Carl Moree was in charge of our small accounts department. When he moved on, I was given the responsibility. In my new position, I occupied a small office shared with Durward Knowles, who seldom used his desk. Durward is now Sir Durward Knowles, having been knighted by Queen Elizabeth II.

Each morning as I entered my office, I always enjoyed a sense of great pride. I usually walked through to Bobby Symonette's office to peer out of his window to capture the picturesque scenery of the marina and Nassau Harbour. In a way, it reminded me of the "forbidden view" from the second floor of our Hawkins Hill home that I glimpsed as a little boy.

I was sitting at my desk and arranging my work schedule one morning, when Louise Sweeting, who cleaned our office, walked in. Following our usual greeting, she offered to make me a cup of tea. She was such a gentle woman that it made it easy to like her very much.

While tea was being prepared, I continued with the sorting of papers and mail. In the midst of the mail was a letter addressed to me marked "Personal." Because it looked important, my curiosity and excitement rose unabated.

I opened the letter carefully with a silver letter opener that was left there by Carl Moree. The letter was dated 13 December 1962. I read the content very slowly.

> Mr. Barry Farrington
> C/o Nassau Yacht Haven
> P.O. Box N-1216
> Nassau, N.P.
> Bahamas
>
> Dear Barry,
> I do not think that I will ever be able to thank you adequately for all your hard work and sacrifice on my behalf during the recent Election campaign.
> The wonderful effort which you and all the other members of the team put into the campaign was a great inspiration to me and filled me with a determination to win.
> You played a vital part in the organization. Without your help I could never have achieved the victory which was won.
> I hope very much that we will be able to keep our organization going during the next five years and that I may count on you for your continued help.
>
> Yours sincerely,
> Geoff

Geoffrey Adams Dinwiddie Johnstone was a young, energetic and highly qualified lawyer with the long-established law firm of Higgs and Johnson, the partners of which were the Honourable Godfrey W. Higgs and Mervyn Johnson. Geoff was a very good friend and just a few years my senior.

I read the letter through several times. The content had great significance not only because the expression of gratitude was so strong but it gave me cause to reflect on my future, politically and within my family. I knew that I was driving myself relentlessly to succeed in my endeavours. Could it be that there was a strong correlation between my experience growing up in our home on Hawkins Hill and the passion and aggression to win whatever the cost?

My father dreamt of doing great things, and when enterprises faltered or failed, he never blamed himself. From a very young age, I wanted to be vastly different. Having experienced a very harsh and unrelenting General Election, I continued my evaluation of the new boundaries of political activity. Quite frankly I was terribly unsettled by the emerging ferocity of the political activists who were promoting racial division. The young men and women I associated with made no such distinction.

Living on Hawkins Hill where families were truly neighbours made the changing political landscape so foreign and quite worrying to me. While so musing, my mind went back to my high school days and I was quite friendly with Edwin "Apple" Elliott, who lived on Hawkins Hill.

"Apple" was an accomplished pianist and musician at an early age. We played softball at the Government High School for Montague House. It was also the time when my mom held a vision of me being a great pianist and in pursuit of her dream I attended piano lessons with Amy Norton Stuart, who lived on Bay Street just east of Armstrong Street. She was an amazing teacher not only because of the highly skilled level at which she taught but also because she was deaf. This was perplexing to me until I learned later in life that Beethoven one of the world's greatest composers was deaf also.

Somewhere along the way my father acquired an upright piano, a Knabe, which he virtually rebuilt. Being an obedient son, I practiced the piano every day for two hours. There was no passion on my part and as a result a clock was atop the piano. At the expiration of my 120-minute practice, I stopped playing. As a pianist I was mediocre at best. "Apple" on the other hand was a natural and his full development was secure.

Around that time of my youth, my mother had created the

Peter Pan Club for young boys and girls. This club thrived under her leadership and every Friday night was dedicated to various activities for club members. The big event at each year's end was the staging of the Peter Pan variety concert. My mother thought that I should debut my piano playing skills at such a concert. What a frightening thought for me! And then through my creative thinking, obviously self-centered, an idea of some brilliance came to me. Why not play a duet with "Apple" Elliott? Obviously, "Apple" would be leader.

We practiced frequently and we were included in the programme.

On the night of the concert, "Apple" and I were introduced with a certain flourish. There is no recollection of the piece played but Apple was brilliantly magnificent and my supporting role was error free but only adequate.

As we bowed in acknowledgement of the applause, there was for me, relief and at the same time considerable pride.

"Apple" was very kind to me.

"Barrie, you played very well."

He was certainly a great guy.

My first and only public appearance on piano was an illuminating experience. I did not pursue a piano-playing career. Although my mother never expressed her disappointment in my lack of interest, I can candidly say at this moment that I was probably Amy Norton Stuart's most notable failure.

And so it was with life on Hawkins Hill. And so it was with me throughout my life and that was I looked at the piano only as a development phase. In any event, with the United Bahamian Party, the youngest element of which I was one, sought to effect change that brought widespread economic and social development for all Bahamians going about their daily lives with dreams in their hearts as we did. We were making progress.

* * *

While in the midst of this meditative state, Louise interrupted me by placing my cup of tea on my desk. I said, "Thank you, Louise" and almost immediately she left my office, closing the door silently behind her.

My mother taught me a long time ago that ingratitude was sinful. I therefore always say thanks to everyone who assists me irrespective of how big or small the helping hand.

As I was sipping my tea, Wilfred Rolle, nicknamed "Raggy," came into the office. Wilfred was the company's messenger but this position in no way diminished his high intelligence. He never learned how to drive a car and therefore made all his deliveries and trips to the post office on his bicycle.

"Mr. F. Today is going to be very busy. Is there anything special you want done?" he would ask.

"Nothing other than the usual, Wilfred," I replied. "But tell me, tomorrow is race day at Hobby Horse Hall. Do you have any hot tips for the Daily Double?"

Wilfred just laughed and added, "You know how things go there. For the jockeys, the favourites are the ones they want to win."

Wilfred loved going to Hobby Horse Hall because he loved horses and had a long association with jockeys and trainers at the track. Another part of Wilfred of which little was known was the existence of his son who sang and sounded just like Nat King Cole. If you had your eyes closed while he was singing, you would swear that it was Nat crooning.

Another feature of Wilfred that I will always remember is his deformed right ear. As was told to me, the deformity was not natural. He once had a brutal fight over some relatively trivial matter. During this encounter, the guy he was fighting bit off a sizable piece of Wilfred's ear.

He told me that the pain felt like his head was being shattered.

Kiddingly I asked, "What did the other fellow look like after the fight."

Raggy only laughed but there was a look of mischievousness in his eyes. We orbited in different circles but that was by purely unintended circumstances whereas the strength of our friendship enriched our Bahamian existence.

* * *

As with most things that happen in our lives, there is a beginning, middle and an end. Having lived through many episodes that affected my life and the lives of many, I can attest to this truism. There are two stages that are evident namely, the beginning and the end. However, the middle state is determined retrospectively and is an important determination in that it completes the certainty of an event in an historical perspective.

In time following the 1962 elections, I attempted to rediscover my position in life and to remain true to the pursuit of being a positive contributor to Bahamian way of life.

Lee Rose struggled with our togetherness which by any standard was fragile. Our past family demons were consistently attacking our psyche and, yet, we had times of family happiness and peace. I would seek to understand what made me tick but I knew deep down that despite Lee's near brush with death in 1962, she could not reconcile her deep and seemingly unchangeable resistance to being a part of my public life.

I remembered on one occasion when we sat talking on the patio of our home, talking with a kind of honesty that most of the time escaped us.

"Barrie, I wish I could bring myself to be selflessly involved with your way of life. You are an excellent provider but there is much more to our being together."

And again the unsaid question was *"what are we going to do?"*

"My very dear Lee, we made vows to each other on 13th December 1957, with every sincere intention possible. You were just sixteen and I was a very young twenty-one-year-old and we loved each other with the passion of youth. It seems that life has accelerated at a speed that exceeded anything we could have expected. In just a few short years we grew intellectually, spiritually and emotionally and in so growing parts of our beings changed. I think you know that in some fashion I wanted to be integral to nation building."

Lee then said something that startled me but gave me pause for introspection. "Barrie, you think that these people accept you but they don't."

I am sure this was said without rancor. To myself I repeated her words and dwelled on them for several days as I examined my motives, albeit somewhat undefined as to the exact reason for pushing on with my professional career and my political aspirations in the face of a difficult family life.

In the end, I was sure that my resolve was unshakable and that the only acceptance that was important was recognition of me as a Bahamian who was committed to doing good for my country and its people. It was an important reality check for me and made the way to the future clearer and purposeful.

I continued on the path that I had set knowing the risk of an untimely and unwanted end of my life with Lee Rose.

The ensuing years following 1962 were quite eventful.

I was viewed by the Executive Council of the United Bahamian Party as a promising torchbearer of the conservative philosophy of the party. I had worked hard and possibly deserved the recognition but I wanted most to remain a significant member of our young group of aspirants who knew full well that change in the way we governed was badly needed. The "hard backs" of the party were not inclined to move quickly in the direction we were advocating but it was our very strong belief that we could, through perseverance and with determined and deliberative pressure on the leadership, influence meaningful change.

Nobody could deny that the economic template for the country was strongly flawed because the extent to which Bahamians could participate was limited. In fact the two pillars of our economy remain the drivers of economic stability, that is, tourism and financial services. Following the General Elections of 1962, I was selected to serve on the Executive Parliamentary Committee, which I did for a number of years. We met every Friday for lunch at the Montague Beach Hotel in a space located on the mezzanine level.

It was here that I began to learn about how Parliament functioned. Being a young and inexperienced participant, my contributions were limited. However, I do recall a discussion regarding the placing of a Money Bill to the House of Assembly, which they seemingly failed to fully appreciate was going to create unwarranted controversy with the opposition.

Thus I piped up a little hesitantly. "It seems to me that, given the aspect of a huge debate arising following presentation of the Bill, the Minister of Finance could, through his office, issue a special money grant and thus avoid such aggravation."

Sir Stafford Sands, Minister of Finance, looked about through his one good eye and said, "Darn it, Barrie is right."

On another occasion a discussion was held at great length about the police report that the Progressive Liberal Party was planning a massive demonstration outside of Parliament and all precautions had to be taken to ensure safety of members and the public at large. Roy Solomon said that the police had intelligence that indicated the possibility of an attempt to blow up the House of Assembly.

Donald D'Albenas added, "That does not seem logical because the Opposition would still be in the Chamber and thus equally exposed."

Bobby Symonette, the then Speaker of the House of Assembly, said with a smile, "I am sure that if this were true the Progressive Liberal Party members would march out of the Chamber."

Trevor Kelly then quickly chimed in, "Well we should get up and march out of the Chamber with them."

It was all very serious business but the exchange entailed a certain humour that could not be ignored. This situation was another clear signal that the political landscape was on the verge of being dramatically altered. At the conclusion of the meeting, Sir Roland in his own inimitable Eleuthera vernacular said, "Gentlemen, it is expected that as many party supporters should be in the Chamber at the next sitting of the House, which is set for Tuesday, 23 March 1965.

In order to access the public gallery when the House was in session, one required a special pass issued by the Speaker's office. On this fateful day I made my way to the House of Assembly. The crowd on Bay Street was enormous and a substantial police presence stood in Rawson Square and within the precinct of the House of Assembly. It was evident that it was going to be a day of palpable tension with the outcome being anybody's guess. However at the time, other than the noise of the crowd, there was order. Even though I got to my appointed seat without incident I was very nervous and the armpits of my jacket were a little wet with perspiration.

And then came the moment when all Parliamentarians were seated and the House was called to order by the Speaker. The chaplain gave his blessing upon Members. Preliminary matters were attended to without incident but following this was the submission of the report from the Boundaries Commission.

Prior to every General Election, it was a government policy that a review was made of all boundaries to try to ensure that the distribution of the voting population would be as fair as practicable aligned with members or representatives for the constituencies that would be established and having regard for boundaries to reflect equitable results.

There was a degree of science in the work of completing the report, including a review of updated lists of voters.

As to be expected, this was a burning issue for the Progressive Liberal Party in that, having failed to carry the day in 1962, they would use every possible means to change the outcome in 1967.

The report was presented in the Committal Stage, that is, for adoption by Parliament. As I recall it was at this stage that the leader of the Progressive Liberal Party, the Honourable Lynden O. Pindling, arose to speak. He was deliberate and eloquent in his address, all without notes. While speaking, the voices of the crowd on the outside were reaching a crescendo. That was a very emotional moment. I had a sense that history was on the verge of being made—for better or for worse.

While speaking Mr. Pindling walked over to the desk on which the Speaker's Mace was cradled. He picked it up, walked just to the right of Bobby Symonette's chair on the raised platform and continued to speak. He was precise in his movements, while passionately speaking all the time. He walked to the window that looked towards Queen Victoria's stature, opened the window and at the point of finishing his speech, pitched the Mace out of the window. It ended up on the concrete below broken into a number of pieces.

At that moment, Milo Butler sped as fast as his size permitted to the Speaker's desk, grabbed the timer that was used to limit exaggerated and lengthy speeches, and with a flourish threw it out of the window in pursuit of the Mace. The result was the same, completely destroyed.

With "PLP all the way" filling the Chamber, members of the Progressive Liberal Party left the Chamber. The crowd gathered on Parliament Street and Mr. Pindling was hoisted to the top of a car from which he gave a most passionate speech. The people were adoringly ecstatic.

The House reconvened and finished the Agenda. The crowd dispersed and except for minor confrontational issues with the police there was a pervading calm.

I think I was the last to leave the House of Assembly not because there were no more events to witness but there was a residing concern that I was alone and thus somewhat exposed to remaining pockets of protest. As it turned out, I walked away from the House of Assembly through the post office and to the parking lot in front of Higgs and Johnson law firm.

My drive to my home was slow and meditative. Having considered the events of the day, I renewed my commitment to work increasingly for the furthering of the improvement in the quality of life for all Bahamians. For me, being Bahamian was the essence of my existence.

When I walked through the front door, I was happy to see Lee Rose and the children. It was an evening of recognizing that our destiny was charted by powers that far exceeded our mortal understanding.

CHAPTER 20

EVEN MORE POLITICS

In the days and weeks that followed the massive protest by the PLP, it was not by evidence but it was certainly through intuitive reasoning that The Bahamas was evolving into a society of a divided people. For me, it was cause of grave concern only because growing up on Hawkins Hill there were absolutely no advocates of separatism based on colour or wealth.

I reflected again on the interview with Dick, the successful comedian, how when asked, "How did it feel growing up poor?" he replied, "It was good because I never realized that the family was poor."

And so it was on Hawkins Hill and with most of the people and families who lived elsewhere. We never knew that we were poor. We accepted what life had to offer and yet lived with a kind of energy and appreciation that kept us whole and spiritually united. I remembered vividly that without a government scholarship, my parents did not have the resources to pay the ten-pounds-per-year school fee at Government High. Any thought of going to college following graduation from GHS was not remotely a possibility.

My mother and father in their own way wanted the best that the world had to offer. But instead I learned more about life where I was, learning that became embedded in my way of life—honesty, integrity, respect, dignity, doing what was right, observing Christian principles and values, using my brain power to advance, and fulfilling commitments to family and friends.

Did I ever tell a lie? Of course I did but through the experience I learned to always tell the truth. Once you do this without wavering, you never have to struggle with remembering what was said previously.

My fellow political friends came together to discuss the future—Rudy Key, Reg Lobosky, Bernard Dupuch, Pierre Dupuch, Donald Sands, Tony Key and Gene Toote. A future from our perspective warranted the substantial change in the way the country was being managed. We also had the ear of Basil T. Kelly, Geoffrey Johnstone, Cleophas Adderley, Durward Knowles and Bobby Symonette.

We did not intend to promote radicalization of the Party but to bring change that promoted a strong conservative centre, which could encompass developments benefitting Bahamians throughout the length and breadth of the country.

Did we succeed in our endeavours? History seen dispassionately would say that we came up short very badly.

"The winds of change" blew like a level 5 hurricane that left the country facing an uncertain future.

The year 1965, with the Boundaries Commission Report now legislatively adopted, marked the start in earnest of the preparation of the next Election to be held in 1967.

In the meantime providing for a family, working long hours, engaging in various sports, and serving the country on the Road Traffic Authority and the Bahamas Sports Commission left little time for me to devote to having a happy marriage.

Except for rare moments of happiness the slippage in the marriage caused Lee to try to find a release in things she could enjoy. She returned to playing basketball and relished every minute.

"Barrie, why don't you come to the game tomorrow might? We are playing at the Nassau Stadium."

"Lee, I wish I could but I have several meetings tomorrow evening which I expect to run late."

She stared at me with an intensity that made it evident that my reply deeply hurt.

Another chip off the foundation of love we vowed in December 1957 to preserve forever.

Soon enough, the time arrived in late 1965 for the selection of candidates to contest elections in the thirty-eight seats specified in the Boundaries Commission Report. The selection of candidates was performed according to an inexact science. There was, however, a selection committee appointed with the responsibility of finding electable candidates for the General Elections.

A slate of candidates was presented to the Executive Committee and voted upon by attendees. I received the nomination to run for the Winton constituency, one of the largest in New Providence but not densely populated.

This was not an outcome that I took lightly; in fact, deep within my heart there resided a kind of nationalism that is so hard to describe. My irrevocable love for my country was embedded in my soul. I believed that I would be able to contribute much to our country if elected, including the furtherance of opportunity within the economic framework on behalf of many of my fellow Bahamians.

I also understood clearly that the road ahead was not going to be easy—much to the contrary, there were likely to be many craters to maneuver around.

On the evening of my nomination, I stood outside of the building smoking a Salem cigarette and talking with Bernard Dupuch, my second cousin. He was also a candidate but as a parliamentarian already, he was seeking re-election.

"Barrie, I know that you feel elated with your nomination. For us younger members of the Party, we need to stay close to each other and without fear make our voices heard. The 'old' guard must be persuaded to change the style of administering the affairs of the country."

I absorbed what Bernard said and felt a shiver go through my entire body. With a puff on my cigarette, although I did not smoke very much as I knew that it was bad for my health, I thoughtfully said to Bernard, "Undoubtedly, the task ahead is most daunting. We need to move forward on a number of fronts. I have to build an election team and with resources being controlled by the Finance Committee and with my limited personal resources, it will be tough sledding. I am up to the challenge."

"I expect for the PLP to be more invasive with their efforts to unseat the UBP," Bernard added.

Since I had recently witnessed the events in the House of Assembly, which subsequently became referred to as "Black Tuesday," I agreed and added, "The PLP will do things that are politically expedient. Also, the PLP will work to divide the country along racial lines." This would be unfortunate but despite Uncle Etienne's resolution in 1956 in the House of Assembly ending racial discrimination there lingered too many bad memories.

For one quiet moment, my mind returned to my days of growing up on Hawkins Hill where we were all one. Was our Hawkins Hill life of good neighbours and friends a complete oddity?

I guess we both became occupied with our own thoughts, which moved us to bid each other good night.

It was late when I got home and except for a security light, the house was in darkness. After letting myself in, I sat in my special chair in the Florida room and thought about the future—a future I believed was going to be as uneven and crazy as the Rocky Mountains. For me, there was only one way forward. For better or worse, my destiny would be left to the unknown.

I opened the sliding door, stepped out onto the patio and looked up at the universe. The stars were shining brightly and feeling a slight wind blowing from northeast, fresh and clean, I inwardly offered a prayer for peace within the country and that I be given the wisdom and strength to always do what was right.

Then I walked into the children's bedroom where John, Bruce and Scott were sleeping soundly. As I stood there, I was overcome with a feeling of hope and happiness. Here were my children with their future ahead of them. I am so lucky. Will I be able to give them a life of fulfillment?

This was a question yet to be answered.

Lee was not surprised that I had received the nomination to contest the Winton constituency. In a way I could understand her resistance because going forward the burden of caring for the family would rest heavily upon her shoulders. But she also knew that there was no turning back.

She wanted to hold her tongue but spoke with a tremble in her voice. "Barrie, this will be hard for us and our marriage will be even less stable, but I still want you to win."

How do you answer such a mixed message?

"Lee, in a way I wish it could be different. It is important for me to satisfy this burning desire within me to serve my country. Stand by me."

The days and weeks that followed were filled with non-stop campaigning and planning. My slogan was "If you want things done, vote for Farrington."

Rudy Key, my campaign manager, worked tirelessly.

There was so much to do—vetting voters list; reviewing posters, and when printing was done, having them put up on lamp poles and other prominent places; developing messages for distribution; preparing radio commercials and newspaper interviews whenever possible; and dealing with correspondence from prospective voters. UBP central provided a lot of administrative power needed for sustaining the campaign through to election day and beyond.

This campaign was going to be quite difficult compared to all previous elections.

Early in the game it became obvious that public meetings were all but impossible to hold. However you may attribute responsibility, the fact was that there were squads sympathetic to the PLP that waged a war of intimidation. And except for the couple of mass rallies that were made into games of war, there were no public gatherings of the UBP.

In the absence of being able to hold public meetings in Winton, I made it a commitment to walk the length and breadth of Winton and to visit the homes of all voters. A daunting task.

There were some good and memorable experiences, as I was able to hold a few meetings in homes where I had some support.

One such person was Gertrude Knowles on Minnie Street. She arranged for friends to come to her house to talk about the country and what I thought could be done to further the development of our people.

When word came that the PLP squads heard about my meeting and were searching the streets for the meeting, Mrs. Knowles had a couple of her friends keep watch on the outside to be ready to warn us should we be invaded.

I will always remember Gertrude Knowles, who was incredibly kind and thoughtful toward me. In her parting words, she said, "Thank you, Mr. Farrington, for working so hard and wanting to serve your country. We need more young men like you."

And so each day with Rudy and others, we walked the streets, visiting homes and talking to voters until we were hoarse. At the same time there were volunteers working in other areas.

One night after campaigning all day, Rudy and I went to the Elbo Room located in Bank Lane for a milkshake. When the waitress took our order, Rudy ordered a milkshake and in the same breath said, "My dear, make sure it is chocolate and not vanilla." We laughed but it was symbolic of the division that was being promoted within the country.

The UPB decided to have a mass rally at the Eastern Senior School on Mackey Street on the eve of the election. There were several thousand supporters in attendance with sufficient police around to ensure that we would not be invaded.

I spoke confidently that evening, as I had grown accustomed to speaking publicly. As I stood and looked out at the crowd, I felt a sense of extreme exhilaration particularly as they responded wildly when I made an emphatic statement about staying the course with the present government. A certain feeling, a power circulated within my being.

Later when I reflected on that surging feeling of power, I could understand how men who hold sway over millions of people must feel invincible when being adored while on a public platform. I have watched a video of Adolph Hitler speaking at Nuremburg to a million or more Germans shouting *"Sieg Heil"* with the drama of the beams of searchlights reaching to the clouds. Such power almost destroyed the world.

It was at this moment as I felt the euphoria of the prospect of being elected to parliament and the UBP being returned to power that I made my commitment to work tirelessly to make every day better for all of my fellow Bahamians. Given the chance I will not be deterred.

Sir Stafford Sands was the final speaker and his delivery was energetic and forceful. He ended by saying, "As sure as the sun will rise tomorrow, the UBP will win the election."

And with that declaration resonating through the country, the voters went to the polls on 10 January 1967. Generally, the UBP felt that they should win the election despite the many acts of intimidation by the PLP because the country had advanced economically significantly since the 1962 Elections.

January 10th was a long day for everyone who worked the polls and who had to be on hand for the count. My opponent in Winton was Mr. Carlton Francis, a well-respected teacher and religious leader. I spent my time at the polling station at the Bahamas Seventh Day Academy on Wulff Road. During the count it soon became evident that victory was not going to be mine.

Carlton Francis was at the same polling station, so before I left to return to my headquarters at the Nassau Yacht Haven, I congratulated him on his victory.

Although I was not physically attacked while leaving, the abusive language hurled at me was horrific. Rudy and I walked away with dignity.

Once back at headquarters there was much conversation about what happened and the suggestion of wrong doing at the polling stations.

CHAPTER 21

THE FALL

Bitterly disappointed with my loss, I could not refrain from saying out aloud to my friends, "The people of Winton have made a terrible mistake. I know within myself that I would have provided strong and sustained leadership." Unashamedly I shed some tears but once done I knew life would go on. To my election workers I gave heartfelt thanks for all their hard work.

The days following were most interesting because the final tally of the elections had the United Bahamian Party with eighteen seats, the Progressive Liberal Party with eighteen seats and two independents.

Negotiations began in earnest to persuade the two independents to come with the United Bahamian Party. Alvin Braynen always wanted to be Speaker of the House of Assembly and this was offered to him. Randol Fawkes, the Labour Leader, was a perfect fit for Minister of Labour. The Progressive Liberal Party made the same offer, which was accepted. One can only assume that the two independents felt that the mood of electorate going forward would be fully in support of the Progressive Liberal Party.

And so it was that Mr. Lynden Pindling, with a slim majority, was called upon by the Governor General to form a Government. Mr. Pindling was made Prime Minister, Mr. Arthur D. Hanna named Deputy Prime Minister, and my Winton opponent, Mr. Carlton Francis was appointed Minister of Finance.

For me there is a footnote to history. Immediately following the announcement of the election results and the independents facilitating the formation of a new government, I received a call from Sir Stafford to meet him at his office. I had no idea why such a meeting would be convened.

I attended his office at 309 Bay Street, which was deliberately kept very cold by him as he was not inclined to have long meetings. The cold discouraged lingerers.

After exchanging pleasantries he looked me straight in the eyes. A little known fact was that Sir Stafford had only one good eye, having lost one in a shooting accident early in life while bird hunting. He was terribly upset that we had lost the election but felt that there was a way to claw back the government. He advanced the argument that we had the economic strength to reverse the tide quickly if we were prepared to take some drastic steps. I told him that I could not support such action.

The meeting came to an end and I left.

It can be assumed that other members of the party were consulted in a similar way. There was apparently no appetite for recovery in that direction, and it suitably passed away.

The Senate seats had to be filled. At that time and as a result of Constitutional advance in 1963, the composition of the Upper Chamber was called the Senate. It comprised ten permanent members, five government appointed members, two opposition members and a President. Of the ten permanent Senators, Sir Etienne Dupuch, whom I called Uncle Etienne, even though we were second cousins, was one.

After the General Elections, in addition to returning to full-time work at the Nassau Yacht Haven and Pilot House Club, I started playing rugby again.

It was a Tuesday afternoon and I was on the Eastern Parade practicing rugby with my teammates when Geoffrey Johnstone, who had been elected to the Montague Constituency, drove his

Jaguar alongside the pitch and parked. He got out of the car and beckoned me to join him.

Without hesitation he said, "Barrie, my man, the parliamentary group has unanimously agreed to appoint you to the Senate. Congratulations. You are most deserving of this appointment."

I was at loss for words and with a wide smile replied, "I am delighted to serve as a Senator."

He added that "the Honourable Eugene Dupuch will serve in opposition with you."

"Oh my gracious! What an honour."

Eugene Dupuch was a brilliant man in so many areas. I could not hide my joy. Eugene was Etienne's brother and also my cousin.

Within ten days I received an official declaration from the Governor General, Sir Ralph Grey, appointing me to the Senate. Imagine, from that appointed date I was to be referred to as Senator, the Honourable J. Barrie Farrington.

My being appointed to the Senate came as quite a surprise to me. My friends and family congratulated me enthusiastically. My mother, father and siblings were lavish in acknowledging my political recognition. Lee was equally surprised and despite our tenuous relationship she was very pleased with my appointment.

Lee put her arms around me and with feelings said quite earnestly, "You have worked hard for party and country and deserve being recognized in this way."

She then looked at me wistfully and added, "I know, Barrie, that you will pursue this dream that you have held throughout our time together. I want you to live your dream."

I was truly moved and in a way it caused a degree of emotional conflict.

What could I say other than, "Lee I want you to have a good life and I want our children to be happy with us."

As we held each other for a few minutes, many thoughts on our marriage raced through my head. I knew that destiny was now dictating the path that we would travel.

Rudy Key continued to be my close friend, supporter and advisor. There were matters to be attended in preparation for the big day. For instance, dress code for Parliament and in particular the Senate was formal morning dress.

Rudy and I flew to Miami to find clothes appropriate for the occasion. I could hardly afford to purchase an outfit of any quality but finally found a bargain. Imaging having to wear "top hat," formal morning coat, including a vest, striped trousers and a matching cravat, plus shoes. My young sons could not understand why I had to dress up in this way. Rudy on the other hand was ecstatic.

And then came the big day when the House of Assembly would be convened and parliamentary business conducted.

The Members of the House led by the Speaker walked the short distance to the Senate Chambers where Senators were assembled. It was in this setting that the Governor General gave his speech from the Throne and members of both Chambers were sworn in officially.

I remembered the day so clearly. Uncle Gene had collected me from the Nassau Yacht Haven, where I had gone earlier so that I could greet friends and colleagues before going to the Senate. The crowd on Bay Street was enormous and although boisterous and jubilant because it was the dawn of a new day in the history in the country, I have no recollection of any incident that could have marred the wonderful occasion.

Once the official swearing-in had been completed, I walked out onto the balcony overlooking Rawson Square and the statue of Queen Victoria. As I stood there in the background, Mr. Lynden Pindling, Prime Minister, and Cecil Wallace-Whitfield were waving to and greeting the adoring crowd. For some reason both turned, saw me, and took a step back to warmly congratulate me on my senatorial appointment. I in turn congratulated them on their victory and wished them good fortune in governing the country. For me, my country came first and being of service in a positive way would be central for me going forward.

Once the excitement of the morning had passed, Uncle Gene drove me back to the Nassau Yacht Haven. After spending a while with Rudy and some of my supporters who had worked so hard for me during the campaign, I made my way home.

It was a happy day of unimaginable proportions but it also represented a change in my journey in life that would have profound consequences.

The Hon. Eugene Dupuch greeting Bahamas Rugby team prior to start of Rugby Festival with Billy "Red Top" Lowe, captain, on his left

Robert Hallam "Bobby" Symonette
President/Owner of Nassau Marine Services Ltd. and Pilot House
Club, mentor, friend, Speaker of The House Of Assembly,
and renowned sailing competitor of 5.5 Meter class boats

CHAPTER 22

A FRESH DIRECTION, PERSONAL AND POLITICAL

My work at the Nassau Yacht Haven and Pilot Club House was intense. There was so much to catch up on, business that had been largely neglected while I devoted my time and energy to campaigning.

Bobby and I had many talks about what had happened at the polls and what was likely to be the new government's plans for ensuring that the development of the economy was sustained.

In one conversation, Bobby informed me of a development that I found surprising and at the same time encouraging.

"The Prime Minister has reached out to me to advise the government on matters being addressed by the Bahamas Hotel Corporation. Most mornings I meet with Mr. Pindling to discuss various issues that are not always directly related to the Hotel Corporation of the Bahamas. In fact, I have access to the Prime Minister at virtually any time."

I said to Bobby, "Could it be a sign that the Prime Minister is more interested in nation building rather than allowing partisan politics to be a continuing divisive force within Bahamian society?"

Bobby paused for a moment and replied, "I am hopeful that there can be common ground for putting country first, but quite frankly given aggressive bitterness that emerged throughout the General Election campaign I believe that it will be some years before the wounds inflicted will be healed, which could then be the basis of a collective reconstruction of our country."

Bobby was a great person with enormous intellect that allowed him to properly rationalize our best hope was to look forward to a better future.

He was my mentor in so many ways, which enabled me to grow. Bobby was a MIT graduate possessing an abundance of confidence that allowed him to mingle comfortably with the rich and famous in all continents. And most importantly, in all that he did, he never abandoned his Bahamian roots.

I was also fortunate to work along with Captain Durward Knowles and we formed a friendship that lasted throughout the years. I admired him most because he always told you what was on his mind—an unvarnished truth that on occasion caused some discomfort.

The chemistry between the three of us, Bobby, Durward and me, was absolutely unbelievable. We were completely at ease with each other nearly all the time. There was only one occasion when Durward and I exchanged angry words. It all had to do with rugby.

Durward played for the Sea Scouts and although he was almost at the end of his playing days, he was still quite a skillful player. On the other side, I was captain of the Buccaneers even though I was still relatively new to competitive rugby.

Durward had reason to have a disagreement on the Eastern Parade one Saturday afternoon in early spring. The cause was silly but the effect was for us to retain an angry silence toward each other for a couple of weeks. In the end we apologized to each other and ever since, have been the dearest of friends.

Bobby, Durward and I didn't like losing the General Elections but we recognized that we belonged in our country and would continue to do our part. History can attest to our collective contributions throughout the years.

On the other hand, Sir Stafford Sands could not accept the loss of the government at the polls. This feeling was too deep-seated and troubling to Sir Stafford that he decided that he could no longer live in The Bahamas. Within weeks he transferred the ownership of his law firm located at 50 Bay Street to a group of lawyers who worked for him. The new firm was Carson, Lawson, Sawyer, Klonaris and Knowles.

I was astounded that he had moved to London and was never to return and yet he could not completely sever his relationship with The Bahamas.

One evening I was visiting with Bobby at his home "High Folly" when the telephone rang. It was Sir Stafford for Bobby. They talked for at least thirty minutes. At the end, Bobby looked at me and said, "That was Stafford. He called me out of pure loneliness." Hardly the testament to a man who despite many personal shortfalls, contributed so much to the economic development of our Bahamas. In fact the financial model he created in the 1950s still forms the foundation of our economy—tourism and financial services/private banking.

When the Senate convened for its first meeting of the new legislative year, freshmen senators were given liberty to make maiden speeches.

As a true novice in this elevated chamber, I suffered considerable anxiety in anticipation of preparing a speech that should contain sage statement about the affairs of the country and out of duty as senators to make judicious decisions designed for all Bahamians. While so engaged in trying to develop an outline of what I could offer to fellow senators and to the country at large, a story came to mind that was cause for pause—in fact the circumstances of the story in a perverted way were somewhat apropos to me.

The story was about a young man elected to Parliament for the first time and upon taking his seat, discovered that he was seated next to a senior and well respected House member. The young member, realizing that he was required to make his maiden speech, decided to seek advice from his senior colleague.

"Mr. Smith, as the newest member of this Chamber and lacking any experience in speaking in this forum, I want your advice as I am expected to speak but uncertain about how to approach this situation."

He replied without hesitation, "Young man, it is better for you to remain silent and for your colleagues to think you a fool than for you to open your mouth and remove all doubt."

And so I pondered my dilemma. In the end I took my own counsel and decided that I should speak.

I prepared my speech carefully. With sincere belief in the collective effort being the principal ingredient in economic and social advance, I did speak and the newspaper reports granted recognition for my contribution. Included in my address was the fact that the Progressive Liberal Party campaigned on the promise of maintaining a stable and business-friendly environment. Our General Elections were scrutinized by the *Wall Street Journal* and statements of unveiled support of the Progressive Liberal Party were expressed fairly frequently. However, when the dust from the General Elections had settled and the government made certain pronouncements of limitations on foreign employment in the country, the *Wall Street Journal* reporting changed.

Noticing this alteration in support, I said in my speech that "prior to the Elections Mr. Pindling was shaking the hands of investors but given recent declarations, the Prime Minister was now shaking their confidence."

My appointment to the Senate had a constitutional element that was, for me, historic.

In order to be appointed a person had to be at least thirty years of age. I was thirty-one and at that time the youngest man ever to be appointed to the Upper Chamber.

Even though governing with a slim majority required careful navigation, the government had at its disposal the talents and administrative skills of Sir Foley Newns, Secretary to the Cabinet. Sir Foley had been contracted by the previous government and his familiarity and knowledge of all matters associated with the Westminster ministerial model of governing was of incalculable value. A number of other imported senior and civil servants formed the backbone of administering the bureaucracies of the civil service.

As with all things in life, there is no absolute certainty attached to the future, a fact that Sir Stafford unfortunately discovered after predicting the outcome of the 1967 General Elections. And in keeping with destiny, the unpredictable in the political setting happened.

Uriah McPhee, the Progressive Liberal Party parliamentarian who represented the Kemp Road constituency, died in March 1968. It was expected that the Progressive Liberal Party would call a Bye-Election to replace Mr. McPhee; however another unpredictable event happened and this changed the political landscape substantially for many years.

The Prime Minister, in a masterful stroke of opportunity, in recognizing the mood of the Bahamian electorate, dissolved Parliament and moved for new Elections. General Elections were held in April 1968 and the Progressive Liberal Party ended with a huge majority in the House of Assembly. The United Bahamian Party wanted me to run again but I decided against doing that.

My term in the Senate lasted for about thirteen months and rightly or wrongly, I lay claim to being the youngest person ever to be appointed a Senator and for having the shortest term. Nothing really to brag about, but for me it is a small footnote to history in Bahamian politics.

Hence my involvement in frontline politics came to an end. Unfortunately, my marriage also came to an official end.

The grounds for our divorce had to be fabricated because the law in those days was intolerant of divorce unless based upon the most serious violation of the sacred vows of marriage, more particularly, adultery.

In the face of a world for me that was disintegrating, it was still necessary for us to work out the best solution for settlement with the best interests of the children being primary.

We decided that John and Bruce should go away to Boarding School. Lee did the research and found a British-modeled school—Appleby, west of Toronto. Resources available for this change were limited but through determined efforts and prayer, arrangements were made. The boys were not happy but at least they would be together.

Lee was of the mind to move to Mexico City and would take Scott with her. This ending was certainly not the kind you would find in fairy tales. Both hearts were heavy and mine felt as if it were breaking apart.

While this emotional upheaval was in the forefront of my daily life, there were other significant events unfolding.

Bobby Symonette, whether in the face of a dramatic shift in the political structure of the country or for other personal reasons, decided to remove himself as the president of Nassau Marina Services Limited and owner of the Nassau Yacht Haven and Pilot House Club. At that time, there were two minority stakeholders, Donald S. Andrews and Major Lawrence Kimball. (This was a little-known fact.)

Thus I was promoted to president of Nassau Marine Services Limited and Donald Andrews succeeded Bobby as director with control on behalf of shareholders. Being president was indeed a new role for me but it reflected the confidence that Bobby had in me to continue the work he loved doing for so many years.

More changes were on the horizon.

Within the next twelve months, several significant events occurred with the business. Bernard Perron, owner and operator of Buena Vista, and Konrad Zeilman, developer, negotiated to purchase the Nassau Yacht Haven and Pilot House Club. As a part of the deal, I stayed on as vice president, treasurer, secretary and director of the new company, Condotel Bahamas Limited.

One significant objective was achieved fairly quickly: Bernard created a gourmet restaurant within the Pilot House Club, which in our opinion was the equal to Buena Vista.

The club and the marina together did not produce acceptable financial margins. Once recognized, the Nassau Yacht Haven was sold to Juan Fernandez and his wife, Carol.

Konrad Zeilman was not satisfied with the future prospects of the Pilot House Club and the opportunity to improve the asset substantially. He and Bernard decided that the partnership should be dissolved. Fortunately, Bernard and I were able to persuade Hans Vander Schoot, president of British American Insurance, to acquire the interest of Konrad. It was from this new ownership platform that Bernard's creative juices were flowing with exciting and visionary development plans.

In our first meeting with Hans and his team, he made it clear that the investments being made were a declaration of confidence primarily in Bernard.

I can recall Hans saying, "Bernard, we are making a major investment in an area where we have very little expertise but we feel confident you can get the job done. Our shareholders expect success, financially."

Bernard unhesitatingly replied, "Hans, I am putting all my money into this enterprise with you, and I have no intention of failing."

Not long after this new beginning, another investment opportunity arose which when considered with potential developments could not be resisted. The magnet was the acquisition of the Fort Montague Beach Hotel built in 1927 containing 176 rooms of which sixty were built in 1960. With the hotel came thirty-seven acres of land and a prospect of acquiring the 14.4-acre tract known as the Silk Worm Farm that adjourned the western property boundary of the hotel, now Harbour Bay Shopping Centre.

Thus 1969 began another part of heady changes with our company, Condotel Bahamas Limited. Unfortunately, our dreams were not realized but the story of effort and determination is worthy of telling.

Josephine Elizabeth Gemmill

CHAPTER 23

JOSEPHINE ELIZABETH MERLIN MACKENZIE

Emotional upheaval in life can leave wounds that are undecipherable to your friends, family and any other people who occupy a place of importance, such as a confidant. However, there are moments when you lower your defenses and then you are vulnerable.

When Lee Rose and I arrived at the painful and ultimately irreversible decision to separate permanently, I discovered a bitterness erupting within me like a volcano that, after being dormant for a long time, suddenly comes to life with incredible force and fury.

I remember the day when the unexpected feeling overcame me. It was late one afternoon and the sun was still fairly high above the horizon. I was alone in the house on Prince Charles Drive. Alone! Lee was gone taking Scott with her. John and Bruce were in Canada. Feeling a painful aloneness, I started drinking until I was totally inebriated. My directionless anger had to be expressed in some physical way. I stood on the steps just outside of the kitchen and the small utility room looking to the west but shielded by the bush of an adjoining lot, undeveloped. At my disposal was a pile of Chinaware and glasses I had placed nearby for easy access. So overcome with alcohol, a sense of mortality and blindness to human existence, I smashed every piece while screaming like a severely injured lion. And then emotionally spent I went back into the house.

Sitting on the top step just outside the Florida Room, I continued to drink. My anguish was so great that I thought of suicide as the only acceptable alternative. What an ugly thought. Philosophical dissertation held for me only a passing interest but at that moment I remembered something written by Friedrich Nietzsche on suicide. He said in essence that suicide is the ultimate answer to any emotional situation that might drive a person beyond the brink of hopelessness. Further, he added that when one has the ultimate answer there is no need to take the final step at that moment in time. Instead, the dawning recognition that life itself is a treasure to be highly valued, that one has the power to live each day going forward until the fortitude to live is fully restored and suicide becomes a memory. For one who possesses undeniably the final solution, it provides them with life.

It was an epiphany.

At that very moment I made two resolutions. I would live each day striving for its new purpose, and never allow myself to live in an unhappy environment.

Sleep was evasive but it did come eventually. As I opened my eyes to a new day, I felt refreshed but still aware of the wound. Freedom from the bonds of marriage can be uplifting or it can be a quicksand and therefore unsuspecting. Although I was still working at the Montague Beach Hotel, I found myself drawn to Paradise Island for entertainment. Along with Jerry Lewless and Gordon Carey, many evenings were spent in the Trade Winds Lounge featuring live entertainment and lots of opportunities to connect with the opposite sex. With dark days of my previous life receding albeit slowly, I felt more alive and more comfortable with daily living.

It was during one of my visit to the Trade Winds Lounge that I met Jo. What was the attraction? On this particular night I was introduced to her by LeRoy Bailey, the General Manager of the Loews Paradise Island Hotel and Villas.

I had seen Jo earlier. She had a great pair of legs and was otherwise very attractive. Added to this, she was wearing white boots and hot pants. We connected immediately and engaged in mild flirting. I learned that she worked as an executive private secretary to the General Manager. I also discovered that she was married to Brian MacKenzie, an American who also worked at that hotel.

I did not have an expectation of our initial meeting going anywhere but the next day while I was in my office at the Montague Beach Hotel, my secretary Helen Weech announced that Jo was there to see me. What a surprise, a very pleasant one. Fate had obviously intervened. We began dating and fell in love. Jo proceeded to divorce Brian and declared quite suddenly, "Barrie, I want to devote my life to you."

While our romance was blossoming, the business of the Montague Beach Hotel was getting bad. With the outlook being bleak, there was no future opportunity for me there so Bernard and I decided that I should move on to other employment.

I joined Paradise Island Limited on 1 December 1971 as Vice President of Paradise Realty Limited, which owned the Paradise Island Casino. My new job allowed us to be much closer together. Even though we did not intend to rush to the altar, we nonetheless married on 14 July 1972, the anniversary date of the French Revolution—Bastille Day. Robyn Melinda was born on 12 January 1973 which was the same day as my mother but that year was 1906.

Jo's parents, Bob and Adeline, who travelled from Hallandale Florida, adored Robyn and were eager to spoil her without limitation. It was during this adjustment period that I received a letter from Scott who was living in Mexico with Lee Rose. I opened the letter tentatively, not knowing what to expect but glad that it was not written in Spanish. I read the letter.

> *Dear Daddy, John and Bruce,*
> *How are you all? I am doing well in school. Has John and Bruce got me anything. Daddy I would like a bicycle for my birthday please. I went on the small roller coaster. It is crazy. I want you to go with me on the big one because I am afraid. Daddy, I have some friends. I miss you all very much.*

I loved Scott and the letter touched me so strongly that I could feel the hot tears gently coursing down my cheeks. I sensed his loneliness and pain living so far away amongst people he did not know. I decided that I would go the Mexico City to see him.

When I broached the matter with Jo, she was unhesitating in her support.

"Barrie, whatever you need to do for your children, I stand behind you and beside you to get the best result for them." And then she added, "We need to be a complete family."

To me, it was obvious that she knew it was very important to me to take care of the boys.

I travelled to see Scott unsure of how Lee would react to my presence. It turned out well. When I mentioned the prospect of Scott returning to Nassau, she did not resist—in fact she understood the importance to Scott.

I flew back to Nassau on Pan American and while I sat there immersed in thought, I pulled out Scott's letter and read it for the umpteenth time. I was moved to put pen to paper and composed this poem "Oh, Mexico" for my son.

No Poet am I—But words come;
Wings stretch from my side, my heart throbs too slowly, too sad.
Sleeping lady passes by, my son too behind must be, but why?
Strange words surround me—I care not
Warmth and happiness must be got, but how?
When love is lost, only work remains.
Sweet kisses too pass by—just memories.
Endure the search, but how long?
We pray. We look. We…go on.

Jo did not want to be a stay-at-home mom. She was employed this time as the executive secretary for Irvin "Jack" Davis, President of Resorts International. Even though I worked in the Executive Suite there was no conflict, at least not immediately.

A lot of pieces of the puzzle started to fall into place, which to me was a huge relief.

Jo insisted that the entire family should be together. Scott was to come home from Mexico and John and Bruce were to leave Appleby College in Canada and return to the family home on Prince Charles Drive.

Scott, at ten years of age, had to travel as an unaccompanied minor to Nassau; I remember meeting him coming through Immigration and Customs. He looked so small in his black raincoat that he wore because it was cold in Mexico City during the early months of the year. I couldn't stop hugging him.

Scott was enrolled in Queen's College as were John and Bruce after they returned home. The boys were good athletes. John and Bruce loved tennis and soccer and Scott gravitated towards swimming where he excelled. He swam for the Barracuda Club with Greg Geiselman.

There was peace in the Farrington household.

Upon completing high school, John attended Miami Dade Junior College, where he continued with his tennis playing in addition to pursuing his academic studies.

Bruce was enrolled in Riverside Military Academy in Hollywood, Florida. During the summer he attended the school's Georgia campus.

My mother of course made sure the boys were confirmed in the Anglican faith and attended church with her regularly.

Scott transferred to Bolles College in Jacksonville and participated in the nationally recognized swimming programme there. But when he became bored with swimming, we moved him to Montreat-Anderson School in North Carolina. Wanting to be in the hotel industry, he transferred to the University of Houston Hilton Hotel School.

I was invited to speak to Scott's class about tourism. It was indeed a very proud moment for me. Scott was thrilled to have me there.

Robyn, ten years younger than Scott, attended St. Andrew's School and from the very beginning applied herself diligently. She was recognized as a very bright student headed for an outstanding future of academic achievement.

My mother provided Robyn with much love and nurturing as did Jo's parents. In fact they did much to instill in Robyn a strong desire to excel and she responded wonderfully.

Even still for some reason, cracks began to appear in the

foundation of our marriage. We lacked the capability to cope with our differences and continued with our daily living in a dysfunctional manner. Having grown up in such an environment I subconsciously recognized a foreboding of a future that would contain dark days.

Jo and I shared an outlook with entrepreneurial content realizing that our economic well-being required engaging in business enterprises outside of our normal jobs.

A series of businesses were embarked upon with varying degrees of success. Our very first undertaking was the establishment of "Serendipity," a store selling touristic souvenirs located in the small shopping centre on Paradise Island. There were four partners—Eddy and Gladys Darville, and Jo and me, and then came Paradise Splash.

In 1986, Jo and I started Fashion Hall with the opening day occurring on my birthday. The first store, started in the Prince Charles Shopping Plaza, was an instant success. Through the years, we established the Fashion Hall brand in the Town Centre Mall, Top of the Hill Mackey Street, Marathon Mall and the South West Plaza Shopping Centre, Carmichael Road.

We experimented with different types of products under our flag and when they failed for one reason or another we closed them.

For me, it was an age of discovery on how perceived success was dealt with within the Bahamian society. I was startled at the depth of envy of and/or dislike for a fellow Bahamian who seemed to be on the cusp of making seemingly meteoric strides in business. Imagine my disbelief when I was informed that, in view of the number of shop licences I held in my country, the licencing authority would be disinclined to grant any more licences.

Disbelief changed to anger. I found a way to infiltrate this regressive attitude and was finally able to have that policy reversed.

Jo and I faced success and failure with equal realism—understandably that like in tennis, you win some and you lose some, but if you are passionate about competition, you train harder to reverse loses.

Another venture came our way but in the end was fraught with quicksand situations. Through an unusual sequence of events I acquired Bahamas Sportswear Manufacturing Company, a sportswear company deeply immersed in debt. The cost of operating and managing a business that was uncompetitive was prohibitive. In a moment of depression I decided to close the company and to absorb a substantial debt that was held by the Bank of Nova Scotia. However, while discussing the situation with Victoria Gibson, a senior and loyal member of the team, and having advised her of the decision to close, she looked at me intently with her eyes brimming with tears and said, "Mr. Farrington, I beg you not to close the business. I truly believe that we can make it. Give us a chance to get the better of this awful situation." She added, "Mr. Farrington, trust in the Lord."

I heeded the words of Victoria and kept the business open and our fortunes began to improve. Victoria had a job for life.

On the home front, Jo and I maintained a fragile relationship against all odds. We travelled, played tennis, and as usual enjoyed a week at Wimbledon. For reasons which probably cannot be adequately explained, the charm between us worsened. This in many ways was regrettable but there was no turning back.

There were some important developments in our lives that made lasting impressions.

Robyn, after graduating from St. Andrew's, spent time at the Bolletttieri Tennis Academy before moving on to Blair Academy in New Jersey. She applied to Vanderbilt University in Nashville, Tennessee, and because of her outstanding academic achievements was accepted. Robyn graduated Magna Cum Laude, which was outstanding. Although she wanted to be a doctor, it was difficult getting into medical school. As an alternative, she attended the University of Miami in pursuit of a degree in nursing and administration. Here again, she excelled.

Bruce was not happy at home for a number of reasons and understandably so. The family's dysfunction, which haunted me even after marriage, was continuously present in my own family. He was sent away for Boarding School at a very young age, followed by military school and so when he was eighteen years old and finished with high school, he left home. I didn't know of his whereabouts. And then one day in late November, I received a most surprising call from him. "Dad, I thought that I should let you know that I am leaving The Bahamas. In fact, I am at the airport now about to board a flight to Miami."

I felt a stab in my heart and a sudden sadness but there was nothing I could say that would make a difference. He then added the final blow. "Dad, I am getting married."

I feebly responded, "I wish you every good thing. Be happy. I love you."

This was 1976 and too much was happening that required my attention. Destiny would be in control of the future with Bruce and me.

John finished school and continued with his tennis career. He got married young to a Jamaican girl, Mary Ann who was pretty and gentle. In due course, John was hired as director of tennis at the Ocean Club.

Scott, once out of university, worked in several U.S. hotels, the last one being the Loews Regency on Park Avenue. I spoke with Bob Tisch, one of the owners I knew because his company had leased the Paradise Hotel and Villas in 1967 from Island Hotel Company, Limited. He arranged for Scott to be employed in one of his New York properties.

No one wants to admit failure even when the life to which you are committed has lost the ardour that ordinarily would be the lynchpin of the union. In avoiding this reality, I hung on to a thread of affection while inwardly wondering how in the world I could reach resolution when there was no apparent answer.

Jo and I continued on with our lives together trying to live with normalcy. We decided in this unstable time to purchase a home in San Souci as the home on Prince Charles Drive was now bordering a busy thoroughfare and losing value. The new home needed a lot of work, which we tackled with enthusiasm.

Robyn loved having her own bedroom and Scott was working at the Holiday Inn on Paradise Island.

Unfortunately for Jo and me, the time arrived for us to take the final step to separate after twenty-two years of marriage.

While contemplating divorce, I spoke with John Carson, a lawyer friend who was soon to enter the priesthood. He understood my dilemma and suggested that I remain in the marriage. I was about fifty-four years of age. He said, "The older you get, the less remedial your actions are." In my thoughts, I replayed his recommendation dozens of times. In the end I rejected that advice and was, in due course, happy that I made a contrary decision.

Once I realized that a permanent separation was the only option to be pursued and which Jo accepted, we agreed that Jo would select a lawyer who specialized in matters of divorce. Even though it was an uncontested divorce, there still were legal formalities to be dealt with including financial considerations for Jo. These were unhappy days but we managed to get to the finish without any acrimony. Fortunately, the law had been amended which allowed "irreconcilable differences between the parties" to be the basis for the Court granting a divorce.

We owned a house in the Plantation, Florida, which was where Jo wanted to live, added to which were other assets. She could survive financially.

Jo left on the Paradise Island Airways plane on a Friday morning with a one-way ticket. Several good things happened—I did not get drunk, and I did not despair. Jo travelled for a year, met Mike and married him. Robyn moved to Plantation and stayed with them for a while.

As for me, I felt that I had done the right thing and there were many things swirling around me that every day was fully occupied. And yes, there were many moments living with regrets, always wondering if I could have made everything different.

Soul searching is so fatiguing, emotionally and spiritually.

Ira Willis Farrington

CHAPTER 24

IRA WILLIS FARRINGTON

My father was born on the 12th March 1901 and died on the 1st June 1980. Buried with him were the unrealized dreams of successful business ventures. He possessed a complex personality which I think, on reflection, resulted from an upbringing within a household dominated by an extraordinarily strong-willed mother, Rosamond Alice Farrington née Dupuch.

I was quite young when she visited our home on Hawkins Hill and my only personal recollection of her was the lack of affection or interest in me.

My father demanded obedience much along the lines of what I was to learn were the rigid lines of family interactions best described as belonging to the Victorian age.

Being so young and not understanding the ways of some married folks, I could sense that there was an undefined uneasiness in the marriage of my mom and dad. At times that unease changed into harsh exchanges, which for my mom was so totally out of character given her unalterable subscription to the loving principles of the Anglican church.

My father laid down the law in our house, one which surely must have been out of the Victorian era and possibly originating in his upbringing by his parents. In any event, for me it must have been a re-enactment. "Barrie, come here, I want to speak with you!" came my dad's command.

"Yes, Dad," I answered when I reached him at his desk

"Starting tomorrow morning, you must come to me in my bedroom and wish me a good morning."

"Yes, Dad, I will," I responded.

This was perplexing to me but I knew that if I failed to comply with that directive I was in jeopardy of the leather belt being applied to my rear end with some force. Disobedience was not tolerated.

As the years passed, my father's attitude mellowed and there was some normalcy. After I got married to Lee and produced our two sons, initially, dad was definitely moved to spend time with them. They played a special game they improvised called "Two Square."

And then my dad became ill, which at first it was not determined to be serious. A sore on his lower lip—which my brother Earle, a doctor, thought had been caused by too much exposure to the sun—would not heal. When examined by an oncologist it was determined that it was cancerous.

In those early days the treatment for cancer was limited but the consensus was that surgery in all likelihood would be required in conjunction with radiation.

Earle made arrangements for Dad to attend a specialist at Mount Sinai. It was anticipated that he would have to spend time in an apartment near the hospital.

Dad flew to Miami on Chalk's Airline, which operated from Paradise Island. Flying a fourteen-seat Mallard, a seaplane, was cause for fearfulness as dad had never flown before and here he was at seventy-six years of age about to commence his journey in an aircraft that took off from and landed on the water. After all the treatments, including surgery, dad was scheduled for the return to Nassau with the hope that his cancer was to be cured.

And this is when the human, spiritual and emotional parts of his existence came to the fore.

When the Mallard was propelled out of the harbour onto the ramp and came to rest very near to the terminal building, my dad said, "Thank God I am back in Nassau."

As he got to the bottom of the stairs on the tarmac, he fell to his knees and with tears in his eyes, he kissed the ground. I heard him say "I am so glad to be back in my country."

The battle with cancer was far from over. Although progress had been made, in the months that followed it was evident that the battle had not been won. The cancer spread to his neck, requiring additional surgery and radiation. Once more the disease appeared to be in check but his health was declining ever so slowly. It was determined that more surgery was needed in a final attempt to hold the cursed disease at bay.

It was terribly distressing to witness his struggle against insurmountable odds. He tried valiantly to put on a brave face but there was fear underpinning this facade. He often said that he was not afraid of dying; however, he never embraced God and the way of the church, so it was difficult to accept his declarations.

Survival and comfort were derived from regular doses of morphine. Notwithstanding a negative prospect, the decision was taken to try another surgical procedure in a final attempt to arrest the disease.

So it was back to the hospital for another surgical invasion of his earthly body. Alas, it was to no avail. The cancer had spread into his chest cavity so the procedure was halted.

For us, the light of hope was being extinguished incrementally.

I was experiencing much difficulty in trying to reconcile my feelings in a way with the history of my very uneven relationship with dad through the many years.

On a night at my home on Prince Charles Drive, I had a deeply penetrating dream about my father. It was as real as you could imagine. I knew that our spirits connected and that there was a mutual need to put everything right.

The next day when I went to see him, I sat next to his bed and said, "Dad, you were with me last night."

His reply was immediate. "I know."

I was emotionally moved with a sadness which lacked

definition. Could we be at peace at last? Two days later he died in the night with no one by his side.

The funeral of my dad was a very simple affair at St. Matthew's Church. My mom was saddened by his death but remained composed throughout the final earthly goodbye. Dad was buried in the Farrington plot.

Following my father's death, I placed a photo of him as a young man on my desk where it has remained ever since. I continue to feel that our relationship remains unsettled. Whenever I gaze upon the photo, I hope for an answer as to why he was so removed emotionally from me. My question continues to be, "What was the cause of his unhappiness that persisted for decades and was there another side of him that was unknown?"

My deep interest in my family's history has been resolute through the years. My curiosity guided me to examine all of my dad's papers, business and personal. And only recently while so engaged I made a most surprising and pleasing revelation: my father, Ira Willis, had possessed a side of him that was romantic, soft, and poetic.

The handwritten letter to my mother dated January 27, 1926, timed as Wednesday, 7:00 p.m., revealed a depth of love that moved me to tears. It possessed a kind of Shakespearean quality.

The discovery of the letter written to my mother some 91 years ago was reason enough for me to realize that it was an unfettered expression of love. In fact it was a clear indication of their commitment to their sharing a future life together.

And, Yes, it did come to pass that mother at 20 years of age and my father, 25 years of age, were married on the 27th October, 1926 in St, Mary's Church on Augusta Street.

I know within my heart that they were happy together in those early years. While writing what might be described as a fairy tale ending, I reminded myself that the years of the 1920s, 1930s, and 1940s were extremely hard as the world was grappling with enormous economic hardships and at the same time trying to survive in a very hostile environment caused by a raging World War. And, for the Bahamas there was no escaping from these realities.

Wednesday 7 p.m.
Jan. 27/1926

Dear Girl,
 I am very sorry — but I shall be unable to come down tonight, on account of the tooth-ache.

It is hurting much more tonight, and it has the gums swollen a bit.

You see, if I came down, I would only be suffering, so I think it would be wise for me to stay home

(2)
to-night. Will you please let Nennie know?

I am sure to see you to-morrow night, if not to-morrow day.

See, girl, can you imagine how much I shall miss you tonight? Say Pearl, won't you let your thoughts come to me home? ~~××× ×× ×g~~!

Sincerely your's
Ira.

CHAPTER 25

RESORTS INTERNATIONAL AND PARADISE ISLAND

When Steve Norton and I began discussing the possibility of me joining Resorts International, I had no idea where and how I might end up should I be employed there. We negotiated a deal but Steve needed to get Jim Crosby, Chairman, and Jack Davis, President and CEO, to consent to my joining Resorts International.

My time at the Montague Beach Hotel and the association with the Nassau Yacht Haven and Pilot House Club was nearly at an end and there was no turning back. And so, waiting for the phone call from Steve was a time of anxiety. As we know, in life there are no absolutes.

Mid-November 1971 the telephone rang at my house on Prince Charles Drive and Jo, who was nearest to the phone, which was red, answered it on the third ring.

"Barrie, Steve Norton is calling for you." Jo handed the phone to me with a smile that brightened her face. My palms were slightly moist as the call represented my future.

"Barrie, I have good news for you. I have talked with Mr.

Crosby and Jack Davis about the prospect of you joining the company and they wish to speak with you further. We believe that we have something that would be of interest to you. Can you come to our office later today?"

I can still hear Steve now because he had a distinctive voice that contained a little of the South. My enthusiastic reply was "I certainly can. What time do you want me there?"

"Let's say 2:00 p.m. Does that work for you?" he asked.

I replied, "Yes, and I presume that the meeting will take place in the corporate executive office."

"That is correct," Steve answered.

I hung up the phone very slowly, but my heart was beating pretty quickly. Even though my position with Resorts International was assured I began thinking *what was it that I would be doing?* It was well known and accepted that Resorts International was an aggressive company with a casino and was focused on growing the company as quickly as possible.

Wrapping her arms around my waist, Jo said, "I am proud of you and I know you will be great."

The meeting with Jim, Jack and Steve went very well and my engagement was confirmed. I accepted less money than I had been making at the Montague Beach but I knew that once I proved my worth, more money would be forthcoming.

On 1 December 1971, I crossed the bridge to Paradise Island to start a business relationship that would last more than forty-one years. And yes, I was going to Paradise Island, the Island that I viewed from the second storey of the family home on Fair Wind Lane, Hawkins Hill.

As Vice President of Paradise Island Realty Company Limited, owner of the Paradise Island Casino, I realized at once that I was moving into an area that was totally alien to me.

My job had two parts to it—to learn and understand the casino business and to be the liaison between the casino operation and our corporate executive committee. Ordinarily, this is not the way the casino would be operated but the casino was without a General Manager. It was decided that management by committee was the quickest way of getting inside knowledge of all aspects of the casino.

It was important for me to understand how the casino became a part of Paradise Island.

The casino licence was originally held by the Bahamian Club, a small casino on West Bay Street that operated for the winter season each year when the wealthy visitors would challenge lady luck at the tables.

The Bahamian Club commenced operating in the mid-1940s and since casino gambling was illegal the government issued a Certificate of Exemption, which allowed gaming at the Bahamian Club.

In the late 1950s, Stafford L. Sands recognized that the economy of The Bahamas was beginning to expand and that tourism was the industry that could underpin the economy of the country. As Chairman of The Bahamas Tourism Board, he created the two pillars of the economy—tourism and financial services, which have sustained the country for many years.

Stafford Sands understood that in some way, the offering of a fabulous and memorable vacation in The Bahamas—aside from sun, sand and sea—needed an exciting ingredient that was not available anywhere else except in Las Vegas, Nevada, and in states that operated outside of the law.

A casino in The Bahamas was going to be a crowning accomplishment!

How was this to be done without having a confrontation with the broad religious community? In 1964 and 1965, the die had already been cast.

Huntington Hartford, who bought Paradise Island (then known as Hog Island) in 1962 from Dr. Axel Wenner-Gren, the Swedish industrialist, did little to make the Island the Mecca for tourism.

The name Paradise Island came in to being when Huntington Hartford realized that Hog Island had absolutely no appeal and a name change was essential. He made application to the government for the name Hog Island to be changed to Paradise Island and by an act of Parliament, Paradise Island came into existence.

Hartford, the A&P Supermarkets heir, although having substantial financial resources, lacked the vision and management/developer skills to make Paradise Island the Mecca of Bahamian tourism. By 1964 his resources were substantially reduced and development had stalled.

Stafford, who had engineered the creation of Freeport, Grand Bahama, with Wallace Groves, realized that the purpose for which the Hawksbill Creek Act was passed in 1955 could not produce the kind of economic activity needed for sustained growth. Through creative thinking it was decided that this Freeport and West End, Grand Bahama, could be economically energized through tourism. However, for there to be strong economic growth a special stimulating initiative was essential. A big part of the stimulus was the introduction of casino gambling.

Thus the wheels were in motion. Huntington Hartford was persuaded to sell his interest in Paradise Island. Stafford and the government wanted a casino on Paradise Island but how to overcome the outcries of opposition that would pour out from the religious communities? Stafford masterminded a plan that satisfied the opponents of casino gambling and the inclusion in the Paradise Island development.

The owners of the Bahamian Club wisely agreed to sell their interests and this paved the way for the transfer of the licence—Certificate of Exemption to Paradise Enterprises Limited, the entity created to have operating control of the casino. In this way there was still only one casino in Nassau allowed to operate.

In July 1965 the government signed a number of agreements with Paradise Island Limited, the development company. Hartford retained an interest in the casino ownership company, Paradise Realty Limited, but due to a series of events, he decided to sell his interest to Resorts.

There was rapid growth. The 500-room Paradise Island Hotel and Villas was completed by early December 1967, coinciding with the completion of the casino, which included an elaborate Las Vegas-styled showroom, Le Cabaret Theatre, gourmet restaurants and bars. The 250-room Britannia Beach Hotel opened in January 1969. And so began my career with Paradise Island. There were many times when I would think back to the day I was officially introduced to Paradise Island.

During the years of Huntington Hartford's ownership, the means of getting to and from the Island was by ferry—a service introduced by Hartford with the Nassau landing site, Mermaid's Tavern being located at the harbour side of Deveaux Street and on Paradise Island at the Café Martinique dock.

When Resorts International acquired Hartford's interest in 1965, a development agreement was made with the government which included the commitment to construct a bridge to connect Paradise Island with Nassau.

The bridge was constructed and officially opened in March 1967. Being a Senator, I received an invitation to attend. It was a momentous occasion for it marked a significant milestone in our tourism history.

Following the ceremony at the foot of the bridge, a reception was held at Café Martinique, the tone of which was definitely upbeat, but for parliamentary members of the United Bahamian Party in attendance, it was bittersweet. The UBP responsible for the Paradise miracle was defeated at the polls in January 1967.

I knew Steve Norton through tennis and basketball as well as being acquainted with him while he was the Financial Controller for the Montague Beach Hotel, operated by Hotel Operators Limited, comprising creditors who had taken control when the hotel encountered serious financial problems. Bobby Symonette was president of Hotel Operators Limited. Steve Norton, as Chief Financial Officer, had to come to the Nassau Yacht Haven from time to time to obtain his signature on cheques and various documents.

While at the Café Martinique reception, Steve Norton introduced me to Jim Crosby. It was a short encounter but Jim did congratulate me on my appointment to the Senate to which he added, "Senator, we are poised to be a significant player in the development of tourism in The Bahamas."

I replied, "Mr. Crosby, the country is pleased that we have the opportunity to be a part of your project which will substantially grow the economy."

After being with the company in a senior position for several years, I discovered that in the 1965 Development Agreement it was originally the responsibility of Paradise Island Limited to build and operate the bridge. But in the end this did not happen. Jim, through his company, Paradise Island Bridge Co. Ltd., undertook to build the Paradise Island Bridge, which was to be a toll bridge.

Steve Norton in a conversation explained, "After deciding that the development of Paradise Island was going to be very substantial and finding adequate funding was to be no easy task, the Board of Directors concluded that a different approach was necessary." He added, "Having a toll bridge included in the development—one that was directly associated with the Bahamian government by way of a ninety-nine-year lease of the sea bed connecting Nassau and Paradise Island—there would be a conflict in the reporting requirements to various authorities in the U.S.A." To avoid potential complications, Jim became the principal owner of the Paradise Island Bridge with Colonel Walter Blum, a longtime friend and minority shareholder.

Steve Norton possessed a very agile brain and was Jack's source for financial analysis of the business. He prepared projections using several scenarios and served as a valuable advisor to both Jim and Jack. Steve's skills were to be tested, as casino gambling for The Bahamas at this level was very new for the entire Caribbean region.

Since I knew nothing about casino operations, Steve provided me with a rough road map for gaming to help me to gain knowledge of the business.

On that first morning, Steve showed me the office that I would occupy, made sure all the essentials were in place and then introduced me to Penny Powell, personal assistant to Jack and Jim. He asked her to take good care of me. She welcomed me cheerfully. "Barrie, you can call on me any time to assist you. I do wish you success in your work."

"Thank you, Penny. I am looking forward to being a part of the future with Resorts International."

Steve then sat me down at the glass-topped table in Jack's office to give me a run-through on what I would be doing. As he began to speak, I once more had a nervous sensation in the pit of my stomach coupled with the realization that for me, I had to look deep inside to rekindle the competitive spirit that guided me on the rugby field to success. I remembered the advice given by my mom repeatedly: "You can only do your best."

The words from Steve brought me out of my brief reverie.

"Barrie, the casino business is a complex one in which honesty is of paramount importance to gamblers. We, therefore, must be forever vigilant and have a full understanding of the numbers, as there is a huge amount of money changing hands every day." After a brief pause, he continued. "I want you to work toward gaining knowledge of all aspects of the operation. The first area of concentration for you will be in the slots department."

He added that he would provide me with the format for evaluating slot play and urged me to remember that the Gaming Board has inspectors in the casino during all hours of operation. They would be on hand to witness and verify the amount of money "dropped" at the tables, including markers denoting advances of credit to substantial casino players.

Steve took me on a tour of the casino to introduce me to the team and to explain my function with employees as well as my reporting lines to the corporate executive committee. I was well received and that pleased me because I did not want them to view me as a spy for corporate management—Joe Manes, the acting casino manager, Sam Landy, Pepi Tirelli, Gerry Grant, and Gino. The casino staff makeup was predominantly expatriates but we had some fellows I knew well—Carl Haven, Roy Rodgers, Ernie Miller, and Kendal Munroe.

Casino gambling in 1971 for The Bahamas was still in its infancy but it represented an incredible and exciting addition to the tourism industry.

Jim, Jack and Steve, with senior executives, were adamant that dress code be near formal for the casino and gourmet restaurants at night—Bahamian Club, Villa D'este, Coyaba located in the corridor leading from the casino to the Britannia Beach Hotel lobby—jacket and tie for men and long dresses for women. It was a kind of elegance that was not to last. All the women definitely had a real reason to be fashionably dressed and enjoyed doing so.

My primary responsibility was to produce detailed information on the performance of each slot machine, all 750 of them. First and foremost I had to understand that each machine was programmed to pay out, on average, a certain amount of money over a specified period of time. Of course I needed to understand the psychology of playing slots. For the uninitiated, the game was easy to play and thus non-threatening but the fact that it all happened within the mystical environment of a casino added enormous excitement for our tourists. This served to favour the players. However, the law of averages applied and it made no difference how long it took the casino to net eight to ten percent of the coins put into each machine.

Gino was particularly helpful in giving me my lesson on the value of slot play and the kind of cheating that could occur—and there were crooks always in the hunt for gain.

Gino explained, "Mr. B., the slot machines are open for play twenty-four hours a day, every day, but for control purposes when the table games are closed for the night, the slots are taken offline to accomplish the following: two employees with keys will open the machine, one at a time, with an inspector from The Bahamas Gaming Board in attendance. When a coin is put into coin slot in a machine, a meter on the inside records the coin. There is also a meter that records the payout for jackpots. Most of the jackpots are paid out with coins during play that accumulate from the machine." He then explained that the coins for the day's activity are taken from each machine and placed in a bucket that is identified with the number of the machine. The buckets of coins are taken to the count room and the process of counting the coins and recording totals begins. For this purpose, specifically designed coin-counting machines are used. Without this automation, counting would take forever.

As my job was to record meter readings, deduct payouts, and calculate the percentage of payout, day in and day out I produced these reports. The obvious question was: *Why the need for concern?*

We need to understand that the business of a casino is based entirely on the exchange of cash predicated upon chance, and as there is no other product in the business there is a tendency to attract some persons who are consumed by greed and the need to beat the system, illegally. And so in the managing of the casino, it is essential to protect, fully, the integrity of all parts of the casino. Detecting cheaters required a vigilance that appeared extreme to me but the need became apparent.

In those early days, the construction and engineering of slot machines were not terribly sophisticated. It was mechanically based and not electronic.

I remember one night Gino came to me. "Mr. B., we have discovered a couple of cheaters who are manipulating some of the larger-denomination machines."

"What are they doing?" I asked.

"They are using a small-sized drill to drill through the exterior of the machine into the exact place where a thin rod is pushed into the machine to trigger the jackpot response. Where the payout requires going to the cashier's cage to collect, the inspector, thinking that it is a legitimate payout, issues a check for the jackpot amount. Also, the cheater never attempts to collect himself, but he gets an innocent bystander to collect the payout for a piece of the payout. The crooks are hard to detect because they have lookouts and if an inspector is heading, generally, in their direction they stop and move away. They are pretty slick."

In time we became more adept at detection. Plus these cheaters were well known in Las Vegas and since we were a part of the Casino Credit Bureau we were given information on their activities and methods for beating the slot machines. It still required constant vigilance.

Casino gaming is all about creating excitement and energy that is truly contagious. When a jackpot is hit in the slots, bells ring and lights flash, coupled with shrieks of joy. Simultaneously, there is the magical sound of quarters falling into a metal receptacle on the outside of the machine. The excitement is hard to describe.

Night and day I spent time in the casino doing everything I could so that I could be a better part of management. I reported regularly to Steve and the executive committee.

The composition of dealers' nationalities was distinctly foreign for two reasons—firstly, they were recruited because they were skilled craftsmen of casino gambling in Europe (especially England and Italy) and secondly, the concept was that tourists, obviously Americans, would be served by international staff—"so foreign and yet so near."

Acquiring knowledge of all aspects of the casino operation

was a relatively slow process as there are many moving parts that are fully integrated. My role kept expanding as the executive committee got more comfortable with my involvement.

Because The Bahamas, in particular, was being identified with casino gambling on a larger scale, the attention of law enforcement agencies in the United States was focusing more intently upon our operations. In the United States, the only legal casino destination was Las Vegas. There was an illegal underground casino operation in Steubenville, Ohio, and since we had a number of staff members from Steubenville who were highly skilled in the operation of casinos, Paradise Island was placed under the microscope of the FBI.

The general belief was that casino gambling was connected to the gangster/mob underworld of New Jersey, New York, Chicago and Las Vegas. To ensure that we were able to withstand the scrutiny of any U.S. crime-fighting agency we formed a Washington, D.C.-base company, International Intelligence a.k.a. "Intertel" for the sole purpose of keeping us squeaky clean. The president of the company was Robert "Bob" Peloquin, a former Department of Justice senior officer and a lawyer by profession. His staff included former FBI, Scotland Yard, and Royal Canadian Mounted Police personnel. Bob had the complete confidence of Jack and Jim.

As I reached a stage of having access to all of our casino records, policies, agreements and the like, I was sure that all parts of the casino operation were above board. However, I was surprised when I was visited by two FBI agents who sealed my files and proceeded to review all information in my possession. I was locked out for several days but nothing untoward was found. It was still sort of unsettling. At the end, the agent shook my hand and said, "Checking your files was necessary as a part of our efforts to ensure that your casino operation is untainted."

What could I say other than "as a senior employee and as a Bahamian national, I am satisfied that nothing wrong or illegal is being conducted within our casino."

Almost with each passing day, my knowledge of casino operations expanded and although repetitive in many respects it was most exciting.

After spending weeks analyzing slot machines results, I gradually became more involved with the gaming side of operations—craps, blackjack, roulette, chemin d'fer. I admit now that I never reached a very high standard of expertise. There was too much to remember.

Promoting casino play required marketing and promotional specialists in this kind of business. To me, Sam Landy, a senior manager, was a reliable source of guidance on how this system worked. Curiously enough, networking between casinos in Las Vegas and Paradise Island was mutually beneficial as it was important for casino management to know which players had good credit ratings and which did not.

As Sam explained to me, "Mr. B., high rollers are a special breed who possess a high tolerance for risk. After all, casino gambling is a game of chance. But, in exchange for this, the casino extends special complimentary services such as hotel rooms, food and beverage in gourmet restaurants, airfare allowances and credit at the tables—and these players enthusiastically play the game."

"Sam, this is truly amazing," I said. "When I consider how hard I work for my paycheck, I cannot fathom spending my money in this fashion."

Given the structure of the high-roller programme, Steve decided that my analytical review and reporting should be expanded. I was pleased to have an additional look into the inner workings of the casino and to prepare reports on events. The way it worked was not complicated but the emotions displayed by a losing player sometimes made it difficult getting to a satisfactory outcome. I soon learned that gambling is addictive. The hope of winning big keeps players on the emotional and psychological hook.

Joe Manes, our principal credit manager, explained to me, "Barrie, much of what we do is on such a personal level. Management, when deciding how to handle an unhappy player, must display great patience and understanding. For instance, if a quality player with $500,000.00 in credit has a bad run at the tables, and at the end of stay is behind by $350,000.00, this player wants the casino to pay for his suite in the Britannia, cover all food and beverage, pay for first-class airfare from New York and return for two persons and—on top of this—discount his losses by 10 percent or more. There are a number of factors to be taken into account with the bottom line being: will the player return, will he pay off his "markers" quickly, and does he have a good reputation in Las Vegas?

"In the end, Barrie, we usually get to a reasonable outcome. But, this is the nature of the business."

This gave me much thought. The executive committee, through Steve, wanted me to prepare a financial snapshot on the casino performance weekly including how much credit was extended, how much money lost, and any discounts given—against which the cost of room, food, beverage, airfare and miscellaneous would be offset. When high rollers won, the cost to the casino was greater. Getting this information required me working with senior staff in the casino.

What we were attempting to do was to be more scientific in designing policies and procedures on how complimentary services could produce better financial results. This approach was not well received by senior management because it flew in the face of how casinos were managed in the early days when the casino General Manager ruled like a monarch dispensing credit on the basis of empirical experience, intuition, through referral or possibly, whimsically.

The model we were trying to create was designed to be a "tool" that could be integrated into the process of extending credit to players on a more scientific basis.

So with assistance and guidance from casino management, I attempted to draft policies and procedures that could form a foundation upon which operational criteria could be developed and implemented.

Security and integrity of the business were critical. There were casinos in the southern islands of the Caribbean that failed to have in place a rigid and enforceable code of business conduct.

In early Las Vegas days, it was fair game for gamblers to try to cheat at the tables and in the slots through manipulation or with the complicit involvement of dealers and other floor personnel. Supervision at each "pit" fell to the most experienced personnel. In addition, casinos were constructed in a way that included structurally sound mirrored ceilings (one way viewing) which allowed special employees to watch all activities at tables. It was known as the "eye in the sky." This was an archaic method that eventually gave way to high-quality monitoring cameras.

At Paradise Island, it was important to physically watch the games as well but at this time casinos were moving into the age of technology and instead of employees being "the eyes," ceiling cameras were installed. Viewing in real time was done in a secure room with a wall of monitors showing all tables and the capability of zooming in on any table. As the quality of camera lenses improved, it was possible to determine the colour and denomination of chips being used by each player.

Personnel working in the camera-viewing room were employed by security, with Intertel being the controlling company. We could not afford for the casino to be contaminated by collusion with players committed to cheating.

As head of our security in the casino we had Lincoln Hercules, a former senior officer in the Royal Bahamas Police Force. He was a no-nonsense sort of manager and it was accepted that wrongdoing was not tolerated. He was highly respected by the staff and had their trust. Lincoln reported directly to Bob Peloquin and also worked closely with Fenlon Richards who generally had responsibility for securing the entire island. He was a native of Texas and formerly worked for the Sheriff's Office in Waco, Texas.

I worked with Lincoln on drafting many of the policies and procedures that we thought would strengthen the casino once implemented. As with all policies and procedures prepared, the executive committee had to review and approve before introducing them into the work place.

Universally it was accepted that the casino was a place for exciting entertainment. Tourists who visited were intrigued and captivated with the experience of being in a casino environment.

There were no clocks visible in the casino and the décor lent itself to constant nighttime—heavy, deep-red velvet drapes were hung around the walls; the tables were dark-stained hard woods with green felt layouts. The psychology was that people gambled more at night than during the day. Obviously a myth but it served to make an impression.

I always had to remind myself that the business of the casino was money and entertainment. To add to the casino image we operated a Vegas-type showroom, Le Cabaret. Tibor Rudas, a native Hungarian and gymnast in his early career, was the mastermind for introducing the most fabulous shows complete with topless models, topless lead dancers, acrobats, singers, comedians and even an ice skater on our own ice rink.

The Le Cabaret was used as magnet to attract tourists from the cruise ships in port a few nights per week. It also served as a showroom for gamblers, casual players, hotel guests, and Bahamians who wanted a night of excitement and entertainment.

Unfortunately human nature being what it is, the temptation to take something that doesn't belong to you, otherwise described as greed, is too often irresistible. And so it was in the casino. Remember it is a money game, lots of money.

In our Bahamian society, secret dealings are not secret for long and through the long established means of "sip sip" it was revealed that between certain employees working the blackjack tables, payouts were being made to particular players on a recurring basis to the detriment of the casino earnings. This situation was fully investigated by Intertel which, in the end, caused Bob to intervene and to terminate all the employees so involved. It was a "black eye" for the casino but essential.

The evaluations of casino players for credit rating, although not complicated, required a lot of time in information gathering plus sifting through the hotel charges to ensure compliance with the arrangements made in advance. In attempting to understand the elements of credit rating, two of our representatives, Sam Landy and Gerry Grant, were most helpful. Although the information was very useful, as far as senior casino management was concerned this kind of activity intruded on their rights to manage freely. So all in all it was an uneasy peace but manageable.

When I met with Steve, I mentioned this to him. "Steve, you should know that the guys in the casino are not thrilled that so much information has to be prepared on each high-stakes player."

Steve answered, "JB, the way the casino was being managed previously made it very difficult to understand how credit was being given and the extent to which the casino benefited once all the comps were taken into account. In any event, you will have to continue with these reports until we reach a level of comfort with the operation."

I added, "Casino management by committee was alien to the veterans but it is a way forward."

The nature of the casino business required an operating structure that was different from the hotel sector. The hours of operation were different to begin with, not to mention the pace of exchange at the table games was very quick and the skills required of staff were at a high standard. For instance, dealers worked six- or seven-hour shifts per night for six days and within each shift there would be forty minutes on dealing and twenty minutes off. This allowed for maximum efficiency at the tables and time for staff to recover from the intensity of the game.

While this system was generally designed to follow the practice adopted in Las Vegas casinos, it was to become a point of contention with dealers.

During the years 1956 through 1967, new hotels were built and many new jobs were created. The government wanted to protect the rights of employees in the workplace and in this regard enacted labour legislation designed to protect employees and employers.

The expansion of jobs created opportunity for workers to be unionized and to be represented on all job-related issues. The union negotiated industrial agreements with owners of hotels on behalf of non-management employees. At agreed upon time periods, terms and conditions of employment were renegotiated and implemented.

Even though the casino industry was integral to tourism, there was no industrial agreement for casino workers and the government understood that control of the work environment within casinos had to remain within the purview of the Bahamas Gaming Board and in keeping with the Gaming and Lotteries Act, which provided rules and policies for the operating control of casinos.

Dealers/croupiers were not highly paid, but the great benefit was that they earned substantial tips (or "tokes" as commonly referred to in casino language) that were given by gamblers who felt generous because they had a good time while gambling, or if they won big their largesse was reflected in the size of tokes given. All tokes were placed in a special box attached to the table with a slot visible on the table surface through which tokes passed.

Given the absolute need to have every act at the gaming table recognized and viewed, tokes given at the table were acknowledged by the game inspector and/or the "pit boss," a manager of a defined area devoted to a particular game. The levels of corroboration were designed to ensure casino integrity and compliance with regulations mandated by the Gaming Board through its official inspectors during the hours of casino operations.

Croupiers/dealers, when coming on to work at a table, would openly brush their hands to illustrate that nothing was concealed going in to service. Similarly, a dealer/croupier when leaving a game for his break would also brush palms openly to signify that nothing was being taken from the game.

At the end of each casino day, tokes were counted and the total was agreed upon by management and croupier representatives. Distribution of tokes to employees, although administered by casino accountants, was paid out in accordance with a formula that the employees agreed upon.

Although casino employees were given terms and conditions of employment consistent with those used in Las Vegas, a significant problem arose with the dealers that caused considerable anguish. By comparison, hotel workers were unionized and as such received the benefits as prescribed by law as well as any which may have been included in an industrial agreement between Hotel Operators and Hotel Union.

Hotel workers, subject to certain conditions, were entitled to premium pay for hours worked on a public holiday. Casino workers, on account of the very different nature of the operation and of the uneven hours worked, did not get public holidays off or premium pay for hours worked on public holidays.

The dealers were of the mind that they were being deprived of an entitlement and were being treated unfairly. A number of meetings with the croupiers ensued but no resolution was reached. I was responsible for reporting to the executive committee on developments. It was recognized that should we change a long-established policy of Las Vegas casinos, we could be creating a situation with substantial financial consequences, as well as removing required flexibility in scheduling shifts of work.

For me, it was all new territory but it proved very important to maintain a line of communication with management and croupiers.

Joe Manes was straightforward with me. "Barrie, this is such an unusual situation. In Las Vegas, a change of such a big departure from accepted practice could present great difficulties in how we schedule games."

Lino Raspantini, who was sitting with us, added, "Remember, croupiers work six shifts per week and they are paid by the shift, which is about six hours per shift with actual work time being about four hours—the reason being that a croupier, in each hour, deals for forty minutes and has a break of twenty minutes. Also, based upon anticipated business, shift assignments depend on how many games are opened during the operating hours of the days."

I interjected, "This kind of scheduling is vastly different from that of a hotel where hours of work are well defined and wherever practicable holidays can be scheduled off."

"Joe, Barrie, we understand but the croupiers seem resolved to press forward with their claim," countered Lino.

"If this is the position, then we will have to await their next move," I said.

Lino chimed in, "We should be reminded that they are also claiming compensation retroactively for public holidays not given or taken."

I could only shake my head because I sensed that this was going to be a situation that would seriously affect working conditions and attitudes in the casino. There could not be a happy ending.

Even though I did not have official contact with the employees, I felt that they were, in a way, always friendly towards me. I sensed that being a Bahamian in a relatively senior position, they felt a certain comfort in talking with me from time to time. For sure I wanted employees to be treated with respect and dignity.

Unhappy with the state of affairs, Steve and Jack were somewhat worried that any disruption in the casino could have an unwelcome impact on financial results. This had to be looked at in the context of Resorts International being a publicly traded company on the American Stock Exchange. The risk to this company was that even a hint of Resorts underperforming financially would have a bad impact on the trading value of the stock.

The problem with the croupiers in particular did not go away but the casino continued operating without any deterioration in the quality of service. At least at this stage, the employees recognized that keeping their jobs and earning substantial tips were very much in their best interest.

Soon the dispute within the casino found its way into the public domain and became the national news story for quite some time. While there was quiet in the workplace, the croupiers engaged Randol Fawkes, former Minister of Labour, to represent them in pursuing the matter through the Supreme Court.

Carson, Lawson, Klonaris, Sawyer, Knowles Chambers (successor firm to Stafford L. Sands) was our company's law firm and for this particular matter John Carson was taking the lead for Paradise Enterprises Limited, the operating company and employer of the casino employees. I worked with John Carson and was thus the liaison with our executive committee and senior management.

As with such matters, all pertinent filings were made through the court. The complaint set out points of contention but failed to quantify the amount of the dealers' claim. After all the preliminaries had been completed, the matter was to be heard by Sir Leonard Knowles, Supreme Court Justice.

John Carson gave the appearance of being a little uncertain of himself and yet extended a quiet and unshakable confidence in his own capacity. In preparation for the hearing, John told me, "You can expect the prosecution on behalf of the employees to be more emotionally based than on what I see can be a strong legal argument. Also, there will be witnesses called to give evidence but the outcome will be strictly on interpretation of the law."

This all being new to me, I enquired nervously, "What do you think will be the outcome?" He smiled indulgently and said, "I expect a good outcome but we must rely upon the wisdom of Justice Sir Leonard Knowles. In this business there are no certainties."

Since it was a civil matter there was no public interest. It required two full days for both sides to present positions. Sir Leonard asked only a few questions of clarification. Once completed, court was adjourned and it was then in the control of Sir Leonard to consider all matters presented and, based upon his interpretation of applicable law, to hand down a ruling.

It was about three weeks later when the parties to the dispute were summoned to the Supreme Court to be given Sir Leonard's ruling. I remembered the words of John Carson as Sir Leonard handed down his written ruling which, bottom line, favoured the casino employees. This was disappointing. In addition, Sir Leonard stated that Paradise Enterprises Limited had a fiduciary responsibility to provide all information required to support the employees' claim and in a form that would enable them to quantify an amount of money for which the casino could be liable.

John Carson rejected this judgment outright and sought the consent of the court to appeal the decision. Consent was granted for the appeal.

A lot of research was essential and once the Appellate Court, which sat quarterly, set a hearing date all written submissions had to be in the possession of the three sitting justices prior to the commencement of the hearing. After all preparatory matters had been dealt with the date was set for the hearing.

I was all excited at 2:00 p.m. on 15 November 1974. The stage was set in Court #4. It was a clear autumn afternoon and the sun was beaming through the west window in the courtroom. I was the only spectator to witness the unfolding drama of an important legal argument that would establish a legal precedent of considerable importance. I thought to myself, *This is like opening night of a riveting play on Broadway and I am the only member of audience.* It was for me euphoric and most memorable.

And there was John Carson in gown and wig, with Lester Mortimer as his junior. Randol Fawkes was on the other side of the room, on his own, with at least six volumes of various law reference books to be used during the hearing.

The bailiff for the justices sat in front of the bench. The justices filed in with dignified silence as we all respectfully stood to accept their impressive entry. Once seated, the bailiff called the court to order with only me as a witness. Yes, only me.

The sun was edging lower and shadows crept across the benches and the marble flooring, lending an even more theatrical feeling to the hearing.

As the proceedings progressed, I was spellbound to the point that I felt as if my presence was essential to the proceeding. The decorum observed was comforting in that it confirmed in a direct way that all society functioned in full compliance with the written law—a structure that had withstood the challenges of those who attempted to abuse a system which gives people security of order.

John Carson presented our company's position with unerring clarity and patience. When questioned by any of the justices, he would respond deferentially such as, "Yes, my Lord, I appreciate the need to expand my position on this point." Whenever Mr. Fawkes rose to speak on a point being advanced by John, he would take a seat until Mr. Fawkes was finished.

To me, absolutely the most fascinating argument put forward by John was related to action started by an architect engaged by the Great Western Railway in 1831. The work by this architect was not completed according to the terms of this contract and Great Western Railway brought the relationship to an end. The architect started an action against Great Western Railway. The matter unbelievably was not completed before the demise of the architect, and the judgment was actually handed down posthumously. Great Western Railway's position prevailed. It had to do with whether or not there was a fiduciary relationship between the two.

I did not understand the similarity of circumstances in our matter, Croupiers vs. Paradise Enterprises Limited, but it appeared that the croupiers, through Mr. Fawkes, sought the court to rule that the employer had a fiduciary responsibility to reconstruct a detailed report in which the croupiers could quantify what they thought they were owed.

After all arguments and precedents were presented, the Appellate Court ruled that Paradise Enterprises Limited did not have a fiduciary relationship with the croupiers. However, the croupiers did have a right of access to payroll information from which they could build a claim quantifying what might be owed. It had to be borne in mind that for every pay period, each employee received a statement of wages for all time worked.

For me, that afternoon in the Supreme Court is indelibly imprinted in my mind—the dignity, the respect, and the intellectual order was a reconfirmation of faith in the legal system that has survived the many challenges through the passage of countless years.

The croupiers failed to pursue the matter and thus their claim came to naught. My report to the executive committee was well received.

Jack expressed it best: "Had this action gone against the company, it would have been the beginning of non-ending conflict with employees over conditions of employment."

Steve added that "in managing the casino we need to constantly balance financial outcomes with employee support and loyalty to the company."

My concern, which I expressed hesitatingly, was: "It is likely that there will be some lingering resentment by croupiers because of the unsatisfactory outcome for them. Our job is to now establish a comfortable relationship with croupiers and with the staff generally."

So several days later I met with John to review and consider what was to be done next.

"John, your presentation to the court was impressive. Congratulations," I said.

In his gentle way John acknowledged my comments and added, "I am pleased that the justices were cognizant of the application of the legal precedent even though I detected that there was a degree of empathy for Mr. Fawkes and his clients."

On the matter of costs, the croupiers were required to pay our expenses.

I really admired John Carson and wanted to be further exposed to his thinking about the application of law and his interest in the priesthood about which he had intimated in an earlier conversation. I invited John to dinner at my home which he accepted happily.

Later that day, I sat at my desk pondering what approach should be adopted to accelerate the mending of fences in the casino. In the end I decided that the best approach was to continue doing my job by being respectfully involved with casino operations.

Barrie with Steve Norton
First day on the job at Paradise Island
1st December 1971

A photo of all staff while we were manufacturing clothing in the 1990s at SunTee

CHAPTER 26

BAHAMAS SPORTSWEAR MANUFACTURING LIMITED

Of course the '70s was a decade of new beginnings and none more unique and unpredictable for me than the birth of Bahamas Sportswear Manufacturing Ltd. In 1974, Josephine Elizabeth joined Resorts International as Executive Secretary to the President, Irving George "Jack" Davis. Coincidentally, a close friend, Gladys Darville, was in the same office area and served as Executive Secretary to Steve Norton, Vice President of Resorts International.

Jo and Gladys developed a close friendship and were both American citizens married to Bahamians. Highly intelligent, they were keen to venture into a business that could be managed without any adverse impact upon their Resorts International jobs.

It was during this period that John Issa, an entrepreneur from Jamaica, purchased some property from Paradise Island Ltd. on the east side of Casino Drive. Issa built a small shopping centre designed to capture the tourist traffic.

Jo and Gladys saw this as an opportunity to open a shop with the theme being tourism-related souvenirs. They appropriately named the store Serendipity. The girls were overjoyed that they could pool resources to start this business. They had fun running the business even though it was not a big money maker. To avoid conflict with Resorts, they would use their lunch hour to attend to Serendipity matters.

They thoroughly enjoyed what they were doing. Each day when it was time to go to Serendipity, Gladys would say to Jo, "Well it's time to go to our second job." And Jo laughingly would add, "This is good because by not eating lunch we are losing weight."

In the second year of operating Serendipity, another store came available. Jo and Gladys saw this as a chance to expand. And they did so without hesitation.

As the stores catered to tourists primarily, we soon recognized that T-shirts with Bahamian-themed sayings imprinted on them sustained revenue from this stream. As they were buying locally manufactured products, the demand for T-shirts stretched the financial resources of the operators of Bahamas Sportswear Manufacturing Limited.

Jo and Gladys came to Eddy and me with a proposition that we were not excited about pursuing but the girls persuaded us to support Bahamas Sportswear Manufacturing Limited to the extent of investing in the company. Eddy did not have the extra cash so it fell to me to deal with this but with a commitment by Jo and Gladys that they would increase the purchase of T-shirts significantly.

Bahamas Sportswear manufactured T-shirts, sweatshirts, and depending upon suitable raw material being available, ladies' beach coveralls. Things started going sideways financially and the relationship with the founders was moving rapidly in the wrong direction. After a number of combative meetings compounded by questionable behaviour of the founders, ownership reverted to me. This is not an outcome that I welcomed.

The business continued mainly because of the contributions of Rodney Husbands and Stephen Slocombe, who were Barbadians and were very competent in the manufacturing of clothing, especially T-shirts. Given the unusual circumstances I had little choice but to intervene to try to save the business.

To Rodney and Stephen I made it clear what confronted us.

"Rodney and Stephen, you two must manage this business, which will require you to dedicate more time to manufacturing than either of you expected."

I trusted these men and in response they declared, "Mr. Farrington you have our full support."

We had a staff of thirty-two of whom twenty-five were sewers and the others dealt with graphic design, silkscreen printing, inventory control, accounting and so on. I felt that this was going to be an enormous struggle but Jo and Gladys relied on this company to provide merchandise. Of course, there were other customers but we were well-structured. There was one person who believed in the future of the business and that was Victoria Gibson who controlled the sewing department. She was indeed a pillar of strength.

Here I was in the middle of an enterprise about which I knew so little. In order to keep them moving forward, it was necessary for me to visit our fabric suppliers in Miami and to negotiate business terms. This was all very informative and the experience gained was valuable and expanded my vision of running a business outside of tourism.

Despite hard work and support from the staff, I was badly overdrawn at the bank with a personal guarantee underpinning the credit line. I had to face what appeared to be the inevitable. By this time Rodney and Stephen had already moved on and Victoria was in charge.

The decision to close the business and absorb the loss in covering the overdraft was gut-wrenching. I called Victoria and asked her to come to see me at my office in the Britannia.

With her sitting opposite to me in my office with my desk separating us, I had to give her the bad news.

"Vicky, you know we have struggled hard to make Bahamas Sportswear successful but the time has come for us to face the impossible," I said gravely.

She looked at me intently as I continued. "I am sorry but I have no choice but to close the business as soon as possible."

Vicky's eyes never left my face. I could see that she was shocked and deeply sad at the same time.

"Mr. Farrington, I am begging you not to close the business. We will find a way to get things turned around." These words were clothed in an emotion that penetrated my soul. Her tears flowed down her cheeks.

She persisted with her pleas for me to continue operating the business. "Mr. Farrington, we will work very hard and make the business a lot better than it is now. I beg you to keep the company operating. The Lord will be on our side."

I finally relented, "Vicky, we will give it another month and then look at it again."

As she left my office she kept repeating, "God will bless you, Mr. Farrington."

Within that month, my son Scott returned to Nassau and he was eager to get to work. I took the decision to let Scott have a go at turning the business around.

Scott did an amazing job and was smart enough to use Vicky's experience and insights. After struggling for about twelve months, we seemed to be lifting ourselves out of the financial quagmire.

Scott convinced me to change our business model. The following changes paved the way to most encouraging results. We got out of the manufacturing business. We were simply not competitive. Emphasis was placed on silkscreen printing. We purchased additional equipment to enable expansion.

We capitalized on the tourism industry with themed Islands of The Bahamas souvenir items under licence from the Ministry of Tourism. We established a department devoted to convincing local businesses to use specially designed promotional items for enhancing business activity.

Piece by piece, revival of the business occurred much to our delight. We then reached a point where we needed more operating space. What was to be the next step?

With hearts beating a little more rapidly than usual, we took a huge leap of faith and negotiated with the owner, Reginald Knowles, to buy the entire building, over 10,000 square feet of space. Fortunately the timing for this move was perfect. Leslie Miller of Sun Burst Paint, who occupied the ground floor, was moving to new premises.

Good fortune kept on smiling upon us. We obtained a mortgage through Commonwealth Bank and ownership passed to Scott and me—a very proud day for sure. And from that moment we never looked back. One of the first things we did was to give the building a Bahamian character. We painted the building a bright orange with a royal blue trim that made an impression on passersby.

I have always had a tendency to question underlying reasons for what happens to us in life. I am a religious person but not a frequent churchgoer. Those who occupy the space around us and of diverse backgrounds generally will attribute events, good and bad, to the will of God. My mother taught me to believe in God and the church, which was a good thing because it is through this persistent evidence that we measure good and evil.

When Victoria Gibson came to my office, she had no idea of the purpose. After all, she did what her boss requested her to do. She received the "bad" news gallantly at first but when fully absorbed she wept. That afternoon with Victoria was a moment of revelation. Had I remained steadfast with my position to close the business, the outcome of this story would be entirely different.

I have repeatedly stated publicly that I owe the success of Bahamas Sportswear to Victoria. Had she not begged me to stay the course and had I not relented there would have been quite a different ending.

J. Barrie sharing a light moment with Tibor Rudas of Tibor Rudas Productions on his birthday in Carmel, California, and Ian MacLaren, general manager of the Le Cabaret Show in the Paradise Island Casino. Tibor was the creator of the Le Cabaret Show.

CHAPTER 27

CASINO GAMBLING: A NEW ECONOMIC MODEL

Being an integral part in the operating management of the Paradise Island Casino was intimidating and at the same time it was the opportunity of a lifetime. By intent it was shrouded in mystery, which added to the allure that many of our tourists found fascinating.

Through discussions with experienced managers and by observation through the performance reports I prepared for the executive committee, it was recognized that casino gambling was addictive. I also discovered that hard-core gamblers were superstitious.

We had one habitual "high roller" who was enamored with shooting "craps"—a game of dice, and who refused to play at a table if a woman was standing nearby wearing a red dress. He would stop for the night. There was no way to help him overcome his superstition.

In and around the casino floor during hours of operating, there was a team of cleaners who swept up cigarette and cigar ashes or other kinds of trash thrown on the floor. It was important to keep the casino area clean and attractive. In the cleaning function, occasionally, a cleaner would come into contact with a player at the craps table. We had a high-stakes player who would stop playing if a cleaner's brush touched his shoes. Needless to say, whenever this player was in the casino, cleaners were kept far away from him.

Then there were the addicts. It is as true now as it was then that once someone is hooked, the urge to gamble is very hard to control. The way the system worked is that a high-stakes player would establish his level of credit prior to coming to Paradise Island. The limit of credit was controlled by the Cage Credit Manager. If a player gambled against a cash deposit, the Credit Manager allowed the cash to be placed in the Cashiers' Cage and the player took chips at the table against the cash deposit. For each advance of chips given at the table, the player signed a chit called a "marker" which went against his established credit line.

Surprisingly the casino in many ways was protective of its high-end players. For instance, a player who established a $50,000 line of credit and then lost the $50,000 over several sessions at the table would have his credit frozen at that point. The casino felt responsible for keeping players within limits; otherwise they would play until they bankrupted themselves. There is always the belief on the part of players that their luck will change if they had more credit.

I once witnessed an overextended player beg the casino manager for more credit to the point where the tears began flowing. He was a longtime credit player. Occasionally, casino management would relent and give additional credit. The risk of a problem was always right on the horizon.

There was an axiom long recognized by casino operators in Las Vegas that was adopted in Paradise Island and that is: "A high-stakes gambler who lives on credit will sooner or later give you some bad paper."

In an attempt to limit this kind of exposure, the system relied on the existence of a central credit agency in which the gamblers who have credit arrangements with several casinos were tracked for performance. If a gambler defaulted on the payment of any debt, this information was shared among participating casinos.

Gamblers understood this exposure and for this reason they tried extremely hard to protect their credit worthiness. For once credit became questionable, a gambler was in effect forced into exile. Of course, playing for cash was always acceptable.

The peculiarity of the casino is that it is a cash business where the product is intangible. There was a place and time in history when it was discovered that imbedded somewhere in the human DNA there is the undeniable urge to engage in risk-taking with the prospect of being rewarded. Losing was irrelevant to the game so long as there existed the opportunity to win. Obviously, losing does carry unintended consequences, but consequences nonetheless.

There is another element that is fascinating. A player who was extended credit for gambling and lost had an opportunity to settle his account prior to leaving Paradise Island or to pay once back home. The casino, in allowing a later payment, maintained an office in the United States for this purpose. And where such a transaction should be straightforward, many times, depending upon the size of the debt, the casino player would seek a discount off the debt. The strangeness of this position is that the player wanted to pay less than what he owed and yet the casino had to pay a gaming tax on the total amount lost.

And then you ultimately get to "sooner or later you will get some bad paper."

The management also had to deal with top-rated players who were always demanding to play for higher stakes beyond those allowed in stated casino policy. To acquiesce, the casino could have had a bad run of luck with any high-risk player. The casino set maximums for each bet made at the tables, but then would come a player with platinum credit who did not want to be constrained by casino-imposed limits. Negotiations were normally short-lived and it was agreed that limits would be substantially increased. In a manner of speaking, the casino (through the casino manager) became a high-risk player, as well.

Once when speaking to Sam Landy about this phenomenon, I "naively" said, "Sam, I am absolutely astounded at how persons are prepared to lose money in a casino. What drives them so ceaselessly?"

"Barrie," Sam answered, with a smile on his lips, "because in part it is ego-driven. Being the centre of attention in a big stakes game is pure adrenaline for them, and consequences be damned." I understood what he said but it failed to convince me that there was any logic to living for momentary thrills and possible monetary gain.

I was in the casino on the day a huge player, with virtually unlimited credit, flew into Nassau in his own jet and was escorted to our best suite of rooms at the Britannia. He was a baccarat player—two-fisted at that. When he arrived in the casino in the late afternoon everyone was put on alert. I did not watch him play because he was in the Salon Privé where special players were allowed to play outside of the direct and inquisitive attention of the curious casino patrons.

Within a three-hour period, this player lost over $2 million. I almost fainted when I was told about this. Unsurprisingly, he settled his account several days later without having reduced his losses.

The public view of the casino maintained that it was an offline business where the "house" always wins. Statistically, as I continued to produce analyses of operating results, one could almost predict what the net win for the casino would be for a twelve-month period. It was uncanny.

Where there was a significant amount of money changing hands between players and the casino during any given day, the question invariably arose and no doubt still arises: is there a way to consistently beat the casino? There is a mathematical element that governs gaming and if that mathematical piece is manipulated then there is a good chance that an expert "cheater" could win consistently.

In the game of blackjack, otherwise referred to as "21," players are playing against the casino. It is the most popular game offered in casinos.

Blackjack is pretty simple. The basic premise of the game is for the player to have a hand value that is closer to 21 than that of the dealer without going over 21.

To start the game four decks of cards are shuffled by the dealer and placed in a shoe with a marker being put about two-thirds of the way in the cards. The reason for this is that the dealer never deals all the cards in the shoe. When he reaches the marker there is a pause in the game and the dealer reshuffles all of the cards.

And then the unexpected happened which changed the outcome of the game at least for a while. Unscrupulous players who were genius-like mathematicians recognized that the odds of winning at blackjack or 21 could be dramatically improved by counting "aces, and face cards in particular" that were put into play by the dealer and before it became necessary to reshuffle the cards.

A card counter would normally have accomplices to help with counting of cards.

It took a while in Las Vegas and at Paradise Island to realize that just a few players were winning big on a consistent basis. With no obvious reason for outcomes, a card counter required stamina because he would have to stay at the same table from late morning until 2:00 a.m. or 3:00 a.m. the next day.

Once the element of chance was substantially removed from the game, the underlying premise for blackjack was destroyed.

The casinos in Las Vegas and Paradise Island were affected with this sort of gaming. In speaking with Joe Manes he said, "This kind of play is not good for casinos and a way must be found to put a stop to it once detected."

"How could you do that?" I asked.

"Barrie, casinos have the right to make rules that will ensure the integrity of the casino operation. We simply cannot allow these kinds of 'gunslingers' to play without control."

"Joe, sounds like a big order to put an end to such play."

"We work with the casinos in Las Vegas and they know who the 'cheaters' are. We will all agree to bar these cheaters from playing in our casinos."

That sounded like a way of putting an end to such crooks. And so the word went out that certain named persons were not allowed to play in any casino that was a member of Central Credit. Thus order was restored and "lady luck" once more reigned supreme.

December 1967, when the casino opened its doors as a place for gambling and entertainment, marked the beginning of another important but uncertain step in furthering the development of our tourism industry. Overall, it was generally agreed that tourism had the amazing potential to be the principal driver of the Bahamian economy. Stafford L. Sands had the foresight for the country to use the beauty of our land and the warm friendliness of Bahamian people together with exciting attractions.

It was now clear that the country was moving on a path without a clearly defined strategy and as a result, there were elements in the development process that in the end were fraught with difficulties.

The Government in 1956 and in the years following had rationalized the need for importing the skills and talents necessary to ensure that foreign hotel developers would be able to operate using skilled, non-Bahamian personnel in order to compete with other destinations. The economy was growing quickly and tourism was proving to be the vehicle for sustainable economic activity. In 1960 and beyond, I had become active in politics and felt deep inside that I could, with the group of young people I associated with, help push the country in the right direction. With a burgeoning economy, Bahamians wanted to play a more substantial role in the growth of the country.

My colleagues and I understood the concerns expressed and accepted that more Bahamians should be participating meaningfully in our expanding economy.

I wrote to Sir Roland Symonette expressing my concerns and those of my colleagues. In essence I said that the Government needed to find a formula for embracing Bahamians who had the aspirations to play a bigger role and who, by and large, had the education to be integrated properly into such economic activity.

Sir Roland replied that he acknowledged what was being advanced but said that "we were no longer a fishing village" and that we were making huge strides to develop the country. He added that we were riding on a wave of prosperity that we could not afford to jeopardize through defective planning.

I remember distinctly adding in a further communication to Sir Roland on the same subject with the following comment: "It would be a sad testament for us if the government should be lost in the face of prosperity." Of course I was looking toward the next election that was to be held in 1967. Was this a premonition?

CABLE ADDRESS:
"THEODORE NASSAU"
TELEPHONES : 3041 - 2730

ENGINEERING PLANT
AND SUPPLIES
GENERAL SHIP REPAIRS
MARINE RAILWAYS

SYMONETTE SHIPYARDS LIMITED
NASSAU, N. P., BAHAMAS

13th September, 1965.

Mr. J. B. Farrington
Nassau Yacht Haven
P. O. Box 1216
Nassau, Bahamas.

Dear Barrie,

I am pleased to receive your letter of September 4th and to know you are offering in 1967 for the District of Winton. I will be glad to help you all I can, and will see you in a very short time.

Reference this portion of your letter which reads:

"Many people of our community are extremely upset by the apparent influx of foreigners into the country and who find employment here without any difficulty. I am being approached often enough to cause me a great deal of concern. I think we should give serious thought to reviewing the position."

This country is no longer a village. Sound and large businesses are now resident here and there is no use us thinking we can run the country with Bahamians only, and you know it. I do not doubt in the least that there are persons, not Bahamians, who are working in the country filling jobs that could be filled by Bahamians but, do we have the Bahamians to fill these jobs?

We have quite a good Immigration Department; my advice to you is, when anyone approaches you on this subject, do not let them talk in a casual way but tell them to name the person or persons to whom they refer, where they are working, the job they are doing and pass this on to me; a file will be made on each individual, the case investigated and a report made. Other than this way I cannot listen to people who cannot come out into the open and make a statement.

On entering politics, one bit of advice I would like to offer, speak honestly and frankly to people, do not dodge issues to gain an individual vote when you know they are wrong, do not try to get criminals released from prison, or try to keep them from going to prison; that's what the prison is for. Do not make any promises that you cannot keep and, more than all, do not let politics put you in the poorhouse.

Sincerely,

Sir Roland Symonette.

RTS/eib

We did lose the government in the General Election of 1967 but my interest in promoting the interest of Bahamians did not lessen. It was against this backdrop that there required balanced consideration on how to have Bahamians brought into the casino in a way that assured success. There are no certainties in life but to the extent that the odds favour the right outcome, the better the chance of permanency.

The PLP Government was pushing for Bahamianization almost regardless of cost. I wanted to be a part of a programme to promote Bahamians to succeed and not to fail. The executive committee recognized that it made sense to begin the search for Bahamians who were well educated and who demonstrated a willingness to learn new skills. And so we began moving forward. There were two areas to be tackled at once—the Cashier's Cage and the Slot Machine Department.

Given the technical aspects of the Slots Department, it was critical that the company appoint the most knowledgeable casino manager to tackle the transitioning process.

Pepi Tirelli, a senior and very experienced manager was given the green light to reorganize the Slots Department and in this regard to transit to a substantially all Bahamian department. Pepi possessed vast casino operating experience and was especially knowledgable and skilled in the management of the slots department.

The Bahamians selected for this department learned quickly and were eager to make a difference. While the transition required careful managing it soon became evident that the stellar standouts were Kendal Munroe, Roy Rodgers, Leroy Storr, Leroy Young and Mark Ferguson.

In tandem with the Slots Department changes, the Cashiers Cage was similarly being Bahamianized under the direction of Joe Manes, senior casino manager in whom the company had complete faith. It was a relatively slow transitional process but the Bahamian trainees adapted quickly.

Once the transformation was complete it was most satisfying to acknowledge the stand-out performers and in particular Carl Haven, Jimmy McKenzie, Gene Cooper and Tony Balfour.

We were headed upon a course of action that would flow into the area then reserved for the highly skilled croupiers who were expatriates. But I envisaged a day when there would be a strong workforce in all facets of the casino operation. Difficult as it may appear, we could not let impatience cloud good judgment.

Through conversations with our experienced casino managers, it became evident that for the persons seeking a little excitement in the casino there existed a psychological barrier that had to be breached.

For one, all the table games such as craps, blackjack, roulette and baccarat are governed by established rules. Unless you are familiar with the rules, sitting or standing at a table to gamble can be somewhat unnerving and basically intimidating.

The other barrier was the issue of summoning sufficient nerve to sit alone at a table to commence gambling. Most people will venture to a table if there are other players—sort of comfort in numbers.

Casino operators understood the dilemma of a novice player. To try to correct this impediment for a new player, the casinos engaged persons, commonly referred to as "shills," to sit at tables and gamble using "house" money and/or chips. This approach helped to build a degree of confidence in a person to venture into the game. This practice was not to "scalp" the unsuspecting player. It was all above board. The practice, however, was never adopted at our Paradise Island Casino.

CHAPTER 28

A CHANGE OF GOVERNMENT IMPACTS PARADISE ISLAND

Although the time spent in the casino was an experience that added another dimension to my career in tourism, I did not see my tenure in this area being extensive because I believed that I could be more valuable to Resorts in another capacity. On the other hand, it was an ever-changing landscape with the most unsettling situation arising when the PLP Government made it abundantly clear that its intention was for the government on behalf of the Bahamian people to own the Paradise Island Casino.

In pursuit of this serious declaration, the government was to use the Hotel Corporation of The Bahamas for this history-making effort. There was cause for consternation among Resorts' lenders and shareholders. Being a publicly traded company on the American Stock Exchange, the fallout amongst shareholders and institutions that provided financing for Paradise Island was indeed worrying. The financial sustainability of a casino-based enterprise relied heavily upon the company meeting financial projections published on Wall Street. A failure to meet expectations generally resulted in the downgrading of the company's stock and the market value of the company.

No one was sure how this scenario would evolve and managing such uncertainty requires steady and confident leadership. Based upon my very limited exposure with Jim and Jack, I did not detect any panic on their part. In fact with Steve Norton and Bob Peloquin providing sage advice to the group, there was a kind of quiet confidence being exuded.

Given the new government's surprising declaration to nationalize casino gambling, I had a quick look at the history of casino gambling in Nassau. In the early 1940s, the Government agreed to the establishment of the Bahamian Club, a small casino to be situated on West Bay Street. This casino operated during a four-month winter season and catered only to wealthy visitors. To legitimize the casino, the Government issued a Certificate of Exemption. The reason for the certificate was that the law prohibited any gambling to occur in a public place. This exemption was issued under Sub-Section (10) of Section 257 of the Penal Code.

The country was moving relentlessly on a path for expanding our tourism industry and there was a strong sense that casino gambling could be central to success.

Earlier in 1965, a development company was formed, Paradise Island Limited with which Huntington Hartfort was associated. This company broadly negotiated a twenty-year development agreement to create a world-class resort on Paradise Island. The interests of the Bahamian Club were acquired and the Certificate of Exemption was transferred to Paradise Enterprises Limited, the current operator and subsidiary of Paradise Island Limited. Paradise Realty Limited was formed to construct and lease the casino to Paradise Enterprises Limited.

The new casino opened on the night of 20 December 1967. The Bahamian Club closed after business on 19 December and moved over to Paradise Island during the night without loss of business due to the move.

An important part of this huge development plan was the construction of a 500-room luxury hotel that would be connected by a corridor to the casino. An agreement was made with the Loews Corporation of New York to operate the hotel. On

1 December 1967, the Paradise Island Hotel and Villas opened for business. This was obviously a most welcome precursor of great events to be introduced in accelerating the development of tourism. Robert "Bob" Tisch and his brother, Laurence, principals of the Loews Corporation were happy with the arrangement.

In reading through some of the notes outlining the plans for the future, it was evident that Jim Crosby and Jack Davis were fully engaged and ecstatic. I determined in meetings I attended with Jack and Steve that Jim was the visionary and thus was not constrained by impediments to progress. He was always undeterred.

The Showroom, Le Cabaret, was completed and for entertainment to add to the magic of the opening of the Paradise Island Casino and gourmet restaurants, Nancy Wilson, world-renowned singer and entertainer, was booked for ten days starting the 28th of December 1967. What a coup for the company. Having first-class entertainment in the casino to sustain the excitement was essential. In fact, in addition to big-name entertainment, the thinking was leaning toward introducing an international revue-type show after the winter season.

Just reading through the development programme made me feel particularly happy that I was a part of an organization that was on the move and that a bright future was ahead. Where would I fit into the company beyond 1973? Once there, for sure I was prepared to work hard and prove my worth.

The 100-room Beach Inn was constructed right next to the world-famous Paradise Beach. It had an upgraded cafeteria to be used by all visitors, including Beach Inn guests. And to add to the splendor of a memorable vacation, a spectacular water show started on 25 December and performances were every evening. The entertainment included several national champion water skiers plus spectacular fireworks.

So much was happening in 1967 and 1968—horse stables were renovated with horse riding introduced. Hurricane Hole Marina with forty-eight slips was fully operational and in January 1968 the Paradise Shipyard was placed under the control of the marina. The Ocean Club was open and operating with fifty-two rooms and twelve cabanas. The original restaurant overlooking the pool and Versailles Gardens had been completely destroyed by a catastrophic fire in 1967 and was not reconstructed. Instead dining was confined to the Ocean Club main building. The Paradise Island Golf Course was renovated and Gary Player, formerly of South Africa and one of the greatest golf champions in the world, joined Paradise Island as the touring professional.

To add more glitter to the glamour of Paradise Island, Pancho Gonzalez, the very talented and world famous tennis champion, was engaged as the tennis touring professional representing Paradise Island and the Ocean Club.

The deal of the century, at least in The Bahamas, was the purchase of Hog Island by Huntington Hartford from Dr. Axel Wenner-Gren on 6 February 1960. The name of "Hog Island" was changed to Paradise Island during 1962 by an act of the legislature.

In one of my talks with Steve, he gave me an insightful look back at the succession of events on Paradise Island from the beginning.

"Barrie, while I was working at the Montague Beach Hotel, I heard about the prospect of Huntington Hartford disposing of his interest in Paradise Island (previously Hog Island) and that the Mary Carter Paint Company of New Jersey was the buyer. I decided that I would find a way to become associated with the development company. As it turned out, I was introduced to Jack Davis and in subsequent meetings he concluded that I could be of value to the new company." Since he hesitated a moment before continuing, I was guessing that he was deciding on how much he would reveal to me. In the end, he went on mainly because many of the events associated with the Huntington Hartford deal were a matter of public record.

Steve went on, "You may recall that the company used for the acquisition of Hartford's interest in Paradise Island was the Mary Carter Paint Company, a company in which the Crosby family had a controlling interest. It seems that the government favoured the Mary Carter Paint Company for developing Paradise Island and encouraged the parties to negotiate a deal. So, in January 1966, Huntington Hartford transferred 75 percent of his interest in Paradise Island to the Mary Carter Paint Company with Hartford retaining 25 percent of the company that was to build and own the Paradise Island Casino. Hartford, for a few years after the transaction, continued to take an active part in company affairs. He later disposed of his remaining interest in a deal with Jim Crosby."

"Well, Steve, that is really a story of 'riches to rags' for Hartford and the arrival of James 'Jim' Crosby and Jack Davis. At what point did Resorts International, Inc., come into being?"

Steve, in understanding my concern regarding the progression of events, explained that in May 1968, merely two years after starting out in Paradise Island, the Mary Carter Paint Company, in addition to selling its assets and business, also changed its name to Resorts International, Inc.

There were more questions ricocheting around in my mind but I wanted the answer to the question regarding the origin of Resorts International, Inc., in the scheme of things.

Steve seemed to remember and added, "Merely two years after starting out in Paradise, in May 1968, Mary Carter sold its net assets, business as well as the name of the Mary Carter Paint division and changed its name to Resorts International, Inc."

"How much more was to be added to this story?"

By the time I started my employment with the casino, the Britannia Beach Hotel of 270 rooms was constructed and had opened in January 1969. The Beach Inn of 100 rooms was operating. The world-famous Café Martinique, an outstanding gourmet restaurant with a French cuisine, and which was originally created by Huntington Hartford, was considered the best restaurant in The Bahamas. The building in which Café Martinique was located was originally the boathouse of Dr. Axel Wenner-Gren and bordered the Paradise Island lagoon.

The thought struck me as I was leaving Steve's office that day in 1972 that I was in position to be a part of an organization that was aiming for the stars. My life had changed. I was now living on my own at my home on Prince Charles Drive. Lee Rose was in Mexico with Scott, and John and Bruce were away at Appleby College in Toronto, Canada. It would have been very easy to use my aloneness to wallow in self-pity but that was not to be; instead I sat in the Florida Room very reflective about where I was in the universe.

My mind drifted to Huntington Hartford and I experienced a certain degree of sadness on his behalf. Even though he had been born into wealth and privilege, his dream of a Paradise-like resort for the rich and famous, through his own mismanagement, had evaporated. And now what he once had resided only in memories.

While in this state, I wondered how far I would be able to go within the company. This was the big leagues. Could it be that my lack of a university degree would be an impediment in my career? My education at the Government High School was very good and with my natural tendency to write pretty well, plus the nurturing given by Robert H. Symonette, I believed that I had foundation upon which to build.

While so engrossed in looking critically at my business and public life, I decided upon one irrevocable approach to every undertaking I proceeded with and that was: "In the pursuit of success I will work tirelessly to obtain that end."

* * *

Little did I know that there were changes for me within Resorts International. There would be exciting moments and at other times there would be demoralizing challenges to be met.

As I was leaving the casino floor following a morning of looking at the results of the previous night and getting a reading on outstanding matters so that I could prepare my usual report on players who had credit with the casino and the extent to which performance related to the comps provided by the casino, I was approached by Steve Norton.

"Barrie, Jack wants to meet with you. Please join us for dinner at the Bahamian Club at 7:30 p.m."

I naturally responded in the affirmative. After all when the President invites you to dinner, you do not decline. Jo would not be particularly happy as she had planned a special dinner for us that evening, but so be it. On the other hand, even though we met regularly in the Executive Committee, I knew this meeting was going to be different. There was no foreshadowing of content so I did have a sudden sense of anxiety.

That evening I arrived few minutes early in keeping with my customary attention to being on time. Shortly thereafter, Jack and Steve walked in.

"JB," as Jack usually called me, "thank you for joining us tonight."

We sat at his favourite table and ordered drinks. I had a soft drink as my rule was never to have an alcoholic beverage during a business meeting or while working, even if attending a business-based social event.

After a few minutes of engaging in small talk, Jack turned his attention to the purpose of the meeting.

"We have been impressed with your efficiency and hard work as the liaison between the casino operations and our Executive Committee. You have accomplished quite a bit in the short time that you have been with the company. The policies and procedures that you and casino management developed for certain segments of the operation have proven to be very useful."

He continued, "We have confidence in you and given your experience in the hospitality business, we need you to take on additional responsibilities in other areas. Quite frankly, we would like for you to eventually move away from the casino into the core operations of the entire resort."

Jack in his very deliberative manner of speaking acknowledged that in representing the Executive Committee as a part of management in the casino, I had proven to be very successful and it was evident that I had been a quick learner. Even though the senior guys in the casino viewed me with a degree of suspicion because I reported to corporate management, he added, "You were able to break down barriers and develop a sense of trust, which contributed to the success of the casino."

As we talked further, Jack and Steve made it evident that operating the casino by committee was not the best approach. They had moved in this direction after early general managers were too autocratic and old school and not very compatible with corporate leadership. Jim, Jack and Steve understood casino gambling but were not familiar with the "nuts and bolts" of how a casino should be managed. And of course, they had to be careful that there was no association whatsoever with organized crime in the United States. In August 1967, the first appointed General Manager, Mr. Edward Cellini, was in place when the Paradise Island commenced operating on 20 December 1967. For some reason Cellini's tenure was not long lived and he was replaced by Mr. Ted Gagliano in November 1971. Mr. Gagliano was relieved of his position for no cause other than he was not as strong in managing the casino as the president thought he should be.

It was at this stage that a decision was taken to manage the casino by committee comprising Steve Norton, Fen Richards (representing Bob Peloquin and Intertel), Jack Davis and me. For day-to-day operations in the casino, Sam Landy was recognized as the manager.

"Jack, I am prepared to do whatever I can to make the company successful."

"JB, let me talk a little about the company and the future."

Without my being inquisitive, in fact it was almost like he was reading my mind. He and Steve outlined several essential steps that would be imbedded into the forward thinking plans of the company.

The company in a progressive and responsible way was moving forward to bring more Bahamians into the business. In this regard, Tommy Robinson had succeeded George Mackey as the Vice President of Human Resources. The expectation was that I, in some integral way, would assist with the process.

Entertainment was to be an important ingredient in making the resort generally and the casino in particular, a high-energy and exciting place to vacation.

The Le Cabaret Theatre was to be the focus and I was to work with Mr. Tibor Rudas, an imaginative producer of variety casino shows. Our model would follow what was being done in Las Vegas.

And at this juncture, Jack impressed upon me that Resorts International was in its ascendancy and desired to build a management team that could deliver on the development plan in conjunction with the operational needs. It sounded complex but my inner self was excited about the future prospects.

Jack continued, "We have a 20-year agreement to operate the

casino and to develop Paradise Island into a multifaceted tourism destination—one without parallel on this side of the Atlantic."

He continued, "We are the centre of considerable economic activity in The Bahamas, which places a great burden on us to minimize mistakes going forward. As a foreign-based company, we must be seen as good corporate citizens."

Steve added, "We are now operating under a new government, and although the relationship so far has been cordial, we know that the government is intent upon Bahamians playing an important part in our growth. Although this is seen as straightforward, we are obligated to our shareholders to balance such issues in a way that still enables our business to operate at maximum efficiency and productivity."

I had to listen attentively as the importance of what was being said did not escape me.

Jack looked at me with eyes that burned with passion, which startled me for a moment because he, in the short time that I knew him, gave me the impression of being somewhat distant from forceful leadership. In this brief encounter he revealed a commitment to success.

Jack concluded, "JB, we want you to continue with your involvement with the casino but we are appointing you Vice President and Treasurer of Paradise Island Limited and in this position we want you to have responsibility for the Le Cabaret Theatre and supervision of the accounting office on Paradise Island in effect within a reasonable time."

My response without hesitation was: "Jack and Steve, I am delighted to be associated with Resorts International and you have my assurance to do my best at all time."

We parted ways about 11:15 p.m. I hardly remembered what I had eaten but my favourites were always a Caesar salad and a prime rib, end cut.

While driving home, my mind was a whirlwind of thoughts and a sense of excitement that was all but impossible to contain. Imagine being promoted after being with the company for such a short time.

I had called Jo before leaving Paradise Island so she was awake and waiting for me when I arrived. The boys were asleep in the bedroom. Robyn was still a baby and occupied a crib in the alcove connected to our bedroom. Even before we started talking, I had a feeling of completeness in my life.

Sitting in the Florida Room with midnight near at hand, I slowly recounted the content of the meeting with Jack and Steve.

Jo was delighted that I had been promoted. She wanted to know the details of my new position. Although not precise, I was able to broadly explain that the accounting office would be reporting to me on day-to-day matters and that the North Miami office would be responsible for the preparation of financial statements, which were essential for monthly reports made to the Securities Exchange Commission (SEC) and for distribution to the many shareholders of Resorts International Inc.

I had to admit that the exposure of the job was daunting but I would have to plow on ahead believing in my ability to learn and cope.

We called it a night and trundled off to bed. My final thoughts before sleep were: "I am going to need all the help I could get and will work to build a good team." Jo would join the company fairly soon as Executive Secretary to Jack Davis and the question which followed was will anything change between us as a result?

The Casino Executive Committee remained in place but the decision was taken to appoint a General Manager. Lino Raspantini was made Vice President and General Manager. He had an engaging disposition and I liked him.

There were changes at the top. When I had joined in 1971, Fred Schock was President of Operating Company—Britannia Beach Hotel Company Limited. He was succeeded by Duncan Rapier, who was previously with the Nassau Beach Hotel. Quite surprisingly LeRoy Bailey, former General Manager of the Paradise Island Hotel and Villas, joined Resorts Bahamas to take over from Duncan.

It was quite strained for a while because Leroy was Jo's boss while we were dating. Unfortunately, Leroy and I had a serious confrontation in the Tradeswinds Lounge one evening over an issue that I don't recall. We were close to fisticuffs but that was avoided.

CHAPTER 29

INDUSTRIAL RELATIONS AND THE BHEA

There have been frequent occasions in my life's journey when I questioned the worth of what I was doing. I viewed myself as existing in a limited universe with complete satisfaction being elusive. Whenever the nagging doubts appeared, I refused to allow them to take root. By the same token, I could not help but wonder if I could have been much further advanced in the business world had I been able to obtain a university education. And then one day there was a fresh realization—the words of Earl Nightingale rang out loud and clear—"Life is a self-fulfilling prophecy." For me, constraints against success were self-imposed and it was in my power to change this condition.

After spending approximately four years with Resorts International I was beginning to feel really comfortable in my surrounding and gained confidence in my job.

Steve Norton was always willing to guide me through murky business areas and at the same time encouraged me to expand my horizons. On one occasion as we were sitting in his office he brought up a subject that surprised me a lot.

"Barrie, as you may know when we opened the Britannia in January 1969 there was no union representation within our operations. Looking back that was not a particularly good position for us to assume in that we were isolated as an employer within the industry."

I immediately asked the obvious question, "Why was that such an uncomfortable position for Resorts International?"

Steve replied, "Before we opened the Britannia, we decided to operate independently of other resorts but that position was the cause of disruptive outcomes. For instance, without consultation with fellow owners we purposely hired persons at higher rates of pay in an effort to recruit the more qualified people."

I inserted my thoughts on this. "I can only presume that this initiative in a number of ways destabilized the industry."

"Yes, you are right and in recognizing our mistake we joined the Bahamas Hotel Employers' Association," Steve admitted.

"And we are now completely unionized, which has made it necessary for Resorts/Paradise Island to be very active in union/hotel discussions and negotiations," he added.

At this point in our conversation Steve said, "Barrie in due course you should insert yourself into industrial relations matters on behalf of our company, along with Duncan Rapier and LeRoy Bailey, General Manager of Paradise Island Hotel and Villas."

In 1976, there were serious difficulties between the Hotel Union led Workers and Employers. Since I was new to the environment, it was necessary for me to take a peripheral part in discussions on the issues being debated. Little did I know where this modest beginning would lead. I was committed to doing my very best with everything that fell into my sphere of influence: making the company successful and at the same time providing support and guidance for Bahamians in their pursuit of advancement within the organization and within the tourism industry generally.

I sat on the executive committee of Resorts International Bahamas and through the successful execution of my duties, which were expanding all the time, I gained the confidence of Jack, Steve and my executive colleagues. The company's relationship with the hotel union was tenuous at best and made all the more difficult because of inconsistency of leadership within the Bahamas Hotel Employers Association. It was vital for direct and forceful intervention to be brought into industry negotiations. The Union was pressing aggressively for better terms and conditions of employment for union members whereas employers were constantly faced with the most difficult task of operating profitably and at the same time being competitive in the market place. And it was against this backdrop that the employers, desperate for a settlement, made a concession to the hotel union which they regretted for many years to come.

The employers were at an impasse with union, which placed considerable pressure on hotel ownership to reach a settlement. Operations and profit margins were sliding backwards. In a last-ditch effort at the invitation of General Manager, the hotel union leadership met at LeRoy Bailey's company-owned house on Paradise Island Drive for a "chicken souse" breakfast—a Bahamian favourite. The outcome was ultimately referred to as the "Chicken Souse Deal."

It was in 1975 when employers acquiesced to the unrelenting pressure by the Union and agreed to mandatory tipping within all food and beverage operations. While this important issue was being debated, the employers were trying to negotiate minimal increases in basic rates of pay, which if too liberal would cause considerable downward pressure on operating margins. In the end, if guests were made to pay gratuities the take-home pay for employees would increase fairly significantly. Rationally, employers felt that by pushing the burden on to the guests, everyone would win but such a conclusion was ill founded.

Not long after implementation there was a downward shift in the quality of services provided by staff. Unfortunately, guaranteed pay through the tipping system diminished the need to provide excellent service to guests at all times. The howls of protest from guests reached a crescendo of substantial proportions that caused an industry-wide backlash. My role in the negotiations was limited mainly because I was a neophyte in this area, but the outcome caused me grave concern about tourism's future.

It was against this backdrop of an uneasy relationship between the hotel union and employers that I decided to put my hat into the ring to vie for the presidency of the Bahamas Hotel Employers' Association. I discussed this with Steve and he was enthusiastically in favour of my doing so.

While I do not recall verbatim Steve's sage observation, in essence he said that "we are poised to enter a new period of trials for ownership and in effect for the entire country."

It was indeed an insightful comment.

In 1979, I was elected President and except for 1982 and 1983 when Peter Hilary and Mike Wallen occupied that office, I was re-elected in 1984 and was constitutionally re-elected every three years for more than thirty years.

Fortunately on the home front, Jo was happy for me even though she knew that the demands on my time were about to multiply. Thank goodness she was working in the hotel industry and surely understood the need for cohesive leadership.

I believed that I was assuming a position that others were inclined to avoid because it required being prepared to apply oneself with a competitive attitude that was unflinching when challenged by adversity and maybe above all would require untiring dedication.

As time and years passed and negotiations with the unions became increasingly difficult and confrontational, I would say to Michael Reckley, Executive Vice President of the BHEA, that "there is a beginning, middle, and an end. We will always get to the end and successfully so. There can be no raising of the white flag in surrender." We always remembered these words every time we commenced negotiations.

Michael would reply, "JB, we understand what we need to do and we will get the job done."

We knew that as we stood in the present trying to plan on how to reach our goal, it was necessary for us to have a clear understanding of the history of what came before.

Let us remember The Bahamas in 1950. A country without natural mineral resources such as oil and precious metals, without a manufacturing industry, and in the main reliant upon fishing and some farming, but we did possess beautiful beaches, crystal clear blue sea, and a warm and friendly people. It was during this time of stillness that Stafford L. Sands created the economic model of the twin pillars—tourism and financial services that have generally withstood the test of time to the benefit of the country as a whole.

In 1954, the Tourism Development Board was formed with Stafford Sands as Chairman and Bobby Symonette as a strong supporting member. From the earliest of days it was understood that stopover visitors had greater value to our economy than cruise ship visitors.

In 1949 there were just 32,000 visitors to The Bahamas. However, early signs pointed to growth and in 1956, 150,000 visitors came and in 1968 we reached the 1 million visitor mark. This was quite remarkable.

As the numbers increased along with the hotel room capacity, there arose the question of how well employees were being treated in an industry where in hotels they were not being represented by a union.

Although there was no labour legislation in place in the late 1950s, a union for workers was formed and headed by its first President, Bartholomew Bastian. The employers formed the Bahamas Hotel Employers' Association in 1958 with Wesley Keenan of the Emerald Beach Hotel elected as its first President.

It soon became evident to both sides that some form of structure for industrial relations was essential so as to ensure, as far as practicable, that terms and conditions of employment were consistent across all properties. With our tourism industry very much in its infancy and representing the potential for economic growth, union and employers both engaged in setting conditions within the workplace with careful deliberation.

The very first industrial agreement was informally structured in the absence of governing legislation.

When Keenan stepped down as President of the BHEA, he was replaced by Sir Oliver Simmonds, owner of The Balmoral. Sir Oliver was the creator and manufacturer of the famous spitfire plane used by RAF in World War II. The hotel union leadership after Mr. Bastian went to David Knowles.

The history-making formal and binding industrial agreement between the BHEA and Bahamas Hotel Union (BHCAWU) covered the years 1968 and 1969. Sir Oliver had made a lasting impression on David Knowles and it was not one that was complimentary. In fact, during negotiations in later years David would find the opportunity to make reference to his encounters with Sir Oliver.

David would say things like, "I hope you will come to the bargaining table with a better attitude than Sir Oliver, who thought that Bahamian workers should not be paid more than a few shillings a week."

He saw Sir Oliver through the lens of dislike. His opinion of Sir Oliver never changed.

It was obvious to government, employers and the union that legislation was crucial for providing ground rules under which unions and employers should function. The Industrial Relations Act of 1970 was enacted and set the stage for the conduct of both parties—employers and union. The first step was for the union, through a defined legal process, to be recognized as bargaining agent for certain categories of workers.

Thus we collectively, union and employers, were navigating albeit somewhat uncertainly in an industrial environment without a reliable compass. At this historical juncture in 1971, George R. F. Myers, General Manager at the Nassau Beach Hotel was elected President of the BHEA.

In the early days of the BHEA, none of the employers had any depth of experience or knowledge on how to engage a union for the purpose of negotiating an industrial agreement that would cover all the elements with terms that not only satisfied the business owners but also complied with the law.

Our first executive director was an Englishman, Trevelyan Cooper, a highly experienced negotiator who brought impressive credentials to the table.

The format was for Trevelyan to negotiate with the union leadership on his own, report to the executive committee of BHEA, and to make recommendations for positions for subsequent meetings with the union. Periodically, hotel owners would be brought up-to-date and their approval sought for changes in positions.

Trevelyan was an outstanding negotiator and had a pleasing personality. He had a single-minded approach. Even when negotiations faltered he would remind us to "keep talking as you never know when there could be a breakthrough that would get us to the end game."

By the time I was elected President, Trevelyan had retired and his replacement was George Muir, another Englishman with substantial industrial relations knowledge and experience. We knew that sooner or later a Bahamian would have to fill that post and we began the process of doing just that. We advertised the position and had a number of candidates with the basic skills required for growing into the top position. In the end, we accepted and employed Michael C. Reckley as deputy to George Muir.

The year 1977 was also a momentous year for industrial relations. The leadership of the Bahamas Hotel Catering and Allied Workers Union (BHCAWU) consisted of David Knowles, President, Thomas Bastian, Vice President, and Bobby Glinton, General Secretary.

The BHCAWU was formally introduced in Nassau and had also established a strong foothold in Grand Bahama. The counterpart to the BHEA in Freeport was the Freeport Hotel and Restaurant Employers Association (FHREA).

Resorts International, through a subsidiary Bahamas Amusements Co. Ltd., operated El Casino in Freeport. Being a member of FHREA, I was the person given the responsibility to represent the casino in the negotiations with the union and in particular, with respect to food and beverage personnel.

In the 1970s, 1980s and the mid-1990s, industrial agreements were negotiated for three-year periods, which did not serve the industry well. It was recognized that three-year agreements were inadequate, that is, too short to enable efficient business management and planning. Also, negotiations were never completed on time so the matter of retroactivity always had to be negotiated.

It was in late 1977 that Michael Reckley and I went to Freeport as negotiations were in progress for a new industrial agreement which included El Casino Food and Beverage employees.

We attended a meeting of the FHREA executive committee in order to be acquainted with progress with negotiations. The chief negotiator for the FHREA was Emmanuel Osadebay. When the current position was revealed, Michael and I were shocked to learn that Freeport was moving toward higher rates of pay than what we had just negotiated in Nassau.

Once we understood the status of negotiations I was obliged to say "Gentlemen, we do believe that the offer on the table is far too generous."

We diplomatically added that it was an unrealistic position to adopt such higher rates. "There is little choice but to go back to the negotiating table." That approach was agreed.

As it happened, a meeting was to follow with Tom Bastian and his team and for which we would remain.

I can recall vividly the afternoon Tom Bastian walked into the meeting room and discovered Reckley and me in the room as well. The meeting went badly. In fact, the employers and the union ended in a deadlock as the FHREA moved to claw back some of the positions that had been tentatively agreed, previously.

Given this unexpected development Tom said, "Gentlemen, we refuse to accept and agree to a reversal of what has been agreed in principle. This is not an act of good faith."

The union and Tom Bastian had no way of saving face and the inevitability of industrial action loomed ever larger on the horizon. And as anticipated the union, within hours following the meeting, had its members withdraw their labour from the member properties of the FHREA.

The legitimacy of the strike was questioned as there had been no strike vote taken. In any event, the parties were required to attend an emergency meeting at the Department of Labour under the control of the Director of Labour, Mr. Bert Edgecombe. This too was expected.

It was in this setting that I first met Mr. Hubert Ingraham, who was representing the Holiday Inn. The meeting was going to last a long time as the Director was determined for the parties to reach an agreement on all differences.

It was about 2:00 a.m. when the Director called for a short break. Hubert and I ended up in the car park to have a cigarette or two. We struck up a conversation that seemed to cover a wide variety of subjects. What I remembered most is that we laughed a lot. He possesses a hearty infectious laugh. The friendship, which came so serendipitously, has not only survived these many years but, in fact it has grown to a most comfortable level. In those days, we did not share the same political beliefs but that was in no way an impediment to our newfound friendship.

Through sheer perseverance and considerable "toing" and "froing," an agreement was reached and the workers returned to their work stations. Because Luis Reynoso and David Hadland were the two senior managers representing Resorts International at El Casino, Michael and I had frequent meetings with them before and during the strike to make sure that all points of contention were properly covered.

We knew that this settlement with the union was very important for Resorts, as the company had given a written commitment to government to build hotel rooms, a second casino and complementary infrastructure in Freeport.

On the way back to Nassau, Michael and I had a chance to chat about his future and that of the industry.

I said to him, "You have a wonderful opportunity to be a significant part of the industry by being the foremost industrial relations specialist in the country. In preparation you need to obtain exposure formally with respect to the science of industrial relations, particularly the negotiating of industrial agreements."

Michael nodded his agreement and added, "I will, in due course, be fully capable of being the Executive Director. I will work very hard to achieve that position and to earn the trust of employers."

While looking introspectively at the future where there should have been a sense of buoyancy, there was instead a nagging, undefined doubt of the future.

The 1979 contract negotiations would turn out to be the most important agreement ever negotiated. None of us could possibly predict an agreement that would hold such enormous benefits for all bargaining unit employers as well as industry managers and other non-union category workers.

Again, David Knowles was President of the BHCAWU, Thomas Bastian, Vice President and Bobby Glinton, General Secretary—a very strong leadership group. Our team comprising

Robert 'Sandy' Sands, Michael Reckley, Keith Duncombe, Legal Advisor, Barry Nottage, Accounting Systems Expert, and me, constituted the nucleus of our negotiating team.

Keith, whom I fondly called "Meredith," would say from time to time "Gentlemen, we are making history and we cannot fail."

There was a fundamental principle that guided us through all negotiations. If the union sought to include an improvement in terms and conditions and where there was a cost attached to the same, the union had to, in effect, buy/pay for the improvement—that is, to take the value into account of any possible settlement.

The employers knew exactly what direct and indirect costs of labour were included in their profit and loss accounts. Employers, through the budgeting process, could also determine to some degree what improvements could be possibly absorbed at once and which would be infinite.

We in fact introduced a scientific formula into the negotiations which did not fail us.

It was essential to always bear in mind that contracts were being negotiated for the future. As we all learned in a most painful way, the future is unpredictable and at times, an economically dangerous place.

As with previous contract negotiations, 1979 was developing into a confrontational zone where "give and take" was almost absent. This was a slow and arduous process. Somehow, as President I became more directly involved. I remember reading somewhere that "we have to be lucky to be able to avoid the constant whirlpool of drama that threatens to suck us in."

It was becoming quickly apparent that more professional assistance was necessary. The industry was continuing to mature and the nature of the business was facing more complex issues, especially in the area of international marketing and an understanding of the ever-expanding competitive landscape. There was one other unknown threat that could have not only had hemispheric implication but also those that were global in nature; for instance, shortage of a vital commodity such as oil caused by military conflict between oil-producing countries.

Given this setting of new dimensions of tourism we engaged legal and financial advisors who could assist us with thorny issues related to contract discussions—Keith Duncombe of Dupuch and Turnquest, a lawyer of vast experience, and Denis Barry Nottage of PriceWaterhouse. These specialists were key to developing information and producing rational recommendations that allowed for the production of financial models that expanded the negotiating landscape significantly.

The hotel union took the position of viewing the industry as a "pot of gold" held only for the benefit of owners and it was only right, in their eyesight, that the workers should share equally. This misconception framed the basis of extended heated exchanges.

Prior to the commencement of negotiations, the hotel union would submit a proposal for changes which under any circumstance could not be agreed. The union did not have to substantiate their claims; they only asked for "outrageous" improvements and relied on the employers to counter with rational positions and hope that somehow an agreement would be reached.

There we were, confronted with a huge battle to get a three-year agreement commencing in 1979. After much debate and public posturing, we arrived at new rates for mandatory gratuities and then got stalled on direct compensation. Employers were definitely in a neutrally entrenched position of "no movement."

And then quite suddenly a solution was revealed. Trevelyan's advice "always keep talking" paid a huge dividend for the industry and the workers.

The union leadership, David Knowles, Bobby Glinton, and Tom Bastian, advanced the idea of establishing a pension fund for workers and to implement it in place of wage increases. The immediate reaction was "no way could this happen." This step forward, if agreed, would have an effect on our benefits and social structure far beyond what any one of us could have envisaged. In the end, the idea took root and the financial implications were analyzed. Advice was obtained from the actuarial firm of Martin Segal of New York.

The debate raged back and forth until there was broad acceptance of such a plan. The employers, however, recognized that to give a pension benefit to bargaining unit employees would cause a most serious problem for non-union/management category workers. After much soul searching and analysis regarding impact, employers finally agreed to the creation of a Pension Fund for non-union/management staff. This was truly an historical event that was to have a lasting effect on the quality of life for many workers in the tourism industry.

And so in the 1979 agreement, history was made and birth was given to The Bahamas Hotel and Allied Industries Pension Fund. The design of the plan was completed but the actual implementation was not until June 1980. It was to be a non-contributory plan, which meant that employers paid all required contributions. It was also agreed that overall governance of the Fund would be placed in the hands of a fourteen-member Board of Trustees with equal representation from the BHCAWU and the BHEA. An independent chairman was also empowered to break any trustee deadlock with a casting ballot. The first Chairman was Father Louis Dames.

The Bahamas Hotel Industry Management Pension Fund came into being in 1980. All trustees were selected from the management ranks of the BHEA members. T. Baswell Donaldson, former Governor of the Central Bank, was the first independent Chairman.

For the years 1978 to 1981, there were disputes to be handled but in the meantime the industry functioned fairly well. However generally, the industry, following the end of negotiations for a new agreement, entered a period free of turmoil.

During the next three years, there was relative peace but during the lead up to an agreement in 1985, relations between the Employers Association and the union took a turn for the worse. At this juncture Tom Bastian, as President, was adopting a more adversarial position in an obvious attempt to maintain a strong support base.

The demands by the Union were totally unacceptable primarily because the economic impact upon the industry would have caused a severe deterioration in company operating margins. The situation worsened to such an extent that illegal work stoppages were being pursued randomly by the Union. Unfortunately, the impact upon tourism was very harmful.

It was known that Everette Bannister a consultant for Resorts International, was recognized as having a personal relationship with Prime Minister Pindling, and upon the request of Jack Davis, President, he arranged a meeting with the Prime Minister for Tom Bastian and me.

On the appointed day we went to the Prime Minister's office in the Churchill Building. The Prime Minister greeted us warmly and then we began the discussion. I realized that the government had long-standing ties with the labour union so I was fearful that the meeting might not go well.

On behalf of employers, I put forward a strong case for minimum improvements in conditions together with financial implications. It was all boring but mostly vital industry information: notwithstanding, I was proceeding with vigor and passion. Then quite suddenly I realized that the Prime Minister's eyes were closing and I had obviously lost his attention. To me, this was not a good sign. Thank goodness he recovered his composure and on I went to complete the employers' story.

It was Tom's turn. He pleaded for improvements in the wage package because the downtrodden workers were being ill-treated. Tom took a deep breath and plunged on with an appeal against social injustice.

"Mr. Prime Minister, you must accept that my hard-working members are the backbone of the industry. Employers disregard this fact and only want to make huge profits for the owners. Prime Minister, our brothers and sisters are suffering."

It was at this stage that the Prime Minister made it clear that employers "had to go beyond what was on the table." In that moment, he was aggressive with his language toward me, which was unnerving. At this point Tom Bastian intervened and assumed a more accommodating position in the negotiations. My respect for Tom Bastian at that moment leapt forward.

The Prime Minister, however, was still in the mode to keep me on the defensive. Finally, I said respectfully, "Prime Minister, if there is strife, we place the industry at risk and the end would probably be a crippling strike."

He looked at me intently for at least sixty seconds but it seemed much longer. He then turned to Tom Bastian and entreated him to adopt a more amenable position that could be good for industry's survival.

There was no resolution to our impasse.

We left the meeting and while standing outside of the Churchill Building agreed on continuing our negotiations.

Surprisingly, some seventy-two hours later the union and BHEA received an official notice from the Ministry of Labour that the dispute between the parties was being referred to the Industrial Relations Board for resolution. This was quite an unanticipated twist because the tourism industry was not considered an essential service and as such could not be arbitrated under this law.

After some discussion, we concluded that the Prime Minister understood the serious nature of the dispute that we discussed with him. With the economy at stake, he decided to issue an executive order for the Industrial Relations Board to deal with the matter.

The Chairman of the Industrial Relations Board, Joseph Strachan, officially informed us of the date set for the hearing and the time within which written submissions should be forwarded to his office.

At the time of the escalation of the dispute, it was evident that employers and union had to change course.

The Board was chaired by Mr. Joseph Strachan with four side members—two representing labour and two representing employers. Ellis Peet was Secretary to the Board.

On the morning that the proceedings were to commence there was an unexpected development that for our BHEA team was reason enough for a momentary pause.

The Board through the Secretary presented a document for our signature which stated that both parties to the dispute would be bound by the decision of the Board.

While the approach seemed unusual, it was quite evident that it was in our best interest to comply. And besides, the Prime Minister had obviously found an innovative way to preserve the stability of our tourism industry and thus history was being made.

For the BHEA, the presenters of the submission rebutting the Union's demands were Keith Duncombe, George Muir, Michael Reckley and me. Presenting for the BHCAWU were Franklyn Wilson of Deloitte and Touché and Tom Bastian.

The proceedings before the Board were conducted in a very formal manner.

The Union in presenting relied very heavily upon the assertion that bargaining unit employees were being denied improvements in compensation and working conditions despite the very considerable growth in tourism.

The BHEA, on the other hand, with Keith Duncombe guiding the narrative, called Barry Nottage of Price Waterhouse Co., to present financial information on the tourism industry's performance and impact upon the economy.

Our team had decided previously that the Board should be given a report on the status of Bahamian tourism by an international expert. For such a presentation we arranged for Joe Gazilli, CEO of Liberty Go Go to appear before the Board. Liberty Go Go was the largest travel wholesaler/ Tour Operator in the North Eastern USA with headquarters in New York City.

Gazilli's presentation was eye-opening in that it described in detail the extent to which efforts are made to drive tourists to The Bahamas.

Chairman Strachan was outstanding with his management of the process. The hearings were protracted and it was evident that a result might not be obtained within fourteen days. Chairman Strachan was a person who observed a custom and practice that he obviously maintained irrespective of circumstances.

Every afternoon at four o'clock the Chairman and side members would withdraw to have tea. Although surprisingly at first, we discovered that the Board provided us with an interlude to review the work of the day. This mid-afternoon practice in many ways reminded us all that dignity and respect should underpin all serious and potentially divisive discussions.

The day was approaching for a decision by the Board which would be binding on the parties. The procedure was that the Board's decision would be held in a sealed envelope by the Chairman and then opened at a specially convened meeting with the decision read to the parties to the action.

Then there was a huge surprise that came like a bolt of lightning out of the blue. One of the employer representatives quietly told us that the Board had decided to accept the BHEA's position totally and further, including approval of all recommendations of the employers to increase compensation for employees, which was a lot less than that sought by the union.

I assumed that Tom Bastian was also aware of this imminent announcement that would favour employers. Although the employers' position was exceedingly strong, we expected some form of compromise to be decided upon by the Board. This presented a huge dilemma for us as employers. Total victory is never ideal in industrial matters especially when dealing with an entire industry.

Given this development, the first imperative was to meet with our negotiating team. I reached out to Michael Reckley, Keith Duncombe, and Barry Nottage and explained the need to meet. They arrived at my home in short order. We discussed at length what we thought could be the way forward. We understood very clearly that the process would require very careful management.

My next step was to reach out to Tom Bastian, President of the Bahamas Hotel Catering and Allied Workers Union, to ask for an urgent meeting to which he agreed. The next call was to Ellis Peet, Secretary to the Industrial Relations Board, to advise that the employers and Union had agreed to meet for the purpose of exploring the prospect of reaching a mutually acceptable industrial agreement. And then I asked that he request the Chairman, Justice Strachan, to hold off on announcing the decision of the Board as the parties had agreed to meet.

Mr. Peet called early next morning to say that the Chairman, while in agreement for a delay, added that "this was highly unusual but that it was far better for the parties to agree on a contract than to have it thrust upon them."

And thus a series of events unfolded in rapid succession, the first being a meeting of our negotiating team with President Bastian and his Vice President, Alex Thompson. We all knew that we would have to tread very carefully through the process. Fortunately we worked out what we thought could be an acceptable position.

Our team then convened an urgent meeting with representatives of hotel owners to discuss direction and to get final instructions. Paralleling our meeting, we knew that the Union was similarly engaged. After a series of meetings, we crafted a new agreement that was accepted by all parties with a huge sigh of relief. And thus what could have been a serious disruption in the industry was avoided.

Chairman Strachan, upon being told of the good news, said, "Thank you for doing the right thing."

The envelope was never opened. The agreement was completed and signed.

From this strange and unexpected account was the beginning of a kind of trust and respect that enabled the industry to deal comfortably with a myriad of difficult matters.

During the years 1979 to 1982, there was relative calm within the industry. In fact industry leaders sought ways to create a harmonious environment. The BHCAWU and BHEA established a working committee to develop ways and means of introducing a programme of activities.

Tom Bastian and I had a relationship that baffled the outsiders and I believe that the insiders too were asking questions about the impact upon the union philosophy. When we were not at the bargaining table, Tom and I would meet fairly regularly to speak about our industry and the future.

On one such occasion, Tom was evidently on a mission.

"JB, we now have an agreement that seems to have a strong foundation. It is important to do some things together that will strengthen the bond between union and employers."

My question in my mind was: *I wonder what Tom has brewing in his very fertile mind?*

"Tom, we need a lasting peace between the union and employers but history works against us. What do you have in mind?"

Through the years of negotiating, Tom's depth of thought was surprisingly futuristic.

"JB, we need to bring employees and managers within our industry together to celebrate and recognize the value of tourism and the role that all employees play in sustaining its wealth."

He went on, "What I propose is the industry having a hospitality day of competition when all employees from all member hotels of the BHEA will participate."

"I think it is a grand idea and if we can do it we will have an industry where employees work in unison" was my reply.

The event was held on the Western Fort. There were a number of races including a three-legged race, an egg-in-spoon race, and bed-making challenges with housekeeping staff proving to competing managers that they could make up beds more efficiently than them. Despite best efforts, housekeeping employees convincingly displayed their skills. It was so much fun.

The event went on for the entire day well into the evening, covering two days complete with hotdogs, hamburgers, conch salad and soft drinks. No alcohol.

On Labour Day, management marched with the union, which was made all the more entertaining because there were dancers and gymnasts performing on Bay Street as we made our way to Workers House. It was truly spectacular and energizing. There were many entertainers from the Le Cabaret Theatre.

Tom Bastian and I stood on the platform together and I was invited to address the attendees. Maybe it is a dictum of life that good things don't last. The following year while I was speaking at the Labour Day march, several employees aggressively attacked me verbally, in essence wanting to know why I was on the podium with the President of the union. It was at this point that Tom Bastian showed his strength as a leader. He came to my side, put his arm around my shoulders and said loudly through the sound system, "J. Barrie Farrington is our friend."

I sensed a change and although the BHEA supported the Labour Day march, I never marched again because I did not wish to be exposed to abuse.

While employers were hoping for an enduring peace with the union it was evident that the focus had to be about bringing a clear and unchallengeable plan for growing the industry with strategies designed to protect the industry from the vagaries of the market and global uncertainties.

On the other hand, the union wanted to maintain member support with almost total disregard of the downward economic pressures that were always confronting the industry.

Unfortunately, the propaganda of the union impressed the members in a way that created a psychological barrier against the possible danger of economic decline. And thus words such as "don't worry we always bounce back" or "the Lord will take care of us during bad times" were frequently uttered by many employees.

A belief in the inevitability of progress is loaded with danger, and when faced with reality we discover that we are unprepared for the impact of decline.

While the Honorable Milo Butler was Minister of Labour, he was readily available to bring the parties relief if it was evident that the industry was under stress by the parties for political reasons or for union protectionism.

He was a devout Anglican and a stalwart member of St. Matthew's Church. On each occasion when he chaired a conciliation meeting, he began with a prayer in which he reminded us of our responsibility to the people of the country and that our Lord God will guide us through the most difficult times.

The Honorable Milo Butler was succeeded by the Honorable Darrell Rolle, who helped us navigate through the negotiations for a new labour contract commencing January 1981. Prior to the industry dispute being apprehended by Minister Rolle, the BHEA and the BHCAWU had exhausted all avenues for a settlement and ended in a stalemate. A general strike was called by the union and chaos ensued. Hotels tried to remain open—a very difficult task indeed. We all knew that there was only a three-day limit within which operating hotels could be sustained.

Minister Rolle commanded the parties to attend his office to continue the negotiations. We were not allowed to leave the premises until an agreement had been reached. The first twenty-four hours were managed reasonably well but with Kentucky Fried Chicken being the main source of nutrition we soon became extremely grumpy. To add to this terrible condition, when nighttime came, about 200 union members holding lighted candles marched outside the front of the Department of Labour singing hymns.

Minister Rolle used shuttle diplomacy in getting us closer together and at opportune times to give advice. Each time he spoke with us he made it plain that he was intent upon getting to an agreement. He was most tolerant and persuasive. "Gentlemen, I am responsible for protecting the country's economy and I will not support an outcome that will create an unsupportable financial burden upon the most important generator of income for the country."

He advised that "you should give what you think you can afford."

During the second day, a thorny legal issue arose on which we needed legal advice before we could agree. We contacted the Hon. Eugene Dupuch, who agreed to see us. It all had to do with the right of the employer in the section labelled "General Conditions." We were convinced that the language being proposed would dilute the rights of the employer. Mr. Dupuch gave us comfort and we returned to the Ministry of Labour.

Time was running out.

At about 2:00 a.m. on the third day, an agreement was struck; however we needed to get it typed. My wife, Jo, the executive secretary to Jack Davis, President of Resorts International, was the only person we could convince into doing this for us. So I called her and told her that "the country needs you, my dear."

A police car was dispatched to collect her from our house and bring her to the Ministry of Labour.

Jo was a most proficient typist. She produced a document by 7:00 a.m. and under the direction of the Minister and Director of Labour the weary parties signed the industrial agreement.

The workers were contacted through radio and they returned to work. Management and the Ministry of Tourism had to work hard on a Public Relations Recovery Programme to minimize the fallout within the market. Some degree of normalcy returned to industry but there lingered amongst many of the employees a deep resentment of hotel operators, even though employee relations programmes were instituted.

While talking with the negotiating team about the future it was generally felt that employers needed to have an arsenal of unchallengeable data about tourism so that we could always be in a position to illustrate to the union leadership that the stakes for survival were extraordinarily high and that frivolous and harmful disruption of the industry could have long-lasting adverse affects.

And so the next three-year period under a new industrial agreement commenced. There were ongoing disputes to be resolved but what was becoming evident was that the financial settlements of the last couple of industrial agreements were causing irreversible financial hardships upon our owners of smaller hotels, members of the Bahamas Hotel Employers Association—restrictive working conditions and mounting costs resulted in a number of permanent closures. This trend continued through the next five years until small, family-operated hotels and guesthouses failed and thus the quaint and intimate properties became exclamation marks in tourism's history.

In this period, hotels were under pressure and we were faced with potential downgrading and reductions in staff. Both sides—union and employers—came together to assess the then current conditions. In the end it was necessary for Tom Bastian and me to meet on our own—president to president.

The Director General of Tourism, Baltron Bethel, made arrangements for us to meet in the offices of the Hotel Corporation of the Bahamas. Paul Adderley was chairman at the time but only infrequently had use of the boardroom, which was made available to Dr. Bastian and me for meetings.

On one occasion we were asked to use a small office as the boardroom was otherwise being used. We kept at the discussions without break until it was lunchtime.

What happened next was, in looking back, funny but fate could have decided a different outcome.

As we entered the hallway, Tom said, "This place seems very empty. Where are the staff?"

We were slightly bewildered.

I said, "Maybe they have gone on strike in sympathy with you."

At this point a female member of staff appeared and a most startled look crossed her face.

She inquired, "Why are you still here?"

We were perplexed.

She added, "There had been a bomb scare in Scotia Bank on the ground floor and the entire building had to be evacuated."

Tom said, "What? Did you all forget about us?"

Obviously, we were out of sight and had indeed been overlooked.

Tom added, "JB, we are here doing the people's business to the point of placing our lives at risk."

I, as I recall, said, "Maybe we should be getting danger pay!"

It was a reminder that uncertainty was our constant companion.

We found a way to give the industry relief from some of the burdens under which hoteliers struggled. Baltron Bethel, when informed of the resolution, expressed gratitude to union leaders and employers representatives for "saving the industry."

Unfortunately, peace was not to last.

A new agreement for 1990 to 1993 had to be negotiated and this was going to test our endurance and will.

On the day before the agreement was to expire, Tom Bastian contacted me and told me that he wanted to be at the table negotiating when the agreement expired. Despite this odd request I acquiesced.

And so, on the evening of 7 January 1990, we met in the executive boardroom of the Britannia Beach Hotel. As the clock struck midnight we began the discussion. Tom Bastian broadly outlined what the union expected to achieve. To me it seemed very ambitious but this was merely the beginning.

After about an hour in this mode, we set some meeting times for negotiating the framework of a new agreement. Having finished the ceremonial beginning of negotiations we went our separate ways.

But before we closed the door behind, Tom had some parting words.

"JB, I might as well tell you now, the association will not have its way in these negotiations." And then with a mischievous look he added, "You are my friend but I can't let you take advantage of me."

"Tom, I know that you will try to do what is right even if it hurts," I answered.

Management and union leadership recognized that this particular agreement would require an inordinate amount of time and patience if we were to get to a good place for the industry.

Negotiating terms and conditions as well as the financial package would take us into unchartered territory. There were two formidable matters that needed to be addressed and which would require the wisdom of Solomon and the patience of Job in order to get to common ground. The two areas to be negotiated were the terms and conditions of the contract and the dispute resolution process.

The BHEA for a long time was most unhappy as three-year contracts were too short when in every instance negotiations extended twelve to eighteen months into the new contract period before agreement could be reached and signed.

The debate was waged energetically and with strong empirical information being provided by the BHEA negotiating team to the union.

After a long and exhaustive struggle by the parties, it was finally accepted that a five-year agreement made sense. Of course, it was a risk in that both parties were committing to live with the agreement for better or for worse. While this change in the term of the agreement was enthusiastically received by the employers, little did anyone understand that this was not the end.

The second most important resolution achieved was the setting of guidelines for resolving limited disputes. The union and employers were very unhappy with the government-operated machinery for the resolution of a limited dispute, which applies only to a matter involving one member hotel.

As negotiations were dragging on, we decided that changing venues periodically gave us fresh outlook. On this very important occasion, we met at the law offices of Dupuch and Turnquest with Keith Duncombe providing, when necessary, legal guidance.

The matter of conciliation and arbitration was central to the discussion.

At 3:00 a.m. with our strength on a downward plane, we mutually accepted, in principle, Binding Private Arbitration. However, in the first instance we would sign a Letter of Intent. The reason for caution was that such an enormous change required special and careful shepherding through the ranks of both sides before it could be finally approved and implemented.

And so on this fateful morning of 17 August 1990, a letter was signed setting out how Binding Private Arbitration would work once put into effect. This was a monumental breakthrough. The signatories were Thomas A. Bastian JP, Alexander R. Thompson, Leonard L. Wilson for the BHCAWU and J. Barrie Farrington,

Robert D. Sands, Michael C. Reckley for the BHEA, Keith M. Duncombe, Notary Public.

The letter was placed in an envelope with the seal signed by Thomas Bastian and J. Barrie Farrington and put in a safe in the office of Keith Duncombe. It was agreed that the letter could not be opened without the consent of the parties and a written directive to Keith M. Duncombe.

This was indeed an historical milestone in industrial relations in The Bahamas. However, the end game might prove to be challenging.

One of the most satisfying realizations of reaching this undreamed of plateau in industrial relations was that leadership from both sides were unafraid to examine creative and meaningful ways to make the tourism industry stronger and more stable. In essence, when committed to nation building, differences could be placed in the background. This may sound philosophical but it was factual.

While Binding Private Arbitration was crucial to industrial peace, there was another burning issue related to employee compensation that required undivided attention. Payroll costs were increasing in a way that impaired financial results of every department. We advanced our considered position on this matter and it was with the weight of our logic and data that we persuaded Union leadership accept the introduction of "one off" payments to employees in specific years.

The concept of this kind of payment was to keep the input of take-home pay for any one year intact. As the description implies, the base rate of the employee was not increased and thus the employer was not faced with paying compounding increases in payroll.

The feeling in the industry was most optimistic about continued growth in tourism, but this was not to last. Global financial difficulties emerged, which caused our tourism industry to be depressed. There was little choice but to seek to reopen the 1990 five-year labour contract.

Unfortunately informal discussion with union leadership on this subject was less than fruitful.

Tom Bastian initially was adamantly opposed to opening the

contract but he soon recognized as did his officers that there had to be meetings with the Employers Association. Tom made it clear that "for the union to make changes would require a miracle."

In any event formal discussions were commenced.

After some discussions about the serious situation between the BHEA and union leadership, it was mutually agreed that formal discussions should take place.

It soon became evident that we needed to make adjustment to wage scales for 1992 and 1993. Tom Bastian readily recognized the difficulties and sought to be cooperative. With the Progressive Liberal Party being voted out of power in 1992, it meant that any government intervention in our negotiations would be led by Prime Minister Hubert Ingraham.

Mr. Ingraham made it perfectly clear that the industry could not withstand industrial unrest. He did, however, grasp the economic dilemma facing the industry and by extension, the country. The solution evaded us for a while but Tom Bastian and his team made it clear that while the settlement numbers could not be altered, there was room for the agreement to be extended by three years to 1998.

Discussions with the union were getting very tense and collapse seemed imminent. I decided that I need to try to get the Prime Minister involved but he was in Inagua. I had no choice but to call Mr. Ingraham.

"Prime Minister, thank you for taking my call," I said. "Our negotiations with the Hotel Union have taken a turn for the worse. We need your assistance."

The Prime Minister grasped the situation and said, "J. Barrie, I will fly in from Inagua as soon as I can."

He rang off and I told the fellows that the PM was coming to Nassau to assist us.

Mr. Ingraham returned to the capital and forcefully guided the negotiations. His intervention proved to be crucial to the outcome.

While the employers and the union through the years continued with negotiating, dealing with disputes, job descriptions and the like, there were several significant events that had a bearing on the direction and survival of tourism.

Resorts International in 1978 successfully entered the casino industry in Atlantic City as the first casino in America outside of Las Vegas.

Jim Crosby, Chairman of Resorts International, died in 1986 while undergoing surgery. The company was left in an untenable position. Resorts International, due to rapid expansion in Atlantic City, was experiencing financial difficulties.

Donald Trump acquired Resorts International, including Paradise Island, in 1987. This was a precursor to many significant changes being made to Paradise Island operations.

In 1988, Merv Griffin acquired the interest of Donald Trump and devoted considerable financial resources to revitalizing Paradise Island.

When I first met Merv Griffin, I was immediately taken with his enthusiasm and energy. A small group of senior managers headed by George Myers met with Merv Griffin in the executive board room in the Britannia, and virtually the first words he uttered were: "Team members, thank you for the musical Bahamian welcome—it was great."

As he looked around the table, you could sense that his Hollywood persona was rising to the occasion. "I have no doubt I will use my resources to make Paradise Island great again," he said.

And thus the beginning of a new era was started.

However, fate was not kind. Severe financial problems forced Griffin on two separate occasions to file for bankruptcy protection under Chapter 11 in the United States.

Survival was threatened and in 1994 Sol Kerzner and Sun International acquired Paradise Island/Resorts International Bahamas.

The future was looking bleak and the profitability of tourism generally was under serious pressure. Sol Kerzner brought energy, vision and resources to the forefront and in 1994 embarked upon an ambitious plan to revive Paradise Island and tourism generally. Other investors also were encouraged to invest in tourism—Butch Stuart and John Issa in particular.

Managing the relationship with the union remained an enduring challenge. The Kerzner era was a time for optimism and commitment to a better way of life for all.

Hotel Union's unrealistic demands force employers to seek government's financial aid to avert economic downturn

Board of Trustees Meeting of The Bahamas Hotel and Allied Industries Pension Fund in the Boardroom of the Britannia Beach Hotel, 1982

Louis R. Dames was the first chairman of this fund

Signing of Industrial Agreement—Bahamas Hotel Catering and Allied Workers Union and Bahamas Hotel Employers Association

Savouring the completion of an new industrial agreement with the Hotel Union, 1985

L to R: JBF, Keith M. Duncombe, Michael C. Reckley, Executive Vice President of the Bahamas Hotels Employers Association, and Luis Reynoso, VP and GM of Britannia Beach Hotel

CHAPTER 30

REBIRTH OF PARADISE ISLAND: A NEW TOURISM BEGINNING

It was not easy to look to the future right after being witness to the demise of the enterprise under the ownership of Merv Griffin, which had created such great expectations. The one unwanted and yet persistent question was: "Will history be repeated under new ownership?" Such negativity was akin to heresy. I pushed this defeatist-like thought from my mind and replaced it with the words of Vince Lombardi, the legendary coach of the Green Bay Packers, who declared, "Winning isn't everything, it is the only thing."

"And so it will be for our team on Paradise Island as we enter the next phase of our history," I concluded.

Thus 1994 marked a new beginning for Bahamian tourism. Nearly $150 million was spent on Phase I of Paradise Island's future, little could I imagine then that our Paradise Island Resort and Casino would be transformed into the well-known legend of ATLANTIS.

In seven months from April to December 1994, Sol directed massive changes and improvements to the Britannia Beach Hotel and the Paradise Island Hotel and Villas, including aquaria featuring a wide variety of marine life.

Once Phase I was finished, Sol immediately moved his focus to the future. A new Heads of Agreement, a legal contract between the Government and a developer, was negotiated with government in 1995. Atlantis was to undergo an expansion of 1200, rooms including a new casino and amenities.

I remember Sol's declaration to expand very clearly. Sitting in the executive boardroom, Sol looked at Butch and me and declared his intention to expand Atlantis substantially.

He said, "I want to create a resort without equal. In fact, Atlantis will be so good that no other resort anywhere will be any better." He added, "The opening up of Cuba will not matter to us."

His reference to Cuba made it clear that Sol's perceptive vision of the future was extraordinary.

Many new jobs were going to be added during construction as well as within the operations once construction was finished.

Getting to a grand opening required the BHCAWU's commitment to support the plan. One way of getting to this stage was to illustrate to the union's leadership the extent of the competition we, as a destination, faced daily.

The decision was taken for a small group of us to travel to Las Vegas via Orlando to obtain a firsthand view of what was happening in other destinations. And so in May 1997, Tom Bastian, Pat Bain and Leo Douglas with Michael Reckley and I started on a journey of exploration and interpretation of other tourism-driven destinations.

On a Sunday afternoon, on Mother's Day, aboard a chartered jet we flew to Orlando and inspected hotels and facilities—Disney and Universal. This was an eye-opening experience.

We then flew to Las Vegas and stayed at Caesars Palace. Drew Goldman, an associate of the Kerzner Group, was our tour leader. All doors were opened to us, even to the extent of visiting all parts of the back of house.

We also met with senior personnel of the Las Vegas Chamber of Commerce. They were effusive when describing the plans for taking Las Vegas into a period of unprecedented expansion; the success was evident.

The exchange with the Chamber gave us a sense of what could be accomplished in a hotel, casino and commercial environment. On one tour, we saw the two latest additions to the Las Vegas destination. It was obvious that the Venetian and Bellagio would be magnificent additions.

It was while we were in Las Vegas that I detected that the relationship between Tom and Pat was somewhat strained. Quite by accident Pat Bain and I had breakfast together.

Pat was very smart, articulate and interesting to talk with. In so many words, Pat expressed ambitions that exceeded functioning in the shadow of Tom Bastian.

"JB, this visit has been amazing. I never envisaged Las Vegas being such a vast destination in the desert. The energy, quality of service and dazzling entertainment coupled with the kaleidoscopic magic of bright lights and glitz is hard to compete with."

This acknowledgement was insightful because it meant that for The Bahamas to compete with Las Vegas, it would require a herculean effort on the part of every industry employee to provide first-class service. Also, it meant that the union and industry would have to function far more collaboratively.

Pat on a more personal note added, "I am not happy about where I am in my personal development. In fact, I am prepared to look within the industry for a management position."

Had I been a little more intuitive, I would have understood that the sentiments given were the indicator of a palace revolt.

Prior to leaving Las Vegas, we discussed the future and a number of action steps.

We agreed that union and management should speak with one voice about tourism and development. We also aimed to expose more industry workers to the vastness of tourism competition. We agreed that arrangements would be made for a contingent to travel to Las Vegas for an introduction to one of our country's major competitors. Once back in Nassau, we'd arrange for a representative group—union and management—to tour the nearly finished 1200-room Atlantis expansion, including amenities.

I recall the occasion of presenting tours for showing off what Phase II—in particular what Royal Towers—will offer to the travelling public once completed. It was obvious to our group of Bahamian workers that no expense had been spared in getting the very best result.

When the tour was finished, a short statement was made by Butch Kerzner. The support by those who had been to Las Vegas was most encouraging, in fact beyond expectation.

My recollection in my mind's eye was of the exuberance of the approval by our industry partners. One person stood and said without reservation, "We are as good as Las Vegas, and we will get better."

The grand opening of Atlantis Phase II on 22 December 1998 was spectacular. The union gave full support and the future looked most promising and rewarding. With investments in various resorts, in Nassau particularly, employment increased significantly. Thousands of permanent jobs were offered to Bahamians. Only success loomed on the horizon.

A new five-year industrial agreement was negotiated and came into effect January 1998 but let me add that, almost inexplicably, the negotiations were very hard indeed and it took some doing to reach an agreement.

The Bahamas Hotel Catering and Allied Workers Union under Tom Bastian's leadership was enjoying growth with an accumulation of financial resources. In fact, he was committed to investing in bricks and mortar, which did not sit well with several members of the union hierarchy. As a result his popularity was losing traction. During 2002, the union in keeping with its constitution held elections for all officers and trustees.

I sensed that Tom Bastian, prior to the election, recognized that his presidency was in jeopardy. Election Day came and Tom was unceremoniously voted out of office. Pat Bain was elected President with Basil McKenzie as Vice President and Leo Douglas, General Secretary.

The change in the BHCAWU executive leadership did not come as a surprise and since we knew the newly elected officers, there was no reason to believe that the union's relationship with the BHEA and the broader industry would change.

The negotiations for a new five-year agreement commencing January 2003 had highs and lows. Unfortunately, the rank and file of the union had huge expectations of their new President.

In 2002, the government changed with the Progressive Liberal Party returning to power. Vincent Peet was appointed Minister of Labour. In a way, this caused the dynamics in the negotiations to be more uneven than could be anticipated.

We spent six to eight hours per day at the bargaining table, which was exhausting. In the midst of it all, Pat and I talked quite a lot about the state of the nation and what could be done to improve the quality of life for all Bahamians.

Unfortunately, negotiations broke down and meetings were suspended. Tensions ran high. Discordant public statements added fuel to issues that appeared virtually unsolvable.

It was while we were faced with what seemed like limited options for resolution that Butch, Paul O'Neil, and I met in my office to discuss the way forward.

Butch reiterated that he was satisfied that the negotiations were being impressively advanced by employers in an attempt to get a fair outcome.

We decided that the time had come to communicate directly with the employees about the issues and the company's efforts to reach a settlement. Having agreed on this course of action my spirits were lifted.

Before leaving my office I received the following email from Butch.

Jbarrie.Farrington

From: Butch Kerzner
Sent: Friday, December 12, 2003 7:52 PM
To: Jbarrie.Farrington
Subject: Union Negotiations
Importance: High

JB. You looked very tired today. Do not let these small people get you down. You have my complete support in this negotiation. I feel quite strongly that we hold most of the cards. And the reason that we do is because our cause is RIGHT. I strongly suggest that you take a 48-hour breather and then come back on Monday rested and ready. I do not believe that Government will do diddly to assist us.

They do not have a clue. It is up to us to sort this out and we must do it by showing resolve. This has been going on for 12 months. Let's make it come to a head. I favor you putting pressure on Pat AND Government. We need Vincent to realize that he is about to blow the negotiation and that he cannot control the process any longer. I favor your idea of soon taking things off the table....On Tuesday we go to the employees with our offer....We have the Nation behind us. JB. You have given Pat every opportunity to behave reasonably. He has not. I am told that you have conducted yourself with your normal dignity and have taken the high road. I would have expected no less. As we have discussed, this is a pivotal moment for Union/Employee/Employer relations. If we handle this right, we will have done something lasting for the future (even though the immediate outcome may be sloppy). Call me anytime day or night if you want to bounce around any ideas. There is almost nothing more important to our Company than to get labor relations back onto the right foot in this country.

Your great friend and supporter,
Butch

Minister Peet explored every avenue to get negotiations back on track. Bishop Neil Ellis stepped into the breach and persuaded Pat and me to meet out of the view of the public. We met several times at the Bishop's home and this represented a big breakthrough.

While in this setting, Pat was relaxed and more open.

"JB, I am determined to find a solution to our impasse. So much is at stake for the country."

I was impressed with his sensitivity to the significance of what our negotiations represented. In response, I assured him that our employers were most desirous of getting to an acceptable solution. "Pat, in the past, mistakes were made by both sides. We cannot afford to make concessions that will burden the industry and the country irreversibly."

Meetings were re-started. Minister Peet was available to us as needed. Finally, Prime Minister Christie stepped in and some very hard decisions had to be made. The Prime Minister clearly understood the risks, which were articulated and strengthened by the constant view of Atlantis from his corner office in the Churchill Building, a reminder that the country was on the cusp of substantial positive growth in tourism.

An agreement for five years was agreed and signed with the start date of 7 January 2003 and expiration of 7 January 2008.

The new agreement was signed on 28 January 2004 at Workers House under the supervision of Minister Peet and the Director of Labour, Harcourt Brown. This was twelve months after the expiration of the prior agreement.

Little did we realize that so many things would change in the intervening years. Pat Bain was ill, very ill indeed, but he did not reveal the nature of his illness. He sought reelection to the presidency in 2005 and won with little resistance. His illness worsened and he could not function well. Stomach cancer was the acknowledged diagnosis in due course. I was personally distraught with this revelation as we had developed a mutually respectful relationship. There was little hope of recovery for Pat.

And so on November 20, 2006, Pat Bain, while in the Princess Margaret Hospital, passed away. This was indeed a sad day for me and in fact a sad day for many persons, particularly members of the BHCAWU. Although for any number of years we sat on opposite sides of the bargaining table, we became close friends. At his memorial service at Worker's House, I was invited to speak as President of the BHEA and also at his funeral service at Christ Church Cathedral.

I thought that with his departure there would have remained a vacuum in unity for developing the tourism industry to remain unchanged.

An election of officers and council members for BHCAWU occurred fairly soon after Pat's passing. Roy Colebrook was elected President, Leo Douglas, General Secretary and Basil McKenzie, Treasurer. As it turned out, Roy and his team were very much in step with the commitment to lift the industry to new heights and had it not been for the global financial collapse of 2008, they would have been instrumental in successfully promoting the benefits of the alliance and the continuance of tourism's growth.

The industrial agreement had a five-year term and would expire on 7 January 2008. With the industry performing well, the future looked very promising.

Sol Kerzner was enthusiastic about continuing the expansion of Atlantis. A new Heads of Agreement had been negotiated with government now led by Prime Minister Christie. And, so construction began in March 2005 on another 1200 rooms to come on stream by September 2007. By this date, there had been another general election and the Free National Movement had regained control of the government. The Cove with 700 rooms added a new dimension to the offerings on Paradise Island as it was designed to be a hotel for adults only, and The Reef with 500 rooms was a condo/hotel.

The Union's constitution called for elections every three years. Roy Colebrook's term as president was slated to run until October 2008. This meant that he would be responsible for negotiating a new five-year agreement that would run from January 2008.

When the union's proposal was submitted to the BHEA, a quick read revealed that the demands, financial and other, were far beyond the reach of the employers.

At our very first negotiating session at the office, we rented on the ground floor of S G Hambros. I had little choice but to say, "Mr. Colebrook, we do not wish to dampen the spirit in which we had hoped we could negotiate and which would have been based upon the realities of what we have learned in the last ten years about the fragile financial nature of our industry. However, I am obliged to say that the Union's demands are excessive."

Mr. Colebrook, with a slight smile and a gentle look of mischievousness, replied, "We believed that the industry can do much more for our members and we believe that we will convince you to agree to our demands."

Seated at the table for union were Roy Colebrook, Basil McKenzie, and Leo Douglas. Also for the union were David Knowles, former President of the BHCAWU, and Bobby Glinton, former General Secretary of the union—both very knowledgeable and crafty negotiators.

We began the negotiations under strained conditions but I also knew that there would be no shortcuts to an answer. In fact I always said to my colleagues as we started negotiations, "There is a beginning, middle and an end." We might not know where to agree in the middle but for sure we will get to an end.

The negotiations dragged on interminably but the search for answers never stopped.

In the end, the matter of money for the workers was the key. We used our most novel way of enhancing take-home pay—a combination of base rate movement, one off payments and a creative addition to housekeeping gratuities, which exceeded anything done in the past. A good part of the gratuities were designed to go into a common pool to benefit back-of-the-house, non-tipped employees.

The year 2008 was to be a year when events would swirl around us like a tornado with a fury that would almost remove our will to continue the fight for a better tomorrow.

Negotiations were at times most hostile but we soldiered on recognizing that no alternative was there to rescue us.

In August 2008, a tsunami swept over the financial market of the world. With lightning speed, the world had been turned upside down and the inhabitants left in the wilderness. The events were reminiscent of the colossal market crash of 1929.

Room occupancies and average rates declined at breathtaking speed. Business dried up and survival was the order of the day. The entire industry was under duress.

Atlantis with the largest workforce, after much consideration, decided that in order to stem the financial outflow, substantial downsizing was needed. The process was painful but some 800 employees were made redundant. The union leadership saved as many jobs as they could, but it was a very dark period in any event.

Efforts were made to soften the financial impact upon the affected employees by providing monetary assistance through the Health and Welfare Fund, a sub fund of the Bahamas Hotel Industry and Allied Pension Fund. Unfortunately, some opponents of the union leadership dismissed this huge effort as being self-serving. At the same time we were still trying to deal with Butch Kerzner's death.

On 11 October 2006, Butch Kerzner was tragically killed in a helicopter crash in the Dominican Republic—a most tragic and severe loss to us all.

Negotiations continued for a new industrial agreement with less fervour than previously but no one shrank from responsibility.

The agreement was concluded and executed on 8 January 2009 more than twelve months after expiration.

Another event occurred which had significant implications for the industry. The BHCAWU by constitutional obligation held an election of officers and trustees on 28 May 2009. Roy Colebrook and his team were voted out of office.

Of course, the world had to continue rotating but this event was to be a turning point of relations between employers and the union.

There were twists and turns involving the new leadership of the union. After much agony, significant financial hardships imposed upon the union and acrimonious posturing by all factors seeking control of the union, Nicole Martin emerged as President of the union with Darrin Woods as General Secretary and Godfrey Brice as Vice President.

History had been made. Ms. Martin was the first woman elected to the presidency of the union. It remained to be seen whether such high office could be administered in a way to maintain cohesiveness between the employers and the union.

For a variety of reasons, a chasm developed between the Union and the BHEA. Unfortunately, in the end there was no emerging peacekeeping force that could possibly remove that which separated the two parties.

I had served as President of the BHEA for thirty-one years and decided that the time had come to pass the baton to Robert "Sandy" Sands who had served as Vice President for twenty-two years and was a successor who could maintain a high level of leadership for the organization.

Sandy and I always enjoyed a most excellent relationship and our ability to work harmoniously for the benefit of member resorts and for the country generally was never in question.

Michael C. Reckley, as Executive Vice President of BHEA was the constant and provided invaluable and sage advice at all times.

Sadly, the vigour and collaboration between the union and employers had almost evaporated, thus causing uneasiness within the industry.

Change in life is inevitable and with this acknowledgement certainty becomes a shadow of what was known in decades past.

A new agreement was to be negotiated and made effective come the 8th January 2013. But the parties, through polarizing actions, failed to act in accordance with the renewal requirements of the agreement. The end result was totally unsatisfactory in that the 2003 Industrial Agreement remained in force and will so remain for three years with an expiration of 7 January 2016.

Nicole Martin made history by being the first woman to be elected to the presidency of the Bahamas Hotel Catering and Allied Workers Union, an organization that for many years was considered the most powerful union in the country. I saw this change as being a most significant opportunity for Ms. Martin to create an environment in which workers and employers could elevate the industry to an unanticipated level of economic activity. However, the global financial crisis of 2008 lingered, making the recovery in tourism very sluggish. Notwithstanding, history will judge the quality of her presidency without regard to gender.

Atlantis Phase II under construction, 1997

CHAPTER 31

NATION BUILDING: LABOUR AND CAPITAL

I have for a long time held a basic belief that human nature cannot be characterized as originating in one society, one culture, one country or one hemisphere. By this I mean that by looking at one's own life experiences and having the chance to observe otherwise through the written word or by video, we recognize that people weep when grieving, express happiness when good happens, feel fear when threatened, and experience distress when civility is disregarded. The connectivity of so many emotions enables us to deal with everyday life and the persons with whom we come into contact.

Are there differences in any stratum of society? Yes there are, but for the moment I want to talk about leadership and the effect upon society, generally and particularly. In a variety of ways while serving as President of the Bahamas Hotel Employers Association and dealing with my counterparts in the BHCAWU there were many observations with respect to behaviour and attitudes that had direct bearing on negotiations and outcomes, most of which had an effect upon our Bahamas to varying degrees.

In my estimation, the most important decision ever made by the BHEA and BHCAWU was in 1979 when we agreed to create a pension fund for union category workers in the industry as well as a pension fund for managers and non-union category workers.

It is very hard to fully measure the impact of this momentous event. However I can say with certainty that the quality of life for retired hotel workers improved significantly and undoubtedly strengthened the underlying fabric of our society.

Looking back through the thirty-five years of existence of both funds, I cannot be too lavish in my praise of the union's leadership in its commitment to all industry workers, and the benefits so widely reaped and broadly accruing to the entire country.

Tom Bastian's presidency was in my estimation, an uncommon dedication to the improvement of the quality of life for hotel workers and to the protection of the principal industry of our economy—tourism.

Under his leadership, the BHCAWU was viewed as the most powerful union in the country. On the other hand while his instincts were all encompassing, his ambition to do it all was to work against him in the end.

Tom believed that creating Union City was his destiny, an ambition not shared fully by his colleagues. Once Workers House was transformed and as such the ultimate union centre, he turned his attention to Freeport and moved to duplicate what he had done in Nassau.

Next came Eleuthera. A substantial complex was constructed at considerable cost. Full utilization of the facility was not realized.

The establishment of Workers Bank was an undertaking that was in due course a reason for much anxiety. I was invited to serve as a director, which I accepted.

I remember the day while Tom and I were discussing a variety of matters when he paused momentarily and then went on to say, "JB, we are moving forward with expanding Workers Bank and I want you to be a director of the bank."

"Well Tom, this is a surprise but I accept," I replied.

My appointment was a statement of significant importance. Tom Bastian was always thinking beyond self-interest as he was driven to make The Bahamas a country that unified capital and labour.

Tom Bastian was exceptional in his grasp of the importance of tourism for our Bahamas. It was therefore not surprising that he took the initiative with the support of his fellow officers to arrange several tourism conferences that brought industry leaders and workers together with two principal objectives: an update on where the country was in tourism, and an insight of a fresh and dynamic outlook on tourism's future.

One such conference was at Club Med on San Salvador. Butch Kerzner was there and gave a presentation on the Kerzner vision.

On the charter flight, Butch said to me, "The good doctor Bastian is obviously fully committed to making The Bahamas a better country." This statement was testament to his desire to be a positive contributor to our society.

Tom Bastian's full support, along with that of his comrades Alex Thompson, Leo Douglas, Basil McKenzie and Leonard Wilson, for the introduction of Binding Private Arbitration was monumental. This mechanism underpinned industrial peace for many years and continues to do so.

In 1994, when Sol Kerzner and Sun International acquired Paradise Island, once more Tom understood the significance of what this change represented. He could see a brighter future for all.

For whatever reason, cracks of dissension appeared in Tom's inner circle and beyond. In what seemed like an inevitable result, Tom was voted out of office and Pat Bain assumed the presidency.

Post Tom Bastian, the relationship with the union was unsettled but what evolved in due course was a relationship with Pat Bain that held unlimited promise.

While negotiating I would take the opportunity to put forward discussions and events affecting our society and the absence of a positive environment in the country.

In one of our exchanges, I said, "Pat, you're President of the BHCAWU and also of the National Congress of Trade Unions (NCTU) which gives you access to about 25,000 workers. On the other hand, as President of the BHEA, I have access to employers through the Chamber of Commerce, Bahamas Employers

Confederation and Bahamas Hotel Association. Imagine what we could do for the country if we constituted an alliance of sorts."

Pat immediately saw the benefit for the nation and responded, "JB, I like the idea of our attempting to influence a meaningful direction within our country. We should look at this from an apolitical position."

It was so gratifying that a powerful union leader would see this future of a society that could be good for all. Maybe it was idealistic but worth the effort.

Our first joint effort was during the period when all nations on this side of the Atlantic were in serious negotiation for the creation of the Free Trade Agreement of the Americas (FTAA). We asked the question: What impact will this have on our tourism and The Bahamas generally and should it be made a reality? The purpose of the FTAA was to reduce or eliminate tariffs which were considered barriers to international commerce. Such an agreement would affect 750 million people in this hemisphere.

Pat and I agreed with the support of our respective organizations to engage Ralph Massey, a resident economist in Nassau, to prepare a paper on Trade Liberalization. The report was prepared and published in 2003. The report acknowledged the support of the BHCAWU, touched on Value Added Tax at that time—ten years ago—and decided and recommended that a Sales Tax be introduced as the more effective revenue generator for the government. The Bahamas Chamber of Commerce and the Bahamas Employers Confederation lent their visible support in the report.

History had been made but I think that the significant importance of what this represented was lost on the government and the public generally. The government and country-minded persons failed to understand that this alliance that had been formed represented the establishment of a launch pad for accelerated and permanent nation building. The report was widely distributed through press releases and presentations to several civic bodies, and every member of the legislature received a copy—the result, minimal acknowledgement and nothing more.

Pat and I commiserated on the less than enthusiastic public response but as Pat put it, "We cannot let one setback be the reason for surrender."

I added, "Maybe there will be those who will see the day when their inaction facilitated the further erosion of an ill-defined purpose on how to grow the economy." On reflection, what we had done together—labour and capital—could have been a template for substantially reducing separatism on important national issues.

We moved on.

While we negotiated a new industrial agreement, we discussed the impediments to employment opportunities. We concluded that a lack of education, particularly the inability to read or write competently as well as poor skill levels, comprised weaknesses that made successful recruiting nearly impossible.

"What can we do about improving education generally in the country?" inquired Pat.

"You are talking about a daunting task but the first step is to bring about public awareness of the deficiencies," I replied.

When Pat agreed, I felt that we could reconstitute our alliance for the public good and use every effort to educate the public on the huge educational deficiency and recommend ways and means of effecting remedies.

Once again, the BHCAWU and BHEA engaged the services of Ralph Massey to put together a compelling and powerfully persuasive case for making education a top priority of the country.

The report "Bahamian Youth—The Untapped Resource" was sponsored by the Bahamas Catering and Allied Workers Union, National Congress of Trade Unions, the Bahamas Hotel Employers Association, Bahamas Chamber of Commerce, Bahamas Employers Confederation, Bahamas Hotel Association and Bahamas Downtown Development Association.

The release of the report received widespread acceptance including the Minister of Education. It was a profound statement of unity when making a presentation to the Minister Carl Bethel that the President of the Bahamas Teachers Union, Belinda Wilson, was there by my side.

The report is still on the website of the Bahamas Hotel Association. The conclusions of ten years ago are still valid in 2016.

There was a commitment by the Ministry of Education to include the principal parts of our Report in a paper on education being prepared by the Ministry.

Here again, no one can point to anything done that indicated that the government took the report to heart.

The report was first issued in 2005 and updated in 2007.

For The Bahamas, labour and capital was indeed a reality but there was no recognition of what this kind of alliance could achieve if fully understood and nurtured.

The alliance we formed was tangible evidence of an opportunity to establish a national platform for tackling important issues affecting our society. In looking at the current economic landscape, it is very unlikely that there will be an another opportunity to form such a broad-based alliance of capital and labour. It is indeed unfortunate.

Roy Colebrook succeeded Pat Bain as president of the BHCAWU and had it not been for the global financial collapse of 2008, the union would have been instrumental in successfully promoting the benefits of the alliance and the continuance of tourism's growth.

After some terrible infighting within the union, Nicole Martin was elected President. Unfortunately too many hangover administrative problems came to roost in the new administration and thus progress regrettably became a non-event.

In our history there was another union that was integral to the tourist industry. The Bahamas Musicians and Entertainers Union (BMEU) was formed in 1946 and by mid-1965 had a fairly large and enthusiastic membership. The union sought recognition in 1974 from the BHEA to represent all musicians and entertainers employed in member hotels of the BHEA.

Accepting BMEU as bargaining agent was very difficult because most of the persons to be covered did not work full time. The one exception was the persons who worked in the Le Cabaret Show, which was owned by the Britannia Beach Hotel Co. Ltd., a subsidiary of Resorts International.

There were many opportunities for employment in entertainment enterprises that catered to the many tourists who came to Nassau by commercial flights, cruise ship and private aircraft. The '60s, '70s and '80s were the halcyon days for those who were in some way making a living in the field of entertainment.

There were night clubs that were famous for their variety of entertainment, which showcased personalities such as Freddie Munnings Sr., Peanuts Taylor, Paul Meeres Sr. and Jr., George Symonette, Blind Blake, Sweet Richard, Ritchie Delamore, Count Bernadino, Pat Rolle, and many others. The clubs had dazzling names such as Cat and the Fiddle, Silver Slippers, Zanzibar, Chez Paul Meeres, and Ardastra Gardens. The hotels had music and limited entertainment but unquestionably the attraction for tourists was to go to the hot spots over-the-hill and to witness and enjoy the exciting and dazzling dancing of Bahamian artists and the unforgettable Bahamian calypso music.

I can remember vividly in my late teens, together with a couple of friends, visiting the Silver Slippers, listening to Freddie Munnings singing, watching some part of the native show and then walking further along to the Zanzibar, which was owned by Felix Johnson.

Oh yes! Moving about over-the-hill was absolutely safe.

One of our friends had a car which made it possible to go to the Cat and Fiddle and then to Chez Paul Meeres. The clubs were always crowded with tourists who were mesmerized with the music and specialty acts.

Tourism was fast becoming the mainstay of the Bahamian economy and the Bahamians in the entertainment field were to varying degrees, prospering.

Marcus Aurelius, Roman Emperor and philosopher, said that "in life we can be certain of change."

As the economy grew, as tourism expanded, and as new and larger hotels were constructed, the entertainment landscape began to change. First, operators of large hotels recognized that there was possibly a way to produce Bahamian shows within these properties and curtail the flow of tourists to the independently operated places of entertainment and thus gain financially for ownership. This trend was recognized by the musicians and entertainers and was cause for much concern. However, the nightclubs still benefited substantially from cruise ship visitors.

The Bahamas Musicians and Entertainers Union (BMEU) began to feel anxious about the impact upon the marquee Bahamian nightclubs and the musicians and entertainers employed there. With tourism continuing on the path of rapid growth, the dynamics of the impact upon the membership of the BMEU were not immediately discerned.

At the end of 1967, the 500-room Paradise Island Hotel and Villas opened together with the start of the Paradise Island casino operations. Within a few short years the room total on Paradise Island exceeded 2000.

It was obvious to the leadership of the BMEU and Ministry of Tourism that the entertainment landscape could not remain unchanged if The Bahamas was to be recognized globally as a significant tourism destination. The expansion of the availability of entertainment within the hotel in conjunction with the casino experience caused the over-the-hill Bahamian nightclubs to lose ground with cruise ship visitors.

Although the change in the entertainment structure was substantially altered, new opportunities for the employment of musicians and entertainers emerged with the Le Cabaret being in large measure the centrepiece.

The BMEU and the BHEA understood that there was a need to find a more formal way to regulate the industry even though it was to be no small task.

In 1974, the BMEU made formal application to BHEA for recognition. After much debate the parties signed a recognition agreement.

During this important initial period of negotiating for a comprehensive industrial agreement, there were many unusual aspects to be considered—for instance, many musicians and entertainers were self-employed, members of bands were employed by orchestra leaders, dancers were employed by the hotel but were subject to special conditions, hours of work were varied and so on.

For the BHEA, Trevelyan Cooper, Executive Director, had the responsibility of working through the variations of engagement, with George Moxey, who was President of the BMEU for a short while.

Leroy "Duke" Hanna was President of the BMEU from 1972 to 1999 and was the most ardent of negotiators but never lost sense of the purpose of his representations nor his wonderful sense of humour, which helped us get through some thorny issues.

As President of the BHEA, I found it essential to be a quick learner because the technicalities associated with the world of entertainment were, for me, outside of my understanding. I did, however, have good advisors.

At various times for practical reasons, it was good for Duke and me to meet on our own in keeping with a practice that originated with the BHCAWU and BHEA: a president met only with his counterpart.

On one occasion I invited Duke to meet at my house and he accepted. We did not want to be constrained by some unwritten law of inflexible formality.

We started about 8:00 p.m. at the dining room table. The discussion was very congenial but no progress was really being made. To break the lack of progress, I said to Duke, "As you know, the water supply from Water and Sewerage Corporation is most unreliable and the quality very bad. I recently purchased a water purifying unit which is attached to my kitchen faucet. The water is now very good. Would you like a glass of water?"

Duke looked at me for brief moment, smiled in his special way and at the same time he shook his legs up and down which caused his belly to shake as well. (He did this at meetings when he was particularly thoughtful). He said, "Yes, Barrie, I would like a glass of water."

I gave him a full glass, which he drank slowly, nodded his acceptance of the quality and added, "This is damn good. Maybe I should do the same thing at home. Joan would be pleased, I am sure." And then without saying anything but obviously having a private thought, he started to laugh.

The meeting continued and we did not conclude until well after midnight. We had wrestled with the rates of pay for musicians playing sets and musicians who could read music, with the latter attracting higher rates of pay. Maybe not surprisingly, there are many Bahamian musicians who are very talented and perform at a very high level who have not had any formal instruction/training in understanding the structure of music. It is important to be able to read music when a musical production is being planned and there is a musical script to coincide with changing scenes. Also scripts changed from time to time to accommodate new acts.

And this was the background against which the negotiations were based. After much back and forth we agreed to an increase of 25 cents per hour for musicians playing sets. We did not go beyond this as the hour was late.

When Duke was leaving and we were saying our good nights, he, with a twinkle in his eyes and a smile on lips, said, "Barrie, you are something else. After hours of negotiating I am leaving with having received a glass of water and 25 cents per hour." I couldn't resist laughing out loud. Duke heartily joined in.

It was with delight that Duke repeated that story to the enjoyment of those who might be included in subsequent meetings.

More formal negotiations were handled by Trevelyan Cooper, an accomplished negotiator with a wonderful sense of humour. He died in 1976 while on holiday with his wife, Alice, in the UK. He was succeeded by George Muir and Michael C. Reckley was appointed Assistant Director.

As with the major labour contract with the BHCAWU, the one with the BMEU was for three years.

When Duke retired, he was succeeded by Percy Sweeting, who was selflessly dedicated to promoting the interests of the members of the Bahamas Musicians and Entertainers Union. Through his straightforward approach to any contentious issues within the hotel industry, he gained the respect and confidence of industry leaders. My every encounter with Percy was mutually respectful. But Fate was unkind to him and he passed away on 11 July 2016 unexpectedly.

Under Duke's presidency, Ronald Simms for several years was the General Secretary. Ronald was smart and articulate but was distinguished more by the necklace he wore that included a charm of a cured pork chop bone. We never learned the importance of this decoration.

Through the years with tourism evolving to an industry that was constantly under pressure by competing destinations that required hoteliers to rebalance the cost of entertainment against the tangible value of such entertainment, the BMEU found itself hard pressed to remain fully included in the changes. There were some significant accomplishments during the decades of covering industrial agreements which should be remembered.

The BMEU and the BHEA comprised members who were forward thinking and recognized the importance of being allies.

In April 1981, the parties to the contract agreed to the establishment of a Pension Fund for BMEU members who worked within properties owned or operated by members of the BHEA.

Employers paid 2% of weekly salaries into the Fund, starting on 15 April 1982. Today, benefits are paid in accordance with those stipulated in the Plan and reflecting the trust agreement.

A Scholarship Fund was started to assist aspiring musicians and entertainers in advancing their careers. The description of the Fund was embodied in the Industrial Agreement. Some good was done through the Scholarship Fund but unfortunately, the viability of economic continuance was absent and after about nine years of operating the Fund it was dissolved.

Following the opening of the Resorts International Casino on the boardwalk in Atlantic City, Tibor Rudas, through Resorts Bahamas, arranged for various groups of Bahamian entertainers to be featured playing on the boardwalk of Resorts' Casino. This was a huge success for the BMEU and the BHEA.

The BMEU had a Musicians and Entertainers Week each year that the BHEA supported. This event was designed to promote musicians seeking to establish a cultural presence in The Bahamas. There was a sense that the contributions of musicians and entertainers to the country and the economy had to be memorialized.

As the number of cruise ships to The Bahamas increased and the practice of keeping onboard entertainment in full swing while in port had an unwanted consequence, support of cruise ship passengers for Bahamian night club tours diminished. The BMEU could not sit idly by while this was taking place and by the same token there was recognition that tourism was the backbone of the economy and needed to be protected. Notwithstanding, strong representation was made to government and following a number of meetings a compromise was arrived at. For the cruise ships in port, onboard entertainment would only be allowed during certain hours. Coincidentally, onboard casinos were not allowed to operate while in port.

This rule was observed for a number of years but was gradually relaxed. As crime in the city became more intense, the flow of tourists to Bahamian nightclubs dwindled until it reached a point where it was virtually non-existent.

Another important and positive milestone for the BMEU was the enforcement of the laws that required users of copyrighted music for commercial purposes to pay annual fees as prescribed by the Performing Rights Society. This organization, although London-based, had as a result of international treaties addressed the legal protection of copyrighted music. For years The Bahamas did not subscribe to the legal obligation and as such did not pay fees.

This matter of compliance gained momentum. The BHEA consulted with the Honourable Eugene Dupuch, Q.C., the preeminent legal brain in the country. He made it quite clear that the law had to be observed and that annual fees had to be paid to the Performing Rights Society. There was a local representative of the Performing Rights Society and each member hotel of the BHEA negotiated fees to be paid annually.

There was and still is no way of determining the financial benefit to members of the BMEU but for sure their rights are now fully protected.

Through the years, many persons directly and indirectly played a part in developing the relationship between the BHEA and BMEU. In particular I mention Ronald Overond, Count Bernadino, Peter M. Krollpfeiffer, George R. Muir, Robert P. Smith, Michael C. Reckley, Robert "Sandy" Sands and George R. Myers.

We also produced world-class band leaders such as Chris Fox and Errol Duke Strachan, both of whom possessed enormous talent. Their contribution to the Le Cabaret revue was outstanding.

Change hits high points as well as low but the spirit of the BMEU remains unchanged.

CHAPTER 32

RESORTS INTERNATIONAL BAHAMAS LIMITED AND J.B.F.

Here I was a graduate of Government High School without a university degree, placed in a job that by its very nature required considerable skills. I was also recognizing that most of my development took place on the job.

Less than twenty-four months after joining Paradise, I was promoted to a position that carried heavy financial responsibilities. My only option was to tackle the job with enthusiasm and attempt to provide strong leadership to my team.

The company was indeed fortunate in having dedicated professionals within the department, and after several meetings we developed a smooth functioning relationship. There grew a fondness by me of our group—Joseph Storr, Ernie Cambridge, Selwyn Estwick, Clara Gibson, Evie Arnett, Carolyn McDonald, Mae Payne, Dimple Davis, Hercules Hanna and Clifford Storr. Without their full support, my tenure as Vice President and Treasurer could have been a journey that would not have had a good ending.

The company had an accounting office in North Miami with the responsibility of preparing financial statements for the entire company covering Paradise Island and Miami for presentation to shareholders and SEC. Getting all the information together accurately required constant integration by the team.

Trying to maintain the integrity of the operations was a huge undertaking. In those early days, there was no electronic capability of recording activity of all operations and transferring to a central computer for audit. Much of the departmental recording of revenue was done mechanically and then consolidated by night audit. Controls were constantly under attack and whenever wrongdoing was discovered and employees were suspended and/or terminated, it invariably resulted in the union getting involved.

I can recall an incident involving a Food and Beverage cashier at Café Martinique who ingeniously was able to manipulate the NCR cashiering machine in such a way that she could retain the cash and inflate signed Food and Beverage checks so that it appeared that all revenue was recorded for the evening. A guest complaint about a Food and Beverage check that had been tampered with started an investigation led by Joe Storr.

After a number of meetings with union officials, the matter was referred to me. Bobby Glinton, General Secretary of the BHCAWU, vehemently rejected the charge of wrong doing. Step by step, I illustrated how this deception was carried out.

"JB, you can't possibly expect us to accept this charge against this long serving and faithful employee and union member."

My response: "Bobby, there is no way that we can overlook this serious infraction of the system. In fact, we believe that this scheme has been in place for some time. You might be wise to accept termination, otherwise the outcome could be much greater to her disadvantage if we decide to dig deeper."

"JB, we cannot agree, we will file a dispute tomorrow."

During the course of the day, the suspended employee decided that she was on the thin edge of the wedge and acknowledged her guilt.

The next day, Bobby came to see me at which time I told him what had happened. He was startled but smiled most mischievously and shook my hand.

Previously, I had reason to deal with the union on several issues, but it was becoming evident that the union leadership's mindset was to try to beat management at every opportunity irrespective of unchallengeable evidence.

This was the beginning of what was going to be a long and uneasy relationship with the union. It was going to take time to build a relationship based upon mutual respect and trust. The union's approach was to initiate industrial action, usually illegally to try to intimidate management into conceding.

My area of responsibility began to expand, a continuing indication of the confidence being placed in me to get the job done.

The next challenge was the commissary.

The butcher's shop, production kitchen and bake shop fell within the province of the Vice President of Food and Beverage. In those early days Max Heuberger, a German national, was in charge of the commissary's day-to-day activities. I had cameras installed in the commissary area with a monitor in my office complete with audio. This enabled me to speak directly with the office and commissary dock. Jay Markley, along with senior accounting staff from the Miami office took care of the accounting, which included supervising inventory taking and reconciliation.

On occasion I would take the inventory sheets and review non-food items just to see what the composition of stock was.

I remember having to stay in bed at home with the flu and to keep occupied I reviewed the last inventory taken of wines—and there emerged a most interesting discovery. Under champagne, I discovered an entry for 100 cases of Ruinart champagne with the purchase date being five years previous. A question was to be raised.

Then on to brandy, we had a substantial quantity of Courvoisier Premium Napoleon on hand. As with the champagne, the brandy had been purchased some time back and merely remained in inventory.

Turning my attention to the linen inventory which was kept in our warehouse in Paradise Town, I unearthed several stockpiled items that had been in the count for a long time—washcloths, blankets and sheets.

A few days later, I returned to work and immediately addressed the issues I discovered. With the Vice President of Food and Beverage together with the Commissary Manager I sought an explanation as to non-movement of Ruinart and Napoleon brandy.

At the time of purchase of the champagne, the price was at such an attractive level that it seemed that a purchase was desirable. And then came the classic comment: "Mr. Farrington, when we brought the champagne the price was $10.00 per bottle. Today, the purchase price is $22 per bottle. We made $12 per bottle over the five years." I almost fell off my chair when he added that for this reason unexplained the Ruinart champagne was never placed on our wine list for sale. In effect, we increased the value of an asset by doing nothing.

"Gentlemen, we are in the business of selling, therefore make certain the new menus are printed and Ruinart included at our established mark-up."

Once available in our Food and Beverage outlets, Ruinart was very popular and within a matter of months we had to order another supply.

With the brandy, the decision had a different twist. The expensive Napoleon brandy was not on the drink menu because the analysis of brandy showed that pouring brands were more profitable. The outcome was that the expensive Napoleon brandy was not on the drink menu. So in inventory we showed a substantial quantity of the premium brandy. This was changed forthwith. Even at the higher price, the premium brandy was being sold.

With respect to the linen, at a meeting called by the hotel operations manager with the director of housekeeping, we looked at the inventory. And then we inspected the inventory at Paradise Town.

"Mr. F., the linen we are holding in our inventory is no longer used within the hotel. There are some tablecloths as well which are obsolete."

This was alarming in that we continued to maintain a value for linen in our assets when in fact there was minimal value.

It was agreed to look at the possibility of using some of the linen in other areas but for accounting purposes the value of the linen was substantially reduced.

For all of us who were involved, this exercise was a learning experience. It is important to examine all parts of the business periodically to be sure that the areas for which you are accountable function effectively.

Being a part of a huge resort operation with many moving aspects, there were no rigid limitations on function. Most of the business was conducted at night and even though there were managers on duty until late into the evening, the coverage required reinforcements. Within the executive committee, the decision was taken for each senior executive to do night duty one night per week.

Thursday night was my night. I would work all day and merely continue on into the shift that generally ended at midnight.

I was particular about walking though the back of the house, especially the kitchens. I made it a point to spend time talking with the staff.

While we did have dishwashing machines, it was still necessary to have dishwashers who were needed to clean the remnants of food off the plates, stack them in the machines, remove any silverware that remained on the plates and then at the end of the wash remove and place them into dedicated storage areas for subsequent use. Accidental breaking of china and glassware was a longstanding and costly problem.

Also, there were general kitchen cleaners who kept the floors clean and free of excess water, which if it remained on the tiled floor could be cause for accidental slipping by staff and possible injury.

These back-of-house workers were, in my opinion, the unsung heroes of our business. They worked in the background out of sight, performing work essential to the smooth and productive operating of revenue-producing outlets. And of course, these kinds of jobs were not by any means the most prized within the company. To reach out and communicate in this way was most satisfying to me.

Thursday nights were made the more special for me as it gave me the chance of having dinner with my wife, Josephine. Every Thursday evening we ate in the Bahamian Club and once over I continued on my rounds.

Jo was pregnant but she still insisted upon eating steak tartare which is a specialty dish with uncooked ground steak being the principal ingredient. On this particular Thursday evening, 11 January 1973, having consumed her usual, she turned to me. "Barrie, I don't feel so good. I am going home now rather than waiting until midnight when you have completed your shift."

I was concerned but not overly so because she had gone through pregnancy with relative ease. "Well sweetheart, you go home. If you need me give me a call."

When I arrived home she was still awake but beginning to feel more uncomfortable and wanted to speak with her doctor, Emi Achara. While speaking with Dr. Achara, her condition was now punctuated with intermittent pains. At this stage Dr. Achara told us that Jo should head to the maternity ward at the Princess Margaret Hospital.

I called my Aunt Lily Thompson, who was to attend Jo during delivery and to be with her until she was settled in at home.

Aunt Lily was a little surprised with the call because she thought that the due date was later.

"Jo! The time has come. Are you ready to make this next big step? Remember, I will be with you." So were the comforting words of Aunt Lily.

Dr. Achara and Aunt Lily were on hand for our check in.

Events progressed pretty rapidly. At 8:30 a.m., 12 January 1973, Robyn Melinda Farrington came into this world, happily.

Whether by destiny or by some special spiritual wish that was put into motion a long time ago, Robyn's birth coincided with that of my mom, Pearl Melinda, sixty-seven years previously in 1906.

Robyn's arrival into this world was a delight that was indescribable. Following the euphoria, I had to return to the reality of my job on Paradise Island.

Quite unexpectedly my responsibilities were expanded to include the Le Cabaret Theatre. This enterprise was very important to the casino as it was the entertainment centre for casino players and guests of the hotel. The concept was not novel in that the company was adapting the model used by the major casinos/hotels in Las Vegas. The showroom was the means of making special concessions to the "high rollers" who frequented the casino.

Although Le Cabaret was owned by the Britannia Beach Hotel, the show was created and managed by Tibor Rudas. In effect, Tibor was under contract to produce a spectacular Las Vegas type revue.

The revue by virtually any standard was quite spectacular. The formula was in a way quite unsophisticated—the principal specialty acts were engaged for three or four months at a time and supported by dancers, acrobats, topless models and an amazing topless lead dancer. I was a little surprised that there was little or no resistance among the religious community to the use of topless models.

The costuming was outstanding and as such contributed so much to the richness of the entertainment. The accompanying music to all the acts and choreographed dances was performed by a most competent orchestra. In the beginning, the orchestra was conducted by an accomplished and respected American-based leader, Don Ragon, and accompanied mainly by musicians from outside. The good thing is that Tibor was intent on introducing Bahamian talent into the orchestra. There were several key changes—Chris Fox, an extraordinary music talent, had the chance to study abroad and upon returning home Tibor groomed him carefully and elevated him to the leader of the orchestra. Chris was also a composer of music and created some interesting music. With the passage of time, the entire orchestra was Bahamian. Edwin "Apple" Eliott—yes, the boy who grew up in Hawkins Hill with me—was the pianist with amazing talent.

The show was very popular—casino players, hotel guests, cruise ship passengers and Bahamian residents found the shows exciting.

The acrobats that included Bahamian boys and girls were superb. Mitzi Chipman became the lead dancer and was marvelous.

Tibor brought specialty acts such as the Gauchos of the Pampas of Argentina and, an Eastern European troupe comprising mostly family members who performed the most daring gymnastic feats with fearless dexterity.

With this new responsibility, I knew that I would be treading into uncharted territory but Tibor was most engaging and passionate about creating new elements of the show that would add enormously to the stature and fame of the Tibor Rudas Production. In every presentation of the show, Tibor was recognized as the producer.

In 1973, a policy decision was taken by Crosby, Davis and Norton to create a new show—an undertaking that Tibor relished enthusiastically. A budget was set of $900,000.00, which was a large amount of money in those days.

Controlling Tibor was impossible but the effort had to be made. Tibor would come to my office for a meeting and would lie down on the couch in my office to discuss the progress of the construction of the show. His enthusiasm was irresistible. He was also very confident about what he was doing.

Tibor cleverly disguised the amount of money being spent by using some of his own money with the expectation of being reimbursed.

Tibor and I had to meet with Jack and Steve to discuss progress.

Tibor to Jack: "Jack, when we are finished you will have a show that will be extraordinary and as good as any production in Las Vegas."

Tibor's delivery was always stilted and his Hungarian accent made the conversation uneven but fascinating.

"Tibor, I knew that you are a genius but we are financially constrained and need to use our resources carefully," Jack replied.

At this point Tibor would remove his thick-lensed glasses and reply with more unintended, hesitant searches for the correct words. His passion and confidence shone through with great impact.

"Jack and Steve, I am building you a show that will bring great success. Trust me to do the right thing."

Tibor provided an outline of what the show would contain which Jack and Steve both liked.

I was nervous not only because I knew that Tibor was going beyond the budgeted limit, but because he was advancing his own money, the degree of overstretch yet unknown.

Tibor went to New York to search for scenery and miscellany for the show. Imagine the horror when he told me that he had purchased an ice rink that had been used in a production at Radio

City Music Hall. He added that he had also lured an acrobatic female skater, Joanne Funakoshi. This ice rink would be used on the stage and Joanne would perform an act that would be perfectly integrated into the show. It was so hard to imagine an ice rink on Paradise Island as a part of a spectacular show.

Tibor was well-insulated in his organization through the meticulous hard work of Colin Wilson and Ian McLaren, both of whom in an earlier life had been gymnasts.

The day I was dreading was fast approaching when a full accounting for the show had to be revealed. Tibor had been thinking ahead and had planned for extending the life of the show by merely changing specialty acts and retaining the core of the production pretty much the same except for some minimal refurbishing, annually.

Tibor came clean and produced a full accounting reflecting the grand total of expenditure at $1.8 million—exactly double the budget. However, he softened the impact by explaining that cost would be amortized over eight years instead of four years. There was some gnashing of teeth but they saw the wisdom of creating a show that would greatly impact revenue and could add another significant dimension to the casino operations.

The show became very popular with the cruise ships and this flow of cruise ship passengers to the show and to the casino was increasing at a very steady pace.

Unfortunately as a result of two trends occurring simultaneously, the downward decline of support for over-the-hill entertainment was noticeable and a cause for concern for the BMEU. One was the introduction of the spectacular Le Cabaret Show and secondly, security in the community just "Over-the-Hill" became more tenuous. The change seemed irreversible. On a positive note, however, tourism was growing, jobs were being created and the prospects for continued development were encouraging.

Once the show celebrated its opening night, I said to Tibor, "Do you realize you almost got me fired?" Tibor took off his glasses, looked at me, chuckled and said, hesitatingly, "I also almost got my walking papers too."

Le Cabaret was the complete showroom attached to the casino. The first show of each night also offered dining with the show;

those wanting to see the show only were also accommodated—two drinks minimum plus a cover charge. The price of dinner also included a cover charge.

In the early days following the grand opening of the resort, it was essential to have highly skilled personnel in Food and Beverage operations which in the main were imported. At Le Cabaret, Fred Roberti was the manager of the Food and Beverage operation and was assisted by two talented Bahamians who were destined to assume senior positions in Food and Beverage—Vernon "Boy" Wilkinson and Vernal Sands. "Boy" ultimately was promoted to Maitre D' at the world famous Café Martinique and Vernal was appointed manager of the Le Cabaret.

Café Martinique was indeed very special not only for its ambiance and the unsurpassed quality of its cuisine but also for its history.

After Dr. Axel Wenner Gren purchased the greater portion of Hog Island (the name was changed in 1962 by Parliament to Paradise Island and for the purpose of the Hotels Encouragement Act, it was declared an Out Island), he built a boathouse abutting Paradise Lagoon (formerly Burnside Pond) from which he could access the Nassau Harbour through a manmade canal.

Huntington Hartford, in his planning of the development of his island, saw the potential of creating a magnificent restaurant featuring French cuisine. There was no Paradise Bridge in 1960, so access to the island was by water taxi owned and operated by Hartford. He established a facility at the Deveaux Street dock and it was from this location that visitors to Paradise Island congregated and were transported to the dock adjacent to Café Martinique.

Café Martinique very quickly gained the reputation as being the epitome of fine dining—a meal consisting of French cuisine was an exquisite experience. Stefano Brandino was the Maitre D'—an Italian who was small in stature but most energetic.

Gonzalo Iturriaga was the head chef who oversaw the preparation of each dish with an unerring eye. I later discovered that Gonzalo had little formal education but through hard work and perseverance achieved recognition as a most talented chef.

As the months passed there were organizational changes that affected the management structure. Fred Schock was replaced by

Duncan Rapier, a hotelier of considerable experience and who had worked at the Nassau Beach Hotel for years.

It was during the mid 1970s into the early 1980s that the operations began to change on Paradise Island and in our Miami office. It was much like a game of musical chairs.

Duncan Rapier departed and his position was filled by LeRoy Bailey, Jo's former boss at the Loews Paradise Island Hotel and Villas. At the time Peter Krollpfeiffer, former General Manager of the Holiday Inn on Paradise Island, was Vice President of Hotel Operations. LeRoy's assistants were Gladys Darville and Judith Burrows. Although LeRoy and I had exchanged harsh words one evening in the Tradewinds Lounge Hotel, we were able to work together in reasonable harmony. In the Corporate Executive Office, Penny Powell and Cathy Glucksman left the company. Gladys moved to become Steve Norton's assistant and Jo, who had decided to return to work, was lured back as Secretary/Assistant to Jack Davis, President of Resorts International and Paradise Island Ltd.

Jo found being a housewife too confining and wanted to be active again in a business environment. Eyebrows were raised and indirect questions posed as to the advisability of having husband and wife working in the same executive suite. The arrangement survived for years with almost perfect harmony.

As my responsibilities increased, it was essential for me to have an Executive Secretary/Personal Assistant. So in 1973, Cleomi Parker joined me. She was extraordinarily talented and smart and it did not take me long to realize how valuable she would become in making my office function with amazing efficiency.

During these years, George Mackey was the Director and Joan Mitchell was his Personal Assistant. Our head of Paradise Island Security was Fenlon Richards. He reported directly to Bob Peloquin, the head of the Resort's subsidiary, Intertel, based in Washington, D.C. Because we were operating a casino that was considerably larger and more active than the predecessor casino at the Bahamian Club on West Bay Street, the company was determined to make sure that the operation was free of any questionable practices—as Bob Peloquin so succinctly put it, "Our casino operation must be squeaky clean."

At different stages, my responsibilities were expanded beyond anything I could have imagined. I felt as if the burden was about to consume me but I relied heavily upon so many fellow employees for guidance and assistance.

In this setting, a Danish proverb that I read and believed in was a way of life: "Better to ask twice than lose your way once."

Either directly or indirectly, I had responsibility for the Le Cabaret, Engineering, Security, Human Resources, Laundry, Transportation, Golf Course, Risk Management, Real Estate, Las Palmas (South Andros). How do you attain success in a business with so many moving parts? The scope was dauntingly enormous and it was abundantly obvious that a multitalented team was essential if the various departments were to function efficiently.

In the natural order of life, which is underscored with good fortune, I was ordained to work with a group of highly motivated associates who were positive and professional contributors to the welfare of the Paradise Island group of businesses.

Even though I may not remember all, I am nonetheless compelled to recognize my partners in the journey to stitch together a mosaic of measurable success. The associates at many levels—Ernie Cambridge, Clara Gibson, Joseph Storr, Aaron Seymour, Iris Baker Smith, Evie Arnett, Selwyn Estwick, Herclues Hanna, Mae Payne, Dimple Davis, Carolyn MacDonald, Clifford Storr—all within the domain of the accounting department. Clive and Suzanne Adamson, Karen T. Carey—Human Resources, Fred Higgs and Leroy Bowe—Golf Course, David Gorlin and Dorothy—Real Estates Sales, Leroy Gay—Transportation and Paul Shealey and Paul Thompson—Security.

Las Palmas, a twenty-room resort at Driggs Hill, South Andros, was the most interesting element within our operations in these early years. Coincidentally, the resort was located in the constituency represented by the Prime Minister, Sir Lynden O. Pindling. Resorts International accepted a proposal to manage the property. Additionally, we constructed three cottages on the hotel's property for the exclusive use of the Prime Minister when he visited South Andros.

Mr. Forbes and his wife were managing the property; however we did bring in a General Manager, Neville LeChoy, a hotelier from Jamaica. We thought that through use of the strength of Resorts' marketing and promotional department we could promote Las Palmas as an out-island resort within our twin destination package. The concept had merit because during the winter season—Thanksgiving through April—when the Britannia was full on weekends, a visitor had the option of a two-night, three-day stay at Las Palmas and then a return to Paradise Island to complete the vacation. The company seriously explored the plan with a number of Family Island boutique resorts; however, the idea never gained traction. Thus we were left with just Las Palmas.

Despite our best efforts to manage the property profitably, it was to no avail.

As a part of overseeing Las Palmas I made regular visits to review financial results and operational matters. On occasion, I would invite a few close friends to stay at Las Palmas and with the tennis court there was a venue for a little exercise and fun.

On one such occasion, crab season had just begun and at nights, crabs were everywhere. Curiously, they found a way to get into the ceilings of the bedrooms. Crabs would climb onto the doors with glass louvers—the sound of these crabs climbing around you while you were attempting to sleep was surreal and quite unsettling. The experience gave us something to laugh about.

The group at different times included Eddy and Gladys Darville (Gladys worked in the Executive Office), Ernie and Sandra Miller (Ernie was accountant for the casino), Peter and Sandra Isaacs, and Carolyn Satter and her daughter, Paula (Carolyn was Office Manager of Resorts International's Miami Office).

Mrs. Forbes, wife of the Manager, was a delightful woman who had the kind of personality that made you like her immediately.

One day while talking with her she confided that she was expecting and that it was to be her fifteenth child. The look of shock on my face was probably enough for her to give an explanation for so many children. She told me that she had a number of multiple births which accounted for the large number of offspring. She then coyly added, "Mr. Farrington, I am deeply religious and believe that it is the will of God that we bring children into this world. However, do you think God will forgive me if I have my tubes tied after this one?"

Without blinking or hesitation I said, "Mrs. Forbes, I am sure God will forgive you. You have certainly done your part." She looked at me for a moment or two before closing her eyes and whispering, "Thank you so much, Mr. Farrington."

It was not unusual for Sir Lynden Pindling to spend weekends at Las Palmas. He enjoyed the environment and privacy that Las Palmas offered and of course, he made good use of his time by meeting with his constituents.

Las Palmas never made a profit despite the company's best efforts to create interest through our Resorts International extensive marketing network for Paradise Island. The day finally came when it was realized that to continue the operation would result in the losses reaching unsustainable proportions. At the time that Resorts withdrew from Las Palmas, the accumulated loss was quite substantial.

Saying goodbye to the staff at Las Palmas and in particular Mr. and Mrs. Forbes was not easy. We had developed a very nice relationship, which made overseeing Las Palmas a pleasant experience.

CHAPTER 33

THE SHAH OF IRAN IN EXILE ON PARADISE ISLAND

There is so much written about Iran during the many years following the forced departure of Mohammad Reza Pahlavi from his beloved homeland.

The Shah's visit to Paradise Island was a totally unexpected occurrence. George Myers, President of Resorts International Bahamas, customarily at night, occupied a table in the Gallery Bar overlooking the casino floor. George, a non-drinker, was a hands-on type of manager and as such wanted to be near the action during hours when the hotel and casino were the busiest.

While at this post one evening, two well-dressed gentlemen of swarthy complexion approached him. Following introductions, one of the gentlemen said "Mr. Myers, we are on a special and confidential mission. We represent His Highness the Shah of Iran and given certain troubling developments in Iran, we are seeking a location at which the Shah can reside in safety for a period of time. Do you have such a place on Paradise Island?"

As can be imagined, George was astounded and fascinated all

at once. "Gentlemen, before I can take this further I need some assurance that this request is legitimate."

In response they said, "Mr. Myers, tomorrow morning we will present you with appropriate credentials which should satisfy your concerns."

Next morning the appropriate credentials with proof positive were presented to George, who called me into his office that was next door to mine and gave me the story. He then called Bob Peloquin at Intertel in Washington and gave him the story. The opinion was that Resorts Chairman Jim Crosby's house was the only suitable place. However, Jim had to agree.

Bob spoke with Jim and got the green light to go ahead. When Bob relayed Jim's response, he did add that when Jim got the story he was in a state of surprise and said, "Well, I'll be damned."

Early next morning a meeting was convened in Corporate Board Room with the senior advisors to the Shah, a representative from Foreign Affairs in The Bahamas, the Deputy Commissioner of Police and several high-ranking officers. George, Fenlon Richards and I represented Resorts International.

This November 1979 was a momentous time for The Bahamas and Paradise Island in particular.

The Shah's representative outlined the timetable for the Shah's arrival in Nassau together with his family. The atmosphere in the meeting was electric—the stakes were very high. We understood, without prompting, that security was of paramount importance. Iran was in a state of turmoil with citizens being killed without appeal to a court of justice. "Sidewalk justice" was the order of the day.

It was made clear that we had just twenty-four hours within which to make adequate preparation. Overshadowing our discussion was the fact that the lives of the Shah and his family were greatly at risk. We spent several hours establishing the schedule of matters needing immediate attention.

In summary, George and I were directed, "Gentlemen, on behalf of the Shah and his family we thank you for being so responsive to our needs, and to summarize—the Shah and the Empress will reside in the house of Jim Crosby at the Ocean Club."

Alterations to accesses to the sleeping quarters were necessary as the Shah and the Empress did not share the same bedroom.

"The villas will be used for the mother of the Empress and the two children, Prince Alireza and Princess Leila Pahlavi.

"The Shah's personal security will assume control of all security matters with support being provided by a team from Wackenhut Corporation, a U.S.-based security firm, added to which there would be a strong Bahamian police presence.

"The Shah and family will be arriving on a 747 Egyptian airline plane at Nassau International Airport and, upon disembarking, will be flown by helicopter to the Paradise Island Golf Course. Transport from that location will be along the secluded north beach road to Mr. Crosby's house."

There were more details given but George and I needed to mobilize our hotel team to get Mr. Crosby's house ready to secure the Shah and to alert all employees of the importance of getting everything right and being aware of the high level of security.

While all this activity was moving at an accelerated pace, the Shah's leadman/advisor arranged for an associate to make all the financial arrangements for all costs associated with the Shah's stay.

George was driving and when we turned into the road just beyond the north entrance to the villas, he stopped the car and turned off the engine. It was at that moment that the significance of the events that were soon to unfold hit us.

George with his left hand on the steering wheel turned towards me and with a wry smile spoke to me very solemnly. "John." George was in the habit of calling me by my first name. "Can you really believe all this shit that is going on?"

With my heart thumping, I could only nod my head in the affirmative.

He went on, "We will be facing danger every moment of every day. I know that security around the Shah will be extra tight but the possibility of an attack is very real."

All I could add is that we can only hope and pray nothing goes wrong while they are here with us.

As George started the car, I reached quickly into my mind and asked the question, "Iran is on fire, the Shah has been deposed and is on the run. How could this have happened in this day and age?"

We got to Mr. Crosby's house. Work was in progress to complete the alternations for the sleeping quarters. The villas were being checked by housekeeping staff making sure all rooms were spotless and properly equipped.

At Crosby's house, we had a brief meeting with the Shah's head of security who explained in broad terms the defensive tactics to be employed in the event of an attack. Logically, if an attempt was to be made on the Royal Family it would come from the ocean side of the house. There were to be three lines of defence while the family was moved to safety with speed, efficiency and under sufficient fire power to repel any attackers. We could only listen attentively but with wildly gyrating thoughts of probabilities.

It was clear to George, the threat and the stakes were extremely high. In fact, we were told that the Ayatollah Khomeini had placed a very high price on the head of the Shah.

A final check was made and then George and I left the operations of the club under the control of the Ocean Club General Manager Steve Sawyer and staff. This Wednesday night was a restless one in bed.

The next day was going to be eventful—it was important that the Shah's introduction to Paradise Island was made without problem. The schedule was set and all the persons involved were in place. The Egyptian Airline 747 landed at Windsor Field at 11:00 a.m., and all went smoothly.

The next part was to meet the helicopter at the Number 1 green of the golf course with transportation to move the party to Mr. Crosby's house. Shortly after noon, the helicopter appeared low on the horizon and was soon hovering over Number 1 making ready for a landing. Once on the ground, we moved to the door and awaited their exit from the helicopter.

The Shah stepped out followed by family. After they were hastily placed into the waiting cars with security well positioned, the procession made its way along the north shore on an unpaved road without incident.

For some reason I was the one to accompany the Shah into the house. We stood in the front room looking out across the beach and into the ocean. Fortunately for a first impression, it was a bright sunny day with a gentle cool breeze blowing in from the northeast—the ocean just slightly choppy and lapping innocently on to the beautiful, powder-like sandy beach. The ocean reflected differing depths with various shades of blue and a sky absorbing white, billowing clouds that appeared to be imprinted against a blue, blue pristine sky.

The Shah stood quietly for a minute or two and then said, "Mr. Farrington, you have a very beautiful country. You should feel proud to be living here."

"Yes, Your Majesty, we do feel blessed that we have been graced with so much natural beauty."

The Shah was about three to four inches shorter than me. He wore a light gray suit, impeccably tailored, with a white shirt and matching tie. His graying hair added contrast to his swarthy complexion. His relaxed attitude conveyed a sense of authority and power. His smile that accompanied his words was genuine and warm and seemed to connect so naturally with his eyes. I assured His Majesty that it was our desire to make his stay with his family at Ocean Club as comfortable and peaceful as possible.

We shook hands and I left him in the care of his senior aide who took control in guiding the Shah through the house.

Once George and I were certain that the Shah and family were satisfactorily settled in, we left for our offices at the Britannia.

On the way George commented that he was very impressed with the way the Shah accepted his sudden change in status and the dignity of his demeanor. I said, "George, when you consider the constant danger in which he is to be continually exposed, and the need for significant security, his serene demeanour is admirable. Can you imagine being pushed out of your beloved country and away from your people? He possesses great courage."

We were quiet with our own thoughts as we made the short drive back to the Britannia Beach Hotel.

I was to return to the Ocean Club at 5:45 p.m. to play doubles with Peter Isaacs, George Carey and Terry North. We played nearly every Thursday evening and had been doing so for many years.

This Thursday night was to be different.

While we were warming up on Court #1 under the lights, lo and behold the Empress appeared with her security and took a seat alongside the court with the intention of watching us play. Of course we were thrilled and at the same time a bit nervous.

Midway into the first set, we were interrupted by the sound of machine gun fire. The sound originated slightly east of the courts in the vicinity of the cabanas. My first thought was that we were going to be caught up in an attempted attack on the Shah and family. At the same time of the gun shots, security swiftly moved the Empress away from the court area to a location which I was sure was predetermined.

Then there was absolutely silence. We were still poised to take flight however the silence remained unbroken. We decided to abandon our match for the night but reminded each other that the following Thursday was still on.

The memory of the machine gun lingered with me. I needed to find out what had happened. Upon checking with Mr. Fen Richard, head of island security, I was told that the machine gun was accidentally discharged by one of the security personnel. For this accident to have happened on the first night at Ocean Club must have been very disturbing to His Majesty and the Empress. Nothing more was mentioned of this event. Thank goodness.

In the days following, there were a lot of activities at the Ocean Club as high-ranking officials of the U.S. Government State Department visited with the Shah. Security remained on high alert.

I decided to conduct a little bit of research on the Shah and his expulsion from Iran. It was confusing that in days, weeks and months leading up to his expulsion, there was a reversal in the relationship between the United States and Iran. The Shah considered the United States as a friendly nation and at the same time Iran was anti-communist.

Incredibly the Shah made many progressive changes in his country and led a pro-Western regime.

The Shah, using oil-generated wealth, had modernized the nation—built rural roads, postal services, libraries, constructed dams to irrigate Iran's arid land making the country ninety percent self-sufficient in food production. He granted women equal rights, thus bringing Iran into the twentieth century. He also favoured peace with Israel and supplied that country with oil.

And then unexpectedly, issues arose regarding human rights with Henry Kissinger. Ted Kennedy was foremost with severe criticism. After a long and unceasing campaign against the Shah's governance, he relented to the pressure being applied. During President Carter's term, he was forced into exile on January 16, 1979. Following his departure, the turmoil in Iran escalated out of control.

The Shah and his family, because of the never-ending threat to their safety, enjoyed very little freedom of movement while at the Ocean Club. He did, however, enjoy playing tennis, and virtually every evening under the lights he would play with John Antonas—the tennis pro, on Court #2. Through the weeks they became fairly friendly to the point that John arranged for his dad to have a photo taken with the Shah.

Getting from the house to the court was to require careful coordination of the security detail assigned to the Shah. It was a short distance from the house to the tennis court, a walk of seven to eight minutes. He was surrounded by armed personnel and while he was on court, security was evenly spaced around the perimeter, always looking outward into the darkness. Of course there were other men in the outer perimeter and basically out of sight.

In the days and weeks that followed, only members of senior U.S. State Department personnel were visiting the Ocean Club to consult with the Shah and his close advisors. With Iran still immersed in civil disorder, it remained a big issue for the U.S. Government to try to find a solution that left the U.S. relatively unscathed from the fallout of the Shah's forced departure from Iran and to which the United States was a party.

In nearly every history-making event, there is some insignificant occurrence which adds considerably to the story.

The casino had on its staff a host, Alan Hirschorn, nicknamed "Jam up" who had great energy and enthusiasm, and who knew how to get things done. "Jam up" found a way to get friendly with Jim and Jack. In fact, they developed a very close working relationship. "Jam up" was the "go to" guy. Somehow he was able to meet the Shah and in his irrepressible way became a backgammon-playing partner. The Shah loved playing backgammon.

George Myers told me that on one occasion, the Shah's aide had made arrangements for the Shah to see a dentist because of a problem he was experiencing but the Shah cancelled because he was playing backgammon with "Jam up." The moral is: "Your position does not determine an outcome; it is your degree of your influence that carries the day."

Jim was very interested in events surrounding the Shah and the quickly organized stay at the Ocean Club. Through a sequence of conversations between the Shah's advisors and Bob Peloquin, a dinner was arranged for Mr. Crosby with the Shah, which was to take place at the house.

About seven to ten days following the dinner, I had reason to meet with Jim because at that time I was overseeing the operation of the Paradise Island Bridge on his behalf.

Jim was very open about the dinner with the Shah. I was fascinated with the story that he told me. The Shah was forced into exile after many discussions with representatives of the Council on Foreign Relations from which U.S. foreign policy emerged. It would seem that under President Carter's administration, the decision was taken to topple the Shah's monarchy.

"Barrie, in the end the Shah had no choice but to pack up and leave, but he had the assurance through U.S. diplomatic channels that if he exited Iran, America would welcome him—that is to say, give him and his family political asylum."

With that assurance the Shah reluctantly left Iran. However, shortly after reaching Cairo, Egypt, the U.S. Ambassador to Egypt informed him that the U.S. could not welcome the Shah to American territory.

I thought that this explained the sudden shift to The Bahamas and the Ocean Club—even this change took some maneuvering as the Bahamian Government would have been somewhat nervous about such a visit.

The most compelling part of what Mr. Crosby was saying to me was the admission of the Shah—that given the level of agitation within his country, he expected that protests would reach a level of substantial violence.

He added quite candidly that the Shah admitted that "I would have been forced to quell the uprising militarily, which meant that there would have been substantial loss of life. However, in the end, history will have to judge whether or not my departure from Iran was good for my country and the world."

After about forty-five to sixty days, the time came when the Shah and family had to leave. A little time was spent in Mexico and there was a report that an attempt was made on his life and he was slightly wounded. One little-known fact that emerged subsequently and which also influenced his departure from Iran—he was terminally ill with cancer. His time in Mexico was short-lived and at the invitation of his friend Anwar Sadat, he returned to Egypt.

Mohammed Reza Pahlavi died on 27 July 1980. His last words were: "I wait upon fate, never ceasing to pray for Iran and for my people. I think only of their suffering."

CHAPTER 34

BUILDING BLOCKS FOR PARADISE ISLAND'S FUTURE

In Bahamian tourism, Resorts International was by far the most significant player. Jim Crosby was energetic and possessed great vision for the development of Paradise Island. The planned growth of infrastructure, facilities and hotels was greatly dependent upon available utilities. Jim and Jack with Steve Norton's input soon realized that the government lacked the capability to provide a reliable supply of potable water. An agreement was worked out with government to allow Paradise Island Limited to build and equip a plant to produce potable water. The one point that was contentious was that government did not want to relinquish a revenue stream, and thus included in this special agreement was a requirement for the company to buy a minimum quantity from the government during each month. Maintaining a balance in this regard was not easy as demand for water on the Paradise Island was directly related to hotel occupancies, new residences and businesses being constructed and operated.

Jim was indeed forward thinking and knew that the water supply and sustained electricity to the Island were crucial. Jim and Jack decided that specialists in this area were necessary if they were going to get it right. Lorne Jenkinson, a senior officer with the Texas-based construction company that had completed the early construction of the Paradise Island Hotel and Villas and the Casino, and Neville "Butch" Carey were engaged to oversee the development of our infrastructure to support Paradise Island operations.

This was a brilliant move by Jim and Jack to remove the absolute reliance on government to provide water to Paradise Island. With regard to electricity, there was little choice but to have the Bahamas Electricity Corporation supply electricity. This too was complicated in that high-voltage cable had to be laid on the bed of the sea in order to connect Nassau to Paradise Island. This also meant that several electricity cables had to be laid on Paradise Island, as distribution was somewhat complicated. Lorne and Butch were central to organizing the construction of a water-producing facility and also to designing and constructing a distribution water system.

Another stroke of brilliance by Jim was his understanding the real importance of water being available for the present users, and as well as those in the future. The situation was complicated by the limitation of available potable/drinking water. To soften potable water demand, he and his team of consultants designed a system for the treatment of secondary water for irrigation and water closet flushing. Unquestionably, the management of water became the most important element in the development of Paradise Island. In short, the Paradise Island Utility Company was created to manage the business of manufacturing and distributing potable and secondary-quality water.

One crucial inclusion in the design of every building to be constructed on Paradise Island was dual plumbing—that is, there had to be one system for potable water and one for the use of secondary water. All used water through sewer lines was returned to the water plant where it was treated and then redistributed for the irrigating of gardens and the flushing of toilets. The secondary water was a lot cheaper than potable water. As a precaution all secondary water contained a blue/green dye that made it discernible from potable water.

For absolute control, all new buildings had to obtain the approval of the utility and development oversight department prior to construction commencing, a necessary control feature.

Jim once told me while we were discussing the water plant and how essential it was for Paradise Island: "If we had not been able to manufacture and distribute water, we would have never been able to develop Paradise Island." What a truly profound statement as we look at the past, present and future of Paradise Island.

Managing the water supply was a very complicated process. The company engaged the University of Arizona to guide the company in putting in place the most efficient water conservation programme imaginable. Lorne and Butch did such a good job that for several years the Paradise Island utility plant was officially recognized as having the best water conservation programme in place for the region.

As Paradise Island grew, the ability to efficiently produce high-quality potable water became very difficult due to the encroachment of saltwater into the subterranean sources of potable water. As demand for potable water increased, the water production problem worsened.

With urgency the plant had to be significantly upgraded so as to manufacture potable water from salt/sea water. And so a sophisticated reverse osmosis plant was installed.

Jim and Jack in looking to the future believed that Paradise Island could be developed comprehensively—resorts, residential community, condominiums, timeshare projects, and marina. After all, the company owned 800 acres of prime land. Opportunities awaited action. But then an unanticipated situation arose which was cause for consternation.

When Huntington Hartford purchased Hog Island, except for several small parcels located immediately west of Casuarina Drive, Hartford received legal assurance that he had clear title for about 800 acres. As noted earlier, the name Hog Island was changed to Paradise Island in 1962 by an act of Parliament.

Inevitably the unexpected occurred. The Burrows family, who was related to Tommy Robinson, Vice President of Purchasing, made application to the Supreme Court to be given title to 32.8

acres of land that ran from the north (ocean) side to south side (harbour). The claim was that the family had undisturbed use of this parcel of land for more than twenty years. The family used the land for farming and the raising of some animals. The law as written allowed for the quieting of title and the assignment of ownership if proof to the court was of a quality that could not be successfully disputed.

Despite a prolonged legal battle, the court ruled that the claimants had proved their claim and thus were given title to the 32.8 acres—the Burrows Tract.

This outcome was a serious impediment to the development of the east end of Paradise Island.

The land at issue was adjoining the Paradise Island Golf Course. Access to the golf course was across the land, which we commonly referred to as the Burrows Tract. The unpaved road across the land was used by many persons, particularly those associated with or employed by Paradise Island Limited. Attempts to reach some kind of accommodation with the "new" owners seemed to lead nowhere except that an element of acrimony crept into the discussions. Tommy was caught in between the standoff and although he did not have a vested interest in the property in dispute, he was related to the new owners of the land. Another oddity was that Eric Lightbourn, head bartender in Gallery Bar, in the Casino, was the principal beneficiary in this parcel of land.

When discussions got bitter, the Burrows family would place barricades across the access road. The inconvenience to the company caused Jack and Steve at the direction of Jim to find a creative way to overcome this irritating obstacle.

The one approach to which a great deal of planning was given involved operating a ferry on the harbour side, which would remove the need to use the road or cross the Burrows Tract. Even though there seemed little choice to do otherwise, the cost to introduce a ferry system was going to be very high.

Then there was a fortuitous development that presented an opportunity that would permanently solve the standoff with the Burrows family. A cousin of Tommy, who coincidentally was one of the beneficiaries of ownership of the Burrows Tract, needed to find a fairly substantial amount of money to settle a private debt, agreed to sell to Paradise Island Limited a part of her interest in the land. The transaction was completed, which meant that Paradise Island Limited held a very small undivided interest in the ownership of the parcel and as such had an equal right to use the road across the tract without interruption. An agreement was also needed that enabled Paradise Island Limited to pave the road.

The final resolution to this situation came about following Sun International's purchase of the interest of Merv Griffin in Paradise Island. Maybe it happened because so many years had passed or maybe the owners were getting older and had no plan for the land. In any event, the owners sold to Sun International for a very tidy sum of money. Eric Lightbourn continued being bartender in the Gallery Bar.

As my areas of responsibility expanded, the workload increased and performance demands were escalating at a rate that caused my life to become unbalanced—a realization that I seemed unable to confront.

Jo, my wife, seemed to sense this addiction to work coupled with strong involvement with other organizations that required more and more of my time.

One day she said to me, "Barrie, do you realize that you are devoting less time to the family and that maybe the foundation of our happiness is showing some cracks?"

There was a part of me that recognized the truth of what she was saying but here I was grappling with personal growth and opportunity to expand my horizon and to contribute to my Bahamas. I suppose being confronted so directly by the woman I married in order to create a better life caused me to answer with a kind of bewilderment.

"How should I treat opportunity? In building our future there must be sacrifices. There is a compelling need to succeed and to contribute to the development of our country."

And then I added, "My love for you and the children is without compromise and I want you to have faith in me and our life together."

We were quiet for a few minutes, each occupied with private thoughts.

Jo was now working for Jack Davis and feeling good about herself and what she was accomplishing as a professional.

Thus we sidestepped the issue for the time being and the thoughts about the condition of our relationship.

And so, the decade of the seventies was turning into a period of putting in place the building blocks for the eighties.

CHAPTER 35

LIFE AFTER DIVORCE FROM JO

After our divorce, and Jo's move to make a new life with Michael Merlin, there was a period of silence. Ultimately, we reconnected and because of common business interests a special friendship evolved.

In 2012, Jo became more reclusive and conversations were generally about Fashion Hall, Robyn and the children. In fact, the relationship was "very civilized," as I liked to refer to it.

Her interest in Fashion Hall remained strong but her stamina for buying expeditions to New York appeared to be flagging. Whenever Susan and I travelled to Florida we frequently stayed at the Merlins' home and time spent there was always pleasant. Through our friendship there was a willingness to accept mail at the house on our behalf or to make special trips to the various shops to purchase specific items for us. All in all there was absolute calm.

On occasion Jo would say, "I don't know how much longer I can continue to go to New York to shop for Fashion Hall. I am not as young as I used to be."

I would laugh and say, "You are just a baby compared to me. You have a lot of good years ahead of you."

And then one day in early 2013, she declared that she would not go to New York again because she had developed a fear of flying. It seemed unusual but there was little option but to accept her statement at face value. Little did any of us know that this change was a precursor to disaster.

Our daughter, Robyn, noticed some disturbing changes but nothing exact. On the way north in September, I stayed at the house with Jo and Mike for one night. She looked thinner and very pale. I was concerned and later told Robyn, "Your mom does not appear to be well. I think you should press her on this subject and see what answer you get."

Robyn subsequently pursued the issue and confirmed that Jo's health seemed to be declining. Robyn did raise the matter with Mike but he did not share the same concern. As time passed, he did admit that Jo's behavior had changed.

Jo and I spoke frequently—mostly about Fashion Hall but also about the grandchildren's activities at school and their performance in softball games.

In December, I decided to spend two nights in Plantation, Florida, before going on to join Susan in New Hampshire for Christmas with her family.

I stayed with Jo and Mike but spent time with Robyn, Javier, her husband and the grandchildren, Nicholas and Elizabeth. Jo complained of having a stomach virus. She did not come out of her bedroom. I did go in to speak with her but she was obviously not well.

Robyn and I spoke later about this but with a sense of futility.

"What are we going to do, daddy? She refuses to see a doctor."

Without a clear resolution I said, "I will write a very stern but sympathetic letter to Jo telling her that those who love her dearly are gravely worried."

The afternoon before I left for the airport, she managed to get out of the bed and sat in the lazy chair in the front room. Little did I know that would be the last time that I would see her alive.

While up north, I did write the letter. We returned to Nassau on 29 December. Brooks was waiting for us at the Lynden

Pindling International Airport and as we were getting into the car, my son John had rung through on Brooks' phone and wanted to speak with me.

"John, I will be home soon. I will speak with you as soon as I am there."

"Dad, I need to speak with you now."

He then added, "Jo died during the night."

My shock was like being struck by a bolt of lightning. Quite suddenly I was extremely angry in a flash and at the same time a great sadness overwhelmed me. Susan was equally affected but more out of the friendship she shared with Jo.

The drive home was a blur. I knew that I had to call my dear, dear daughter, Robyn. Making the call was hard and when she heard my voice all she could say was "Oh, Daddy!" There was no way to describe the feeling.

The next morning, we were on the plane to Fort Lauderdale. Robyn agreed for me to tell Nicholas and Elizabeth of this tragedy.

Jo had succumbed to breast cancer—an illness that she cleverly kept hidden from Mike and Robyn.

The agony she must have suffered is simply beyond what any of us could have imagined. Robyn obtained a photo from the medical examiner. The disfigurement, size and grotesqueness of the growth were hard for the medical examiner to absorb.

And so at sixty-seven years of age, Jo's life came to an unrealistic and tragic end. She was buried next to her mom and dad. I know that this made her feel happy.

Robyn struggled with reconciliation. For quite some time she had hoped that Jo, her mom and best friend, would have left a message of explanation, but no such message ever came.

Sitting alone in my "cave" at home, many scattered images surged through my mind—the moments of shared laughter, the unwelcome intrusion of anger and subsequent regret, the grief of laying loved ones to rest and then, of course, the recognition of the inevitability of God's wishes.

My mind came to rest on one indelible image—setting in the parlour of the funeral home and looking at the profile of Jo in the coffin. It just seemed so unreal. My final thought was: "She deserved something better than this!"

CHAPTER 36

BAHAMAS INDEPENDENCE AND THE COMPANY'S EXPANSION

Cleomi Parker joined my office on 15 May 1973, and it did not take long for me to realize that she was a professional, possessing extraordinary talent—who, along with Judith Burrows, allowed me to function at maximum efficiency. The one skill that she had at her disposal was that she could take dictation in shorthand and transcribe perfectly.

The Transportation Department, managed by Leroy Gay, was not easy to guide as there were so many elements that were the cause of shifting operational mandates. Keeping the company's fleet of vehicles in good condition was most difficult for our mechanics in the company's garage but they persevered under the guidance of Mr. Gay. The company under an industrial agreement with the hotel union was obliged to provide transportation for line staff to and from work during specified hours of each day.

The decision was taken to make an agreement with the Bahamas Taxi-Cab Union to provide staff transportation. Unfortunately, despite best efforts of Richard Moss, Union President, and his executive team to provide a reliable service, the problems were never-ending. As other hotels were subject to the same obligations for employee transportation, I undertook to negotiate a new contract on behalf of the Britannia Beach, Loews Paradise Island Hotel and Villas, Holiday Inn, Beach Inn, Flagler Hotel, Ocean Club and Paradise Island Limited. Contractually, we had identical schedules for collection and delivery of employees.

Out of these encounters, the relationship with the Bahamas Taxi Cab Union became very cordial with Mr. Richard Moss being central to this outcome. I can say that he was a gentleman and a forward-thinking leader.

Mr. Gay once said to me, "Mr. Farrington, we have contracts but I am worried there will be trouble ahead."

"Why do you say that, Mr. Gay," I asked.

"The fleet of buses is old and having a lot of mechanical problems. Also, the drivers seem not to care too much about giving service."

This exchange was not welcome but we knew that we had to press on.

On top of this, the company had to provide transportation for guests between properties on Paradise Island. We purchased several Thomas buses for this purpose. Mr. Gay was ably supported by Wesley Campbell and a good team of mechanics and coordinators but the task was monumental.

Garbage collection was another area that was highly difficult to manage.

After years of diligent trials, the company changed the structure of transportation. The Garbage Collection contract was tendered and a new provider was selected. The result was a win for the company. Reluctantly, the contract with the Bahamas Taxi Cab Union expired and a better organized company was contracted to transport employees. Guest transportation remained within the direct control of the company but we believed that a change would be necessary in the future.

Transportation was an extremely important part of the service infrastructure and as such management had to remain relentless in getting it all right.

Directing our Human Resources Department was very

complex given that there was such reliance on recruiting the right talent for all departments, putting in place sustainable and relevant training programmes, establishing employees appraisal systems, managing employee welfare and benefits and communication models for all levels of employees, and so on.

The strength of any organization is founded on the versatility, skills levels, competency, commitment, and loyalty of its workforce. This is crucial. Composition of the workforce—Bahamian and foreign and getting the balance consistent with needs of the company is a delicate process.

When George Mackey resigned from the company, the Human Resources Department had to be reorganized. Finding a Bahamian to take this position was not easy. Sheila Glinton was appointed. She brought maturity and the ability to navigate successfully with government agencies, especially Immigration. At another stage, Conrad Knowles was installed and due to his training as a senior police officer and subsequently in other areas of civil service he brought about a strong organizational regimen that served the company well.

Jim and Jack had to, with the consent of the Board of Directors, embark upon a substantial expansion to the development of Resorts International in The Bahamas. There was no question in my mind that the future was to be a remarkable shift in the company's business philosophy. Steve in conversation intimated as much. "Barrie," he said, "the company needs to move on despite the difficulty with government. You need to be thinking about creating depth of management skills within the company to meet changes that will be coming."

This was obviously a statement of challenge.

"Steve, this could be the next step to creating a company to an extent that possibly exceeds what the Bahamian community imagined."

Over the next few days, I thought about how to strengthen the company overall and in particular the areas for which I had direct or shared responsibility.

If we were going to grow the business footprint within and outside of The Bahamas, one of the critical areas requiring considered attention was Human Resources Management and

Development. In discussing this with LeRoy Bailey, I put forward the idea of reconstructing the Human Resources Department and in this regard we needed to have very experienced and very knowledgeable persons to lead.

We went outside of The Bahamas in search of the talent we needed. We were fortunate in attracting a husband-wife team with outstanding credentials to join us under contract.

Clive Adamson and his wife Suzanne, both Canadians, were discovered by a headhunter the company assigned to find suitable candidates for the position. It was made clear as well that the position was not intended to be one that lasted a lifetime.

At this time we engaged Clive and Suzanne, we had recruited a young, intelligent, energetic and ambitious woman to work in Human Resources. This was Karen Thompson (now Karen Carey).

Many good programmes were put into place and we were seeing good results. About two years had passed and Karen was doing very well. Clive and Suzanne had been directed to coach her. Karen was restless and wanted the top post. I did not really feel that she was ready and discussed with Clive and Suzanne how best to get Karen fully qualified for the top job.

Karen was not happy with me about delaying her promotion but agreed that she would attend the University of Detroit for two years in order to get her degree in Human Resources Management and Development.

When she and I met to discuss, this she had fire in her eyes. She was definitely angry with me. However, we arrived at a resolution that would in the end see her ascend to the senior position. All went as planned and Karen became Director of Human Resources and ultimately a Vice President and then Senior Vice President.

The other areas needing oversight, which generally required assistance from Steve, were real estate, the Paradise Island golf course, and sales and development.

Jack and Jim were involved in planning future growth as Jim was very particular about what kind of businesses would be allowed to build and operate on Paradise Island.

Jim was fastidious about protecting the Paradise Island landscape and environment.

The decision was to build additional tennis courts at the Ocean Club. Jim was determined to protect larger trees from removal. He was adamant about this. In constructing the fence at the back of Court #9, there was a Kamalamy tree that was in the way. Lorne Jenkinson and Butch Carey wanted to cut the tree down. Jim would not hear of it. So the fence had to be built around the tree. Thereafter, we called it Crosby's tree.

The company wanted a section of the Island devoted to residential development and carved out approximately seventy acres for this purpose—The Paradise Island Colony.

To better understand the opportunities for developing Paradise Island, Jim and Jack had a parcelization plan prepared by Len Chee-A-Tow which reflected existing usage as well as parcels that could be used for other kinds of projects. The one irritant to Jim with respect to this plan was the 32.8 acres Burrows Tract that been quieted and at that time outside of the control of the company. Notwithstanding the plan visibly gave Jim the scope for creating a master vision for the Island.

There were other considerations for Jim and Jack that contained an historical element and which were going to require extraordinarily cautious navigation through unchartered political and bureaucratic terrain. Following the change of government in 1967, the government turned its attention to Freeport, Grand Bahama, which through special legislation—the Hawksbill Creek Act 1955—carved out some 50,000 acres for light industry and tourism. The principal architect of this concept was Wallace Groves, an American financier from Virginia who had taken up residence in The Bahamas in the mid-1940s. He originally owned a lumber company in Pine Ridge, Grand Bahama.

In the 1950s, Stafford L. Sands sought to establish an economy based upon tourism and financial services. All of the essential elements were in The Bahamas, as described in the early days of marketing—sand, sea and sun.

Bank secrecy laws made The Bahamas a safe haven for private wealth.

Wallace Groves found a willing visionary in Stafford. Thus we saw the creation of Freeport, which included substantial incentives to encourage development of light industry and tourism.

It seems that it didn't take very many years of attempting to create an economy on light industry to realize that growth in this area was slow and painful. Recognizing that tourism seemed to be the more powerful engine for growth, resources and energy were pushed in this direction.

As I became more familiar with the company's operation in and out of The Bahamas, I was somewhat surprised to learn that the company owned Bahamas Developers Ltd., which held real estate in Queen's Cove and King's Cove, which was promoted to prospective investors who wanted residential property in Grand Bahama. Quite frankly, what I could discern was that it was not a very active and successful enterprise.

I also learned that Resorts International, through a subsidiary, was managing El Casino in Freeport for Bahamas Amusements Ltd., the holder of a Certificate of Exemption.

At this time line staff members in the Food and Beverage Department were union category workers and as I was gaining experience in industrial relations matters in Nassau, I was directed to deal with union issues at El Casino. I had no contact with the gaming side of El Casino.

Jim and Jack were expansion-minded and wanted to be the major players in the tourism industry. In the mid 1970s, the company entered into an agreement to build hotel rooms and reopen the Monte Carlo Casino, which had closed a few years previously.

It was interesting to go to Freeport to meet with Luis Reynoso, Manager of Food and Beverage Operations, and David Hadland, Administration Director. The hotel union was constantly agitating and the company's effort to keep the staff motivated to do their jobs was not particularly easy.

It was in 1977 and I had just completed negotiations with the BHCAWU in Nassau for a new industrial agreement to cover line staff in the member properties of the BHEA, only to be told that I had to fly at once to Freeport as there was trouble brewing between the Freeport branch of the BHCAWU and the Freeport Hotel Employers' Association, which included El Casino.

Tom Bastian, the Vice President of the BHCAWU, was aggressively leading the negotiations with the employers in

Freeport. Emanuel Osadebay, a lawyer, was representing the employers in the negotiations. Once the status of the negotiations had been presented, I told attending members that it was not a good deal because we had just completed negotiations in Nassau with better terms and conditions. Michael Reckley was with me and recognized that we were, in all likelihood, heading for a showdown with the Union.

When employers re-started negotiations by taking certain items off the table that had been tentatively agreed by the Association, the union leadership became very agitated and contrary.

We had no choice, because to do otherwise would not have been in the best interests of the industry in Freeport.

The union walked out of the meeting and immediately began solidifying their plans for industrial action. We were not surprised when virtually all line staff left their stations without notice.

As anticipated, we ended up at the Ministry of Labour with Mr. Charles Turnquest, Deputy Director, chairing the meeting.

Unsurprisingly the atmosphere was unfriendly and conversation was most contentious. Unfortunately, there was no progress towards reaching a settlement. At about midnight the chairman declared a short suspension of the meeting.

It was in this setting that I first encountered the Hon. Hubert Ingraham, a minister in the Pindling government. As it turned out Mr. Ingraham and I, while on the outside, decided to have a cigarette, which I did with reluctance. We engaged in a conversation that covered a variety of subjects. What I remember most is that we laughed a lot. Thus, began a friendship that has endured more than four decades.

Mr. Ingraham was representing the owners of the Holiday Inn. The year was 1977 and Freeport was striving to regain tourism market share and generally speaking, the residents were optimistic about their future.

In this environment, Jim Crosby obviously felt that it was an opportunity to grow Resorts International through increased investments in Freeport but this was not to be.

Resorts entered into an agreement with the government and the Grand Bahama Port Authority to build a 240-room hotel at Lucaya and to re-open the Monte Carlo Casino. I recall Steve preparing a business model for operating two casinos. He sought to have casino tax relief on the basis that both casinos could be treated as one entity. The other important request was for the government to allow casino management to rotate personnel between both casinos on an as-needed basis. He felt strongly that having this flexibility would produce maximum efficiency and could result in containment of staffing and related costs.

It is hard to determine the source of the resistance to their concept but Steve did not receive acceptance from the Gaming Board.

While contending with Freeport opportunity and the continued development of Paradise Island, there loomed on the business horizon an event that would change the economic landscape of a depressed tourism, but in this case it was happening in New Jersey. The voters of Atlantic City were going to the polls to vote on a referendum to introduce legal gambling. There was no certainty as to the outcome but there appeared to be a prevailing mood amongst the New Jersey voters to support the introduction of large-scale gambling.

Jim and Jack decided to make the biggest gamble imaginable. Resorts bought the largest hotel in Atlantic City, Chalfonte Haddon Hall, which although not in good shape could be upgraded to accommodate a new casino. At the same time, adjacent parcels of land were purchased as well as prime land not too far from the hotel. So on this day, 2 November 1976, the voters addressed the referendum and made a huge leap into the future by voting "yes" resoundingly. For Resorts International, it represented a giant step forward in making Resorts International a major player in the world of gaming.

The euphoria experienced by Jim and Jack overflowed into serious thoughts of increasing the investment and scope of expansion in Freeport.

What emerged was a plan to buy the Holiday Inn and upgrade to a standard that would be attractive to a high-income clientele that could better support the casino. Further, the thought was to commit the new hotel to the Lucaya and the Monte Carlo casinos. However, separating the two locations was the Atlantic Beach Hotel, which was not for sale.

To facilitate easy access to Lucaya, the idea to build a boardwalk along the ocean was born.

Agreements were in place for the purchase of Holiday Inn in Freeport and in fact Resorts International made an announcement to the press about this purchase. And this is when things went wrong. Government refused to give its approval for this transaction and despite our best efforts to reverse this position, the government was intractable.

The disappointment of Jim and Jack was one of complete and devastating surprise. They saw this rejeçtion as a reversal of fortune and it meant that to remain in Freeport was untenable.

A new round of negotiations commenced with government with the intent being for Resorts International to find a way to get to an amicable position that would allow Resorts to withdraw from its obligation to increase its investment in Freeport.

The negotiations covered a couple of years but Resorts paid a penalty of $2,500,000.00 to get to the end. With effect 1 January 1982, Resorts International was disconnected from Freeport, Grand Bahama, except for its real estate development at Queen's Cove and King's Cove, which was inactive.

While negotiations with the Bahamian government were proceeding, Resorts was in the midst of creating the first legitimate casino in the USA outside of Las Vegas. On the 26 May 1978, Resorts International Casino/Hotel opened its doors for business with unbridled excitement.

Jim Crosby was determined not to let the Freeport fiasco stand in his way to expand the boundaries of Resorts International. Jim also had recognized some years previously that he needed an insider with the Bahamian government who could help with advancing the expansion plans for Resorts International. In the late 1970s, Jim had developed a business relationship with Everette Bannister, who was close to the Prime Minister. In due course Mr. Bannister was engaged as a consultant for Resorts International and in many ways made life with the government much less adversarial.

Jim and Jack were now riding a new wave of optimism for making Resorts International into a major player in tourism and casino gambling in the United States and The Bahamas.

Much attention was being directed at Atlantic City by Resorts International as it was reasonable to predict that in due course casino operators from Las Vegas would be attempting to get a foothold there as well.

These were heady days for Jim and his family because they were the majority shareholders of Resorts International and thus their wealth grew accordingly.

I often wondered how Jim connected with Huntington Hartford and what were the common interests that made it mutually beneficial for a business arrangement to be crafted. After all, Hartford owned Paradise Island whereas Jim and Jack were land developers in Freeport, Grand Bahama. Obviously from Huntington Hartford's perspective, given that his substantial inheritance was decreasing he needed to find a way to remain relevant in the development of Paradise Island.

What I did piece together was that the Mary Carter Paint Company was purchased by Jim's father along with other investors. This happened in 1958. Jim was made chairman. He had his sights on other opportunities. In 1968, the paint division was disposed of and the name of the company changed to Resorts International. It was a public company traded on the American Stock Exchange.

When I joined the company in late 1971, I was aware that Resorts International was listed on Wall Street. For as long as I could remember I was not one to take risks that required putting up money. This was especially true because I did not have any excess cash. However, I felt that I needed to show support for the company through the ownership of shares. So I purchased 500 shares of Resorts International at $1 5/8 per share. I had no idea where this might lead as Resorts International languished on the American Stock Exchange and was not likely to be a winner. At least so it seemed in those early days.

Once Resorts started its casino operations in Atlantic City, the interest in the company within the stock market exceeded what Jim could have ever expected. I did not know what to do about getting more shares. Frankly I was scared because I was venturing into uncharted territory—there was simply too much risk but at the same time I needed to be courageous. The reality was that I had a family to support and my annual salary when I started on Paradise Island, $20,000.00, was less than what I had been earning at the Montague Beach Hotel.

Fortunately, I was working directly with Jim and managing the Paradise Island Bridge. I obviously had opportunities to speak with him about Resorts International and the prospects of the share value of Resorts improving and to what level.

When I broached the subject with Jim, he answered with a smile and said, "Barrie there is no way of telling how a stock will perform within the market because there are just too many variables. For instance, you cannot measure the psychological impact upon a potential investor in Resorts. However, I wouldn't be surprised if the stock reached $60 per share." At that time the stock would have been moving between $25 and $30 per share.

I didn't know how to react. Even if I wanted to jump in I did not have the resources. "Jim, thank you," I said, adding feebly, "these are exciting times."

As it turned out, investors on Wall Street anticipated a huge financial windfall through Resorts International's premier position in developing casino gambling on the east coast of the U.S.A.

Believe it or not, the stock rose to $207 per share even though earnings did not support this price. While this was rapidly unfolding in New Jersey, there were happenings in The Bahamas.

The situation in Freeport had moved to a disappointing end but there were development projects being planned for Paradise Island. The 250-room Britannia, which opened in January 1969, was functioning at full capacity. In fact during the winter season there was a huge surge in occupancy and room rates, especially on weekends.

Paradise Island, from the initial entry of Jim and Jack with their alliance with Huntington Hartford, was viewed as an area for touristic development. In 1971, the 533-room Holiday Inn was constructed and 250-room Flagler Inn came on stream in the early 1970s. The future for Paradise Island did indeed appear to be very promising. However The Bahamas government, suddenly in 1973, announced that in 1978 all casinos would be owned and controlled by government. Indeed a shock to the company.

The Board of Directors under the guidance of Jim and Jack

who were influenced by the financial projections prepared by Steve, decided that the company needed to commit to building additional rooms. The stars in the universe were aligned.

The vision for Paradise Island assumed proportions beyond the ordinary. First and foremost was the decision to add a 350-room tower to the Britannia Beach Hotel with additional dining. After all necessary clearances were obtained from government and required financing in place, construction proceeded in 1980 and the hotel opened in June 1982.

While this was in progress, the lease with the Loews Corporation for the 500-room Paradise Island Hotel and Villas had come to an end through mutual consent on 1 January 1982.

The tourism landscape on Paradise Island was evolving. The Grand Hotel comprising 360 rooms was being constructed on the north shore adjacent to the Paradise Island Hotel and Villas. This new hotel opened in June 1982 within weeks of the opening of the 350-room expansion of the Coral Towers/Britannia Beach Hotel.

During the intervening years, my role within the company was evolving. With the company's holdings expanding fairly rapidly, more time was devoted to administrative matters such as liaising with government on a variety of matters for which government approvals were required, wrestling with Hotels Encouragement Act Agreements, and focusing on insurance and risk management, the golf course, security, transportation, real estate, and human resources—with substantial emphasis on industrial relations.

The company had expanded greatly and management of the operations was becoming increasingly complex. The days of the early 1970s were behind us.

Government's decision to own casinos caused grave concern within the company. There was so much to attend to in order to get to a reasonably comfortable place. I assisted Ray Gore, Senior Vice President/Finance, of our parent Resort International Inc. along with Steve in negotiating a ten-year management contract of the casino with government and subsequently making sure there was a smooth transition.

Thinking back to that situation, we were baffled as to the reason government felt it important to own this casino. Our lawyers examined every aspect of the relationship to attempt to find legal cause to prevent such a takeover. The bottom line was that the government was new and inexperienced and driven by an overpowering nationalistic will to diminish the reliance upon non-Bahamian businesses. Fortunately, as the government matured a more realistic approach to business governance emerged.

Ray Gore throughout the negotiating process remained focused and surprisingly calm in the face of this huge problem.

I do not recall exactly the occasion but in talking with Ray and Steve about getting to the end game, which on occasion was exceedingly frustrating, I asked Ray, "Do you feel like the company has been wronged by the government?"

Ray removed his glasses, wiped the lens carefully and then said, "Barrie, what I think is immaterial. Our purpose is to get the best deal we can for the company and to do it with the minimum of acrimony." And that was the voice of wisdom, experience and knowledge speaking.

I was not at liberty to discuss in detail with Jo about was what transpiring but because she was the executive secretary to Jack she was sufficiently familiar with what was happening to allow some discourse.

I was frustrated and thought this government dead wrong with its current approach. Jo would say, "Barrie, calm down, you will get to the end one day."

Amen.

Barrie with Merv Griffin at conclusion of a star-studded weekend at Paradise Island

CHAPTER 37

MERV GRIFFIN

The early years of the 1980s were ones in which the company under Jim Crosby's leadership seemed destined to grow at an accelerated and successful pace. Jim and Jack exuded enormous confidence that was contagious. Resorts International in Atlantic City was producing bottom-line results, which were well received by Wall Street.

Jim wanted to have the largest casino in the world and with the backing of the Board of Directors planned the construction of a 1500-room hotel with a 100,000-square-foot casino. In order to construct such a hotel/casino, which he named the Taj Mahal, Resorts International had to borrow substantial sums of money. The word within the company was that the cost of the borrowings was very high, but the future looked bright.

Jim, at the same time, saw the need to expand the casino on Paradise Island. He wanted to increase the gaming space by 50 percent from 20,000 square feet to 30,000 square feet. To accomplish this, he needed to obtain the agreement of The Bahamas government. Negotiations moved ahead fairly quickly, which was somewhat surprising. The essence of the agreement was that in exchange for the right to expand the casino the company would build or cause to be built 250 hotel rooms within five years of the date of agreement. The expansion of the casino took place as agreed and added substantially to the operating results of the casino.

With the financial resources of Resorts being under pressure, the decision was taken to build 100 rooms of the 250 committed and within a five-year window, to build the remaining 150 rooms subsequently. And then there was a confluence of events that shook the company to the core. Jim was not a well man but seemed to function pretty well. He smoked quite a lot and drank some alcohol but not excessively. He developed emphysema, which affected his lungs and breathing. His condition was getting worse. He consulted the best physicians in New York. As I recall, the story there was a newly developed procedure that enabled doctors to remove the accumulation of tar and other residue from the lungs, the result of which would be a significant improvement in quality of life. Unfortunately, Jim did not survive the operation and died on 12 April 1986. It was a very sad day for all of us. The funeral was in New Jersey and many of us attended.

Knowing the history I could not help but pose the question: *Had Jim lived and continued with his visionary leadership, where would we be today?*

Henry Murphy, Jim's brother-in-law, was elected Chairman of the Board. The Crosby family comprised the principal shareholders of Resorts International and obviously moved in this direction until the future could be discussed and decided upon.

The vacuum within Resorts International created significant interest of potential investors, the most notable of which was Donald Trump. He was in due course successful in acquiring Resorts International. He made it clear early on that he wished to carry on the work of Jim.

Donald Trump travelled to Paradise Island with his entourage of advisors and friends. Bob Peloquin of Intertel and George Myers were instrumental in introducing Mr. Trump to the Prime Minister and key Cabinet Ministers. He assured the Bahamian government in writing to continue with the development plans of Resorts International for Paradise Island.

Being privy to the contents of the letter, we were hopeful that a new beginning was about to be made. This was not to be. Within twelve months, negotiations had commenced between Merv Griffin and Donald Trump for sale of Resorts International to Mr. Griffin.

As a part of the deal, Mr. Trump got the Taj Mahal. We speculated that from the outset the Taj Mahal was the prize he wanted.

The deal was struck and moved to conclusion in October 1988 about twelve months after Mr. Trump had acquired Resorts International.

I can remember the Bahamian contingent comprising George Myers, Keith Duncombe, Giselle Pyfrom and me going to New York for the closing. George was President of our various companies and I was Assistant Secretary and Director of the Bahamian group of companies. The transaction was of a size that many documents had to be executed. Our contingent was very small but one day during the hurrying and scurrying back and forth we counted about seventy lawyers and paralegals in attendance. We were stunned by the number.

Merv Griffin was welcomed to Paradise Island with great excitement. He made it clear that he was sincerely enthusiastic about continuing the development of the Island and making a difference in tourism. By reputation, he was a highly successful businessman and entertainer renowned for his shows *Jeopardy!* and *Wheel of Fortune*.

Mr. Griffin loved playing tennis and with my son John as Director of Tennis at the Ocean Club, he spent much time on court. In fact, he carried John to Monte Carlo to play in a pro-am tennis event. He had very high regard for John, so much so he contemplated making John general manager of the Ocean Club.

The President of Resorts International Inc. was Dave Hanlon, a big man with broad shoulders and penetrating eyes. I recall the first time Merv introduced Dave to senior management at the Ocean Club. Before completing a greeting, Dave said to Mr. Myers, "George, I would like to go and see the kitchen." Even though startled, George promptly complied. And, thus Dave wanted to establish an image of not tolerating any nonsense on his watch.

Christopher Whitney, Legal Counsel, joined the company.

He was always engaging but at the same time not lacking in competence and requiring adherence to company legal requirements and regulatory needs. He was highly influential in maintaining structural order in the company.

When Merv took over Paradise Island, air service between the Island and Florida was being provided by Chalk's Airline with a fleet of fourteen-seat mallards and several Albatross seaplanes. Crosby had purchased Chalk's from Arthur "Pappy" Chalk many years before. For some reason I was fascinated with the sea planes and saw the novelty and commercial aspects of operating the services between Florida and Paradise Island. Merv decided that better service was needed and so he created an airport on the southeast portion of the Island and named it the Paradise Island Airport. The company operated a small fleet of fifty-seat Dash 7 planes. One purpose was to create more airlifts for casino junkets. Thank goodness Ambassador Carol Hallett was able to obtain Washington's approval to make Paradise Island Airport a U.S. pre-clearance terminal—a most welcome outcome for residents of Paradise Island and for those persons living in east New Providence.

Merv wanted Paradise Island to be special and at the same time he desired to grow Resorts' Atlantic City operations, a most difficult task. He always included senior management, particularly George Myers, Michael Williams, Senior Vice President of Operations and me in his social gatherings at his home, previously the home of Jim Crosby.

One evening, we were there for cocktails with his great friend, President Ronald Reagan, and his wife, Nancy. The "great communicator" was in fine form and most congenial. Merv's special friend Eva Gabor of Hollywood fame was always with him.

In December of each year, Merv would invite many of his friends of stage and screen to Paradise Island for a long weekend of pure pleasure, which included golf and tennis competitions. I was responsible for managing the tennis. For me, getting through the day with six tennis courts and eighty participants with everyone having to play in a round robin in the morning and then final competition in the afternoon was not an easy feat. Thankfully, I had the help of Vicky Knowles, Mickey Williams and others.

The one rule that I had to observe and for which I had no specific instruction was that Merv had to win. John, my son, was his partner, which made it fairly easy but not assured. Merv made those weekends wonderful for everyone attending. He was truly outstanding.

The early 1990s turned out to be very hard for the company. The world economy was stagnant and the performance financially of Atlantic City and Paradise Island was mediocre and moving towards being weak. Meeting the company's debt obligations became increasingly difficult. On two occasions the company had to file for court protection under Chapter 11 of the Bankruptcy Law so that it could develop a plan to avoid bankruptcy. There was a period on Paradise Island when the saying of the day among staff was "tings tuff."

It was so demoralizing for all to see room occupancies decline and average room rates heading down hill. To top it off, Mr. Myers resigned as President and COO. For a while there was an office of the President comprising Michael Williams, Vincent Vanderpool-Wallace, Denis O'Brien and Pat McCoy, CFO. Subsequently, Mr. Williams and I occupied the office of the President. Vincent moved to be Director General of Tourism, a very good move for our industry.

And the day came when Merv Griffin threw in the towel because there did not seem to be a way out.

Human nature being what it is particularly when adversity, in the form of defeat, rears its ugly head, we anticipated Merv Griffin's reacting with uncontrolled anger but he accepted the loss with surprising calmness.

Michael Williams and I went to see him at the house to say our goodbyes. We presented him with a very special painting that had been done by Susan Jane Sargent, who was to become my bride. The words of appreciation to Merv seemed hollow but were certainly heartfelt and in response he warmly thanked us for the painting, which he said he would treasure.

I really liked Merv and was very sorry to witness the end of his dream. I don't know how true it is but our company insiders claimed that Merv lost $100 million of his own money in the Resorts International investment.

Executive team of Griffin Resorts International participating in menu testing in the kitchen of Britannia Beach Hotel, 1989

From J. Barrie's left: Vincent Vanderpool Wallace, Gabriel Sastre, Michael Williams, Karen Carey, Dave Hanlon, Michelle Perna, Chris Whitney, Chef Helmut Schmidt, Don Cooke, Brian Webb, Warren Binder and me

J.Barrie, President Reagan, John Farrington, Josephine Farrington Enjoying an evening with Merv Griffin at his home near the Ocean Club. Nancy Reagan was also attending.

*Barrie being most attentive to Henry Kissinger,
Secretary of State of the United States, 1985*

CHAPTER 38

HENRY KISSINGER

In the 1980s while tourism in the Caribbean was expanding generally, The Bahamas was still considered by North American travellers to be the most desirable destination for an island vacation in the sun.

The Caribbean Hotel Association held its annual conference in The Bahamas in January 1985 at the Paradise Island Resort and Casino and industry leaders of the Caribbean and the U.S.A. were attending. The highlight of the opening ceremonies in the Le Cabaret Theatre was an address to be given by Henry Kissinger, former Secretary of State in the cabinet of Richard Nixon.

Having watched him on television espousing the foreign policy of the U.S. and the importance of commencing a relationship with China, which under previous administrations had been avoided, his depth of knowledge and political foresight was inspiring.

I managed to get George Myers to have me invited to the breakfast being held in the Villa D' Este with Mr. Kissinger. This was exciting.

Before sitting down for breakfast, we were standing casually chatting about various world affairs. The conversation turned to India and the economic struggles of its huge population base. Mr. Kissinger had not too long previously published his book about his historical time as Secretary of State, *The White House Years*. I had purchased the book and had briefly looked at some of his comments about India. I don't know what prompted me to mention his book and his reference to India. I suppose he was surprised that I knew of his book. He immediately grabbed my arm and peered at my name tag with the question, "What is your name again?"

In concluding his address to the attending members of the Caribbean Hotel Association on 10 June 1985 in the Le Cabaret Theatre, Paradise Island Casino, he stated:

> "One, we have the possibility of improving our relations on the questions of war and peace with the Soviet Union, but beyond this, we must put before our peoples and the peoples of this hemisphere a vision of a positive future and the hopeful note on which I want to leave you with, is that both of these objectives are within our own capabilities to achieve, and there is no other nation in the world that can make this statement."

And as we look at the global situation today, his concluding assertion is as valid today as it was when he he made this declaration. Of course there remains the unanswerable question of how long will that declaration remain authentic.

His address to the conference was, in my opinion, outstanding. It was fascinating to experience the candor with which Henry Kissinger described how foreign policy of the United States was formulated. He said, "The first thing to remember about United States foreign policy is that when one travels abroad, people usually think it is a homogeneous, long-range, carefully thought-out body of strategic doctrines. The fact of the matter is that until 1945, the United States did not have to conduct any serious foreign policy the way Great Britain had to for hundreds of years. The United States was really isolated from world affairs, by two great oceans, by the protection of the British Navy, by its own preoccupation with expansion across a continent."

Mr. Kissinger also took the opportunity to comment on the aging, complicated, and secretive political structure of Russia. In fact as pointed out, "You also have to remember that of all of the leaders of the Soviet Union, nobody has ever retired voluntarily. All have died in office except one, Kruschev, who made the mistake of going on vacation without taking his colleagues with him." With humor, he added this footnote to history: Leaders should never take a holiday while the Cabinet is still functioning.

Mr. Kissinger further pointed out that the average age of the Politburo was seventy-five and there was never a prospect of rejuvenation. And "the second problem is that of the economy. Imagine running an economy in which the cost of nothing is known, in which every article in commerce moves on the basis of governmental allocation and which all prices are fixed by remote authorities in Moscow. Inefficiency, corruption are endemic and productivity has to be low." To illustrate the extent of the rot, Mr. Kissinger recounted the story that appeared in Pravda, the principal news organ in Russia: "A train with twenty-three cars left in 1983 a station in Central Russia headed for Moscow and never arrived there, and they have not been able to find that, to this day."

Mr. Kissinger was and still is a scholar who made a lasting impression on the world.

A glorious and memorable engagement with Nelson Mandela, 1993

CHAPTER 39

NELSON MANDELA

It was Boxing Day 1993—26th December, and for some reason Susan and I decided to attend Junkanoo. The year before when we attended, the crowd was so dense, and in certain cases unruly, that we agreed that thereafter we would watch the parade on television.

While walking past the spectator stands, mainly occupied by special ticket holders, and located in front of the Queen Victoria statue, we looked up into the seats and saw Prime Minister Ingraham with Mr. Nelson Mandela. The Prime Minister acknowledged our wave and we moved on.

At about 11:00 a.m., the telephone at our home rang and it was Mr. Ingraham. He said Mr. Mandela was in Nassau on vacation and was residing at Lyford Cay. He went on to say that Mr. Mandela wanted something to do as he was bored.

"J. Barrie, I want you to host Mr. Mandela at lunch tomorrow at the Britannia Beach hotel. The group for lunch will include Cabinet Ministers with Mr. Mandela." It was unbelievable that Mr. Mandela, a man who had captured the hearts and minds of people around the world in successfully fighting against apartheid in South Africa, was going to be a guest of honour at our luncheon.

At this time Michael Williams and I shared the office of the President of Resorts International Bahamas and we had only a short while to organize lunch in the Presidential Suite.

On 26 December, 1993, Nelson Mandela with Prime Minister Ingraham and Cabinet Ministers arrived at about 12 noon. The word had spread throughout the resort and so the lobby was filled with tourists and staff.

As Mr. Mandela stepped into the lobby, the spontaneous applause and cheering was enthusiastic, which to me was a clear indication of his life and struggle against apartheid, which was legendary throughout the world. He shook hands with virtually everyone in the lobby including the children. Later on when he and I were on a tour of the resort and there were so many persons pressing around him, I asked him if he minded. He replied, "I am very thankful to all these and other people who gave us their support while we fought for equality in my country. I cannot ever thank them enough. I will shake every hand in appreciation."

For me, his actions were a testament to the spiritual strength of his leadership.

We finally made our way into the elevators and to the special dining area on the eighth floor. With the anticipated change in ownership of Paradise Island, fairly substantial construction work was in progress but this had no effect upon this great occasion.

I had the good fortune of sitting immediately to Mr. Mandela's right. He spoke at length about the transition from apartheid to a majority democracy. He acknowledged that Mr. F. W. de Klerk, his soon to be predecessor, was wise enough to recognize that change was essential and right to do if the country was to survive socially, politically and economically. He also admitted that he had little choice but to tell his followers that "the changes in our society will not happen overnight and that they as a people will have a much better life in due course." He added, "I understand the expectation arising from the change in government but the people will have to exercise patience."

Sitting there with him it was hard to appreciate the depth of struggle he and his fellow countrymen had to endure and the complication of making a transition to a new order.

What struck me most forcefully sitting there listening to him was the total lack of any animosity toward the white leadership. Instead there was a kind of holiness in his demeanour, which was to be his strength in going forward into the future.

In the December 1993 issue of Time, Mr. Mandela and Mr. de Klerk were in the same photograph as being recipients of the Nobel Peace Prize. He spoke with gentleness about this honour. He did not venture into what was still a sensitive area of his relationship with Mr. de Klerk but I got the impression that getting to the end was not particularly easy.

It had to be remembered that at the time of our luncheon, Mr. Mandela was President-designate of South Africa. He would not take office until 10 May 1994.

When our lunch was over, the Prime Minister wanted Michael Williams and me to give Mr. Mandela sight of the concept being developed to turn Paradise Island into a most exciting, family-oriented resort.

We took Mr. Mandela to our Corporate Boardroom where we had a model of the attraction that would have a pirate theme, the name of which would be "Skull Mountain." We also had artist renderings of all support facilities to the main theme. Mr. Mandela was impressed and interested in what was to be done under the Sol Kerzner banner.

I later found out from Prime Minister Ingraham that Sol Kerzner had approached Sir Lynden Pindling about acquiring Paradise Island years before. However, with apartheid still in place in South Africa and Sol Kerzner being South African, there was absolutely no possibility of approving such an investment.

When Nelson Mandela through negotiations with Mr. de Klerk resulted in the elimination of apartheid, the acceptability of a South African investor in The Bahamas was virtually a foregone conclusion.

With apartheid dismantled, Sol Kerzer's interest in Paradise Island was reawakened. Mr. Kerzner and Mr. Mandela were friends and on this basis, Mr. Mandela, when asked about Sol

Kerzner as an investor, endorsed Mr. Kerzner unhesitatingly. In fact, he told Prime Minister Ingraham that Sol Kerzner would be a good partner for The Bahamas.

While we were talking with Mr. Mandela, he made no mention of Sol Kerzner.

Michael had meetings to attend so it was left for me to give Mr. Mandela a tour of the Island. Making our way through the waiting tourists in the lobby was slow.

I will always remember Mr. Mandela saying to me as we entered the limousine to begin our tour, "I owe these people so much. They provided spiritual and vocal support to the ANC's movement for equality." There was only warmth in this statement. The ANC was the African National Congress led by Nelson Mandela.

Mr. Mandela was like the Pied Piper of Hamlin. Everybody wanted to touch him. We went to Paradise Beach, the Paradise Island Airport, the Golf Course, Ocean Club and our final stop was the Casino. He had never been inside of a casino, which was quite understandable given circumstances of his life. He was fascinated with the slot machines.

We made our way back to the entrance where his limousine was awaiting him. We said our goodbyes. I was so elated at being afforded the chance of spending time with such a great man.

There is a Native American proverb which is so applicable to him: "We will be known forever by the tracks we leave."

CHAPTER 40

NATIONAL INSURANCE BOARD AND THE B.E.C.

Following the Free National Movement's victory in 1992, I was appointed to the National Insurance Board and was pleased to serve. I was not totally at ease as to how the National Insurance Board functioned but was committed to learning as fast as I could so that in due course I could contribute positively to its continued development. Rowena Bethel, in-house legal counsel, was especially forthcoming and helpful. The Chairman of the Board was James M. Pinder, who was in the life insurance business and also was a Member of Parliament.

The Board was faced with finding suitable investments in the local market that, based upon actuarial needs, would produce gains in assets which could satisfy the claims present and future made against the Fund.

The National Insurance Board by foreign exchange constraints was limiting its investment prospects to the local market. At one board meeting, I said to the Chairman and members that we must be willing to look beyond the investment criteria currently used.

The Chairman and Ms. Bethel almost simultaneously said, "What are you thinking exactly?"

I responded, "As we are confronted with certain exchange control consideration, we definitely need to be investing in the U.S. Markets to give us a better return on NIB's money."

"How do you propose doing this?" the Chairman asked.

I replied that it would not be without difficulty but given that we were then managing almost $700 million, we could strive to convert some Bahamian dollars to U.S. dollars and make investments abroad. It was definitely unlikely that we could have had a balanced Bahamian/U.S. investment portfolio but it looked like a promising way of strengthening our investment portfolio.

They thought that the idea had merit and should be examined further. Nothing happened mainly because the sums were too vast and any attempt to convert substantial sums of Bahamian currency into U.S. dollars would have had an adverse impact upon our U.S. dollar reserves.

And then about twenty months later, the unexpected happened. My phone at home rang one evening and it was Prime Minister Ingraham. After we exchanged pleasantries he said, "I have a job for you. I want you to be Chairman of one of our government corporations and I will let you select the one that you will feel most comfortable with."

Without appearing to be unappreciative of the offer, I retorted, "Prime Minister, I am honoured that you made the proposition but I should like to think about it overnight."

He replied in the affirmative and rang off.

Since Jo and I had divorced in 1992, the answer would have to be decided otherwise. I called my brother Earle and after telling him the story posed the question, "Do you think this is something I should accept and if so which public corporation?"

Earle was such a rock of logic and common sense that how he responded was to be expected.

"Barrie, you have a good business mind and are very energetic. It would be a pity not to have you working for the country in this way."

"I suppose you are right. I want to serve but would like to be a part of an organization that is managed best," I added.

Earle's comeback: "From what I understand, Peter Bethel, who is General Manager at the Bahamas Electricity Corporation, ran the tightest and most efficient ship."

My mind was made up but I also wanted to speak with Susan, who was now very much in my life.

Without hesitation when I spoke about the appointment, her eyes lit up with excitement.

"I think this is great. Go for it!" she said.

The next morning I rang the Prime Minister at his home. I knew that he was an early riser and was always engaged in the governance of the country.

He answered the phone.

He laughed when I said that I was willing to accept the post of Chairman of the Bahamas Electricity Corporation.

He said, "Fine. The letter of appointment will be issued right away." He added, "I will transfer Albert Miller to Batelco." I had not realized that a change was necessary but it was not for me to discuss this situation.

I knew that Vincent D'Aguilar was to be Deputy Chairman and that was a huge addition, as Vincent had at one time worked at the Bahamas Electricity Corporation (BEC) as a senior electrical engineer and therefore knew the technical side comprehensively.

Prior to starting officially, we met a couple of times so as to establish the right chemistry. My talks with Peter Bethel were at a very high and mutually respectful level. He was the ultimate professional and leader. His reputation within BEC was legendary for that matter within the country.

The Minister responsible for BEC was the Deputy Prime Minister, Frank Watson who had the complete support of the Prime Minister and as such, I would discover as the months passed, he had wide power in governing BEC.

For days prior to my first Board Meeting, my mind was in turmoil because I knew that I was about to step into an arena that was completely alien to me. BEC in the near past was unable to sustain a consistent supply of power, especially during the summer months. Albert Miller assured me that in his opinion, he had the right personnel but lamented the inadequacy of reliable and consistent electricity generation.

Several nights before our first official Board Meeting, I recall reading the words of a writer, Jamie Prolenette who said, "Limitations live only in one's mind. But, if we use our imaginations our possibilities become limitless."

This was a job I could not do alone and would need the helping hand of the Board Members and BEC personnel at all levels.

The first Board Meeting was successful with the help of Albert Miller, who was going to Batelco and the presence of the Deputy Prime Minister. With Vincent D'Aguilar at my right hand I was comforted and with committed support of Peter Bethel there was a sense of optimism.

Vincent and I agreed to divide responsibilities so as to use our time effectively. His portfolio would cover operational matters and administrative matters would be with me.

After the first Board Meeting, Vincent looked at me and with a smile said somewhat cynically, "Now the fun really begins." My rejoinder was, "I only hope that our fun doesn't end up in tears."

Shelly Cooke-Seymour was Secretary to the Board and Legal Counsel. Shelly proved to be very helpful and made sure the Board functioned effectively. Throughout my eight years as Chairman, she strove to make my office administratively complete with the legal requirements of the office as well as overall legal representation of BEC. And then right at the end of my time in office she acted in a way that surprised me immensely. She allowed her political attachment to do something that in effect was like a stab in the back.

Sharon Brown and Wendy Warren formed the core of our Audit and Finance Committee. They were never hesitant about taking on tasks that many times were time-consuming.

For me, it was always comforting to have Rodney Braynen, Philip Beneby, William McDonald, Vantlock Fowler, Yvonne Isaacs, and Brian Moree sitting at the Board table dealing with a multitude of complex issues of the company.

Peter Bethel gave unerring leadership to a very talented executive management team that included Edward McKenzie, Anthony Forbes, Everette Sweeting, Darville Walkine, Kevin Basden, Edgar Moxey, George Knowles, Patrick Hanna, Brian Albury, Bradley Roberts and Freeman Duncanson.

There were a number of serious situations that were facing us with great urgency. The generation capacity of BEC was lacking both in New Providence and the Family Islands. Residents of New Providence experienced electricity outages during the summer. And there were settlements in the Family Islands that never had electricity. Generally, the growth in capacity did not keep pace with demand.

It was suggested by Peter Bethel and his team that we look at every possibility of expanding our capacity while minimizing the capital cost to BEC.

One idea was to contract with an Independent Power Producer (IPP) who would invest in the installation of generation and BEC would buy electricity for twenty-five years, which would enable an investor to recover invested capital and with a profit. Such an arrangement would be covered by an airtight agreement.

Jamaica had instituted such an arrangement and it seemed to be working acceptably. Vincent and I discussed this with BEC senior management who were receptive to the idea. A team from BEC went to Kingston, to examine their system and report back. Subsequently Vincent and I discussed the possibility of a visit of our own.

"Barrie, it is essential that we find a way to remedy our problem in Nassau. Jamaica has installed additional capacity through an IPP and we should have a look," Vincent said to me.

"Vincent, I think it is worth a look to see particularly since the numbers appear to work. I will speak with the Deputy Prime Minister about going to Kingston."

During these initial exchanges, we sought and received the advice of Peter Bethel. His knowledge of such matters was extensive and therefore of great value to our deliberations.

When I spoke to the Deputy Prime Minister, he was enthusiastic as he understood the dilemma at BEC.

His office made the necessary arrangements for us to travel to Kingston, Jamaica, for meetings with our counterparts. Our delegation comprised Frank Watson, Vincent D'Aguilar, Peter Bethel and me. The purpose of the visit was to meet with officials of government, Jamaica Public Service Company and an independent power producer to discuss Jamaica's experience with an IPP and the government's privatization programme.

We met with a number of officials including the Minister with responsibility for Mining and Utilities, the Hon. Robert Pickersgill.

There was one outcome of the Jamaican experience that surprised me. While the IPP performed satisfactorily, there was a "high price to pay." The impression gained was that the price structure was based on a charge for availability and a rate for energy supplied. It seemed a little lopsided but choices for enhancing electricity supply in Jamaica were limited.

On commenting on BEC's position, we said to the Deputy Prime Minster, "In our opinion BEC should install the plant on its own if the funds are available."

While in Jamaica, George Myers' sister-in-law Lorna met us and took us to dinner at the Blue Mountain Inn in the mountains, which was delightful. I do recall, however, that while driving to the restaurant along the narrow mountainside road we came ever so close to colliding with a car going in the opposite direction. In fact the side mirrors of the cars banged each other just enough to cause the one on our car to close involuntarily. This little incident was a reminder that life is very fragile with difference between living and dying being ever so small.

We were disappointed that in Jamaica we could not discover a workable solution to our generating deficiencies in Nassau.

In looking at our ten-year history at BEC, it was evident that the growth pattern was an indication of the overall improvement to the economy and the quality of life of our citizenry. For instance, in 1985, installed capacity was 161.3 MW and in 1994 it was 265. MW with the number of consumers growing from 43,000 to 63,000—about fifty percent increase in a relatively short period of time.

Despite the improvements generally in the capacity of BEC, there were still areas within The Bahamas that had never benefited from a constant source of generated electricity. Given the situation and acknowledging that our generating capability was seriously lacking, our mandate set by the Prime Minister and Cabinet was that all populated areas were to be provided with electricity by early 1998. In addition, we were faced with installing another 30MW of generating capacity in the same time frame, which represented a very considerable undertaking.

Recognizing the urgency of moving BEC to a much higher level of operating efficiency, the Board collectively committed to working to that objective and we were delighted that management joined us in the commitment.

Peter Bethel and his executive team proved to be absolutely supportive of the process and as new strategies were developed and unfolded their total involvement was very much in evidence.

Government was determined to make BEC financially responsible and in this regard imposed more rigid financial responsibilities. For instance in 1994/1995, duty-free exemption on fuel oil for electricity generation was rescinded and in this regard BEC would be obliged to pay duty to a maximum of $7.5 million per year. This represented a big change in operating margins.

In addressing the Rotary Club of East Nassau, I reinforced the intent of Government and the Board to transform BEC through the achievement of certain objectives that would produce a new and dynamic method of operating their public utility.

The concerted efforts of the Board and management culminated in some spectacular results in 1999 and 2000.

It was with a sense of great satisfaction that the very strong financial condition of BEC enabled the Board with the approval of Cabinet to enter into a loan agreement with a consortium of local banks for approximately $60 million to finance the New Providence expansion of generation.

The Power Expansion Programme, Phase II, together with certain distribution upgrades, was executed without a government guarantee for money borrowed. The Board took enormous pride in the fact that for the first time ever the financial strength of BEC persuaded the banks to lend the money purely on the merit of the strong financial results of BEC.

However the installation of our new 30 MW generator was for me bittersweet. Vincent D'Agular was the expert electrical engineer on the Board and as such his wisdom in deciphering tangible and intangible issues connected with generation and distribution to me and the Board was of incalculable value.

In the planning for the purchase and installation of a new 30 MW generator, Vincent expressed some serious concerns about continuing to use a model made by a Japanese manufacturer with ABB Alstom Power SA—Spain being the main contractor. On its own, this did not constitute a problem but Vincent was not enamoured with the performance of an identical engine already in place. The difficulties were real but not necessarily debilitating. His thought was that we should look at other options.

"Barrie, I feel that we are obliged to be more diligent in assessing our options for the purchase of a new 30 MW generator."

"Vince, I have to rely upon your judgment in such a matter. After all, we have had success in moving BEC forward in a progressive and productive way. What are we to do?"

"We should look closely at all the bids that have been tendered by qualified bidders," Vince replied.

I realized that this would cause a bit of a delay but we should feel comfortable with any proposal that we would be submitting to the Cabinet through the Deputy Prime Minister who held ministerial responsibility for BEC.

After much debate with our consultants and internal discussions with our management personnel, we decided to propose purchasing a unit from Hanjung, a South Korean manufacturer. The Board supported the recommendation and all documentation was submitted to the Deputy Prime Minister through his Permanent Secretary.

On the day that Cabinet was to consider the proposal Vincent, Bradley Roberts, General Manager, and I were invited to attend and to present. Vincent was unable to attend.

We thought that the strength of the presentation would carry the day. However, this was not to be the case. The presentation was most impressive, I thought. However, there were other important international issues to be considered and which potentially could produce outcomes that could be very beneficial to the Bahamas. And it was in this context that the Bahamian Government decided that the new generator should be purchased from ABB-Alstrom-Spain.

When the decision was explained, there was a dark silence at our end of the table. Our disappointment was palpable.

Vincent, when told of the outcome, was visibly shaken because he had spent much time in examining the value of the South Korean generator in the context of all bids received. His research was impeccable. It had to be borne in mind that the Spanish tender was one that was approved by our consultants for consideration.

Vincent did not say very much and remained quiet for two days before he called me.

"Barrie, the recent outcome at Cabinet has deeply concerned me. I want to meet with you."

"Of course, Vince, we can meet at your convenience."

Vince came to my office at Paradise Island. I had a sense of foreboding as to what the content of the meeting was likely to be.

We had been friends for a long time and as such there was a comfort with each other. Vince was obviously feeling distress and wasted no time in getting to the bottom line.

"Barrie, the outcome at Cabinet is unacceptable to me because we had put so much effort in arriving at a recommended position, and for Cabinet to cast it aside is a personal affront. And, also I do not think that it is in the best interest of BEC. I therefore will be tendering my resignation from the Board with effect immediately."

I was horrified and mortified with the prospect of losing the sage advice of my friend Vincent.

I begged him to reconsider. "Vincent, we had done so much good work at BEC. Our partnership together with Board members and senior management had elevated BEC far beyond what anyone in the country could have expected. I plead with you to reconsider your decision."

Vince, however, was resolute.

My final plea: "Vincent, we can do more from the inside that we can from the outside."

Vincent left my office with me deep in thought. However, the next day I received his letter of resignation. It made me sad. When I told the Deputy Prime Minister, he was surprised and said that he would speak with Vincent.

I had a serious doubt about his ability to reverse Vincent's decision and my doubt was proven correct.

When I informed the Board there was general disappointment, but as mature, intelligent adults we understood that we had to carry on. In fact I arranged to meet the Board away from the precincts of BEC. Absolute privacy was essential.

We looked at our record through the years. In 2000 there had been no load shedding. In fact I was personally so pleased with this result and the way we had developed a long-term revolving strategic plan to stay ahead of developing electricity demand that I contemplated not replacing my standby generator at home.

We electrified all the settlements in the Family Islands. I can recall that when we turned on the electricity at Cherokee Sound, Abaco, some citizens came out and smashed their lanterns in the street. The words "At last!" still ring in my ears.

We diligently pursued government's mandate to install street lights in all inhabited areas of New Providence. The mandate included new subdivisions as they were developed.

Destiny seemed to favour getting BEC as an all encompassing utility successfully into the twenty-first century. We were indeed poised to make BEC a utility of which all Bahamians could be proud. However, we were confronted with a militant Electrical Workers Union, which made negotiating a new industrial agreement most difficult.

Having spent many years negotiating with unions in the hotel industry, I was not alarmed by the turbulence of the union leadership. Even so, when our proposal for a new agreement was burnt in the parking lot of BEC along with photographs of the Deputy Prime Minister and me, it caused a momentary hesitation in my optimistic outlook.

As negotiations stalled, the degree of militancy increased proportionately. Illegal withdrawal of labour was most distressing but regrettably was compounded by acts of vandalism to portions of BEC's infrastructure.

In such instances the union leadership expects all members of the bargaining union to stop working—the intent being to create havoc and bring BEC management to its knees. However, although causing extreme inconvenience to consumers, BEC was able to cope. Some responsible employees would "cross the line" but at risk of reprisal. There was one incident when one such employee, Paul Maynard, stayed on the job to handle emergencies and for this he was attacked and beaten.

I went to see Paul at his home and it just happened that Shenique Miller, a cub reporter from The Tribune was also there to get a direct report from Paul.

In recognizing the danger, he was exposed to in crossing the line he admitted, "I was afraid of being subjected to physical harm that could be serious."

Paul had indeed been injured and suffered a broken arm.

I had only admiration for Paul, which I conveyed on behalf of the Board.

"Paul, there is no way to fully express our utmost appreciation and recognition of your valour in performing your duty."

What a champion. He put his life at risk.

There were other employees who "crossed the line" but they, thankfully, were not directly exposed to danger while doing their job.

There were several other acts of sabotage entirely beyond the national interest. The next devastation was the shooting of the overhead high voltage transmission lines, which caused much damage. This caused tremendous concerns to reverberate not only within BEC but throughout our entire community. How could this happen? The police recovered several bullets which were badly damaged. The damaged bullets were given to the FBI to see if forensically the calibers of the gun could be determined. Alas, this could not be done. Unfortunately there was more than one such incident.

Another event could have had long and serious impact upon our distribution system in Cable Beach—some persons unknown drained the oil out of a major transformer bank, resulting in a complete blackout in the area.

It seemed to the Board and senior management that efforts of sabotaging the BEC's operations were intensifying. The police undertook to place police officers at critical substations on an around-the-clock schedule.

There was a sense that the union leadership had inside information that afforded them the capability of acting selectively and safely. In light of this possibility, the police arranged with the FBI to conduct an electronic sweep of all executive offices. Nothing untoward was discovered.

Despite the difficulties with negotiations, it was still crucial to reach a final agreement. In an attempt to move negotiations I arranged on a couple of occasions for meetings between management and union leadership to take place in the Corporate Boardroom at Atlantis. A change of environment seemed to have a positive effect. In the end, an agreement was reached and peace entered the workplace.

Through the years we had placed considerable emphasis on employee training. In the year 2000, 350 employees participated in training courses, either full-time or part-time.

The Board was determined that management at all levels would recognize and accept that they were accountable for all actions within BEC. This process began with the approval process of the annual operating budget. Although, it seemed to management somewhat extreme, the audit and finance committee of the Board reviewed the content of the budget in quite some detail.

Everette Sweeting, CFO, subsequently said to me, "To have you and audit committee review the budget in such detail with his team and management was an event that had never occurred previously." He added, "It was eye-opening and gave my team a greater sense of accountability." This was said with a smile gently playing on his lips.

During the year Peter Bethel retired and was sorely missed. He said to me in a humorous way, "Yesterday, I was someone important. Today, I am a nobody." We both laughed but it was the way of life except for the good memories. Peter had been succeeded by Freeman Duncanson, who had a clear understanding of what the demands of the job required of him.

Freeman retired within fifteen months of his appointment. Bradley Roberts, Deputy General Manager, took over the management reins of BEC.

Then came the General Elections of 2002. The Free National Movement (FNM) lost the government and since I was a political appointee as were all the Board members, we were obliged to submit our resignations.

In my resignation I said that I would serve at the Prime Minister's pleasure so as to ensure a smooth transition.

In this time something happened that was so unexpected, I experienced a weak human moment. I had called for a Board meeting because there were few housekeeping matters that required being disposed of and certainly nothing that could be significant or policy-oriented. I had requested Shelly Cooke-Seymour to convene the meeting. Nothing happened and I could not contact Shelly because she had not come in to work. Then quite unexpectedly I received a call from MP Bradley Roberts, the Member of Parliament who was to be Minister responsible for BEC. He inquired about the meeting. I told him of the purpose but he remained concerned. I therefore offered not to have the meeting to which he agreed.

On immediate reflection it was apparent that Shelly had advised Bradley on my intent. For me it was another lesson in life about misplacing trust.

During the eight years at BEC much had been accomplished by the Board, management and staff.

At BEC unveiling plaque for a new generator by Prime Minister Hubert Ingraham, Deputy Prime Minister Frank Watson, J. Barrie, Chairman, and Bradley Roberts, GM

CHAPTER 41

BAHAMASAIR

In the lead up to the 2007 General Elections, the mood of the people seemed to be shifting significantly to the favour of the Free National Movement (FNM). If the outcome were to be the formation of an FNM government with Hubert Ingraham as Prime Minister, I felt the urge to try once more to make a contribution to the country. Because I had served as Chairman of BEC from 1994 to 2002, I thought that it would be beneficial for me to return to BEC and based upon my previous experience I could take up the reins of oversight very quickly.

In a pre-election conversation with Mr. Ingraham, I audaciously raised the matter with him.

"Mr. Ingraham, in the event the FNM is successful in the general elections, I would be prepared, if you so wish, to return to BEC as Chairman. I believe that I could hit the ground running."

"J. Barrie," as he called me, "I know that if you were there again you would do a good job but we have to wait for an outcome. You never know how voters will be influenced when the day of decision arrives."

We left the question open knowing that an answer would be forthcoming one way or the other on the day after the General Elections.

The FNM did win the election and Mr. Ingraham formed a new government.

Some weeks later I was sitting in the International Box at Wimbledon when my cell phone vibrated. I looked at the originating number and recognized that it was a call from Nassau. I answered timidly and was greeted with the voice of Brent Symonette, newly appointed Deputy Prime Minister. I left the Box and moved to the outside pathway. Brent did not waste any time.

"Barrie, I know that you are enjoying your tennis but I am calling you from the Cabinet Office and I have been directed to invite you to be Chairman of the Board of Directors of Bahamasair."

I didn't respond at once because it was so unexpected at which point Brent asked, "Are you still there or did you faint?"

I could hear the Prime Minister in the background saying "tell him to accept."

Recovering from the shock I said, "I accept this serious challenge but I have several requests."

Brent does not waste words. "And what are they?"

Replying I said, "I wish to have Kenwood Kerr, Michael Reckley and Wendy Warren to serve on the Board with me."

He repeated my request to Cabinet and the immediate answer was "consider it done and congratulations."

When I returned to my seat I told Susan the content of the conversation. Because Bahamasair had such a wretched reputation I could not resist saying, "I don't need enemies if I have friends like those in Cabinet."

At any rate the die was cast.

On my return to Nassau, I was briefed by John Fowler, Secretary to the Board and Chief Customer Service Officer at Bahamasair and Henry L. Woods, Managing Director.

The composition of the Board was very representative of a wide range of interests and viewpoints. I assigned responsibilities to members—Ken Kerr, Deputy Chair and Chairman of Operations

Sub-Committee, Disa Campbell-Harper, Chair of Budget and Finance and Michael C. Reckley, Chair of Labour Relations. Other members who were very active and important to deliberations were Carlton Wildgoose, Erma Williams, Archdeacon Keith Cartwright, Dr. Mildred Hall-Watson and Arlington Miller.

Board members convened prior to our official meeting with Bahamasair Executives and in general conversation we quickly arrived at a consensus that Bahamasair needed a lot of attention at all levels.

The common phrase written in the public domain was: "If you have time to spare, fly Bahamasair." The reputation for being late in departing and arriving was cause for a significant defection of airline travelers from Bahamasair. The impact financially was significantly adverse.

My first words to my colleagues were "ladies and gentlemen, the enormity of the task is daunting. However, we are the products of the business world and know that we will have to tackle all situations enthusiastically and try hard to make a difference." The members murmured their agreement.

The question was where do we begin?

Our Minister, the Hon. Neko Grant, who was also Minister of Works and Utilities, in addition to meeting with us privately, also attended the first Board meeting. His charge to us was quite pointed. "Members, there is a big job to be done. I expect you to do it. You will have my full support."

I felt the need to make a subtle statement to executive management at the first meeting of the Board so I changed the seating order of attendees. I sat in the middle seat of the table with my back to the outside and Mr. Woods, Managing Director, sat immediately opposite. John Fowler, Secretary to the Board, sat at the head of the table.

I wanted the executive team at Bahamasair to understand that we were going to travel a different business path and symbolically the change in the seating arrangements was a reinforcement of that intent.

The airline, starting in 1973, lost money in every year of its operations and it was up to the Board to lead by example with respect to reducing costs, however insignificant.

On Board meeting days, the practice was for members to be served a full meal. I declared that going forward, meals would be very modest. If the airline was broke it was important to show that the Board recognized this fact.

Mr. Wood asked if I was sure I wanted to reduce the meal to sandwiches and fruit. To which I replied, "Yes, Mr. Woods, but there may be special occasions such as Christmas where we can be served a meal, not otherwise."

Our agenda which was comprehensive and abundant included a business plan for five years, update on privatization, industrial matters with unions and industrial agreements, capital expenditure, budget for current year starting July 2007, concern about overstaffing, dealing with massive debt, vacation accruals which were out of control, and a cost savings plan.

In recognition of the staggering weight of the work ahead of us, I said to the Board, "While by instinct we might want to tackle all business weaknesses at once, we must be prepared for the long haul. Step by step we will try to reinvent Bahamasair."

The previous Board, at the request of government, had a report prepared by McKinsey (airline international consultants based in Washington) to advise government on the prospects of privatizing Bahamasair.

The report was quite extensive with the cost of which being $1,000,000 with extra expenses amounting to about $250,000. The report was given to government but it was never acted upon. From what I gleaned, selling an airline that was suffering huge losses and which endured substantial overstaffing would have been all but impossible, particularly when considering the potential political fallout.

Ken Kerr, my deputy and I along with senior management, visited all the departments at Nassau airport as well as visiting and holding meetings with the team in Nassau, Miami, Fort Lauderdale and West Palm Beach.

We could understand that there would be certain skepticism because of unkept past promises but we were determined to make a huge difference.

In Miami, Glenda Pletcher, station manager, stood at our luncheon meeting and made a profound statement of support.

"Chairman and fellow employees, I know that we are fighting a very big fight to stay in business but I believe in Bahamasair with all my heart." Ken and I looked at each other and understood that we could get the job done with support like that.

Our familiarization with how the airline functioned took about six months of dedicated study, then came the hardest test of all. How do we confront and overcome operating a bankrupt airline that through the years 1973 to 2007 had accumulated losses of $414,200,000.00 with funding coming from the Public Treasury and in effect out of the pockets of the Bahamian people?

In 2000, fuel cost was 13.42% of revenue and by 2007 it had more than doubled to 27.70% of revenue.

The airline owed government agencies, departments, corporations at 30 June 2007—$51.8 million. From 1990 to 1997 the National Insurance contributions were not paid. Including interest (adjusted) the total owed was $6.5 million. Government settled the debt for $3.269 million.

In the latter part of the 1990s, the airline failed to pay the U.S. government for ticket taxes collected. The government paid $20 million to settle. The airline borrowed a like amount from Citibank and repaid the government.

During the late 1990s up to 2002, the airline operated significant overdrafts with the Royal Bank of Canada which were not formalized. Overdrafts totaling $13 million were converted to loans in 2002.

Labour costs increased by 12.7% from 2000 to 2007 even with a decrease in average number of employees from 837 to 721.

The fleet consisted of six Dash 8s and three jets with maintenance being very high due to the advanced age of aircraft.

Consistency in senior management had been absent. In its thirty-five years history Bahamasair had been headed by seventeen CEOs.

The report prepared for the Board painted a picture of abject failure with the overflow being a cloud of depression and discouragement settling on all the workers.

Within the Board, instead of bowing to what seemed like a similar fate of others, there emerged a determination to make the tide flow the other way.

In speaking with the Board when all had penetrated our consciousness I said, "The challenge is to make this airline one of which all Bahamians could be proud. It will not be easy but we are products of the private sector and we know how to get things done."

Erma Williams said, "Chairman and fellow directors I believe that we can make a difference."

In a note written to Ken Kerr, once we were satisfied that we were pushing Bahamasair in the right direction, I said, "We are by far the most progressive and task-oriented public entity in the country."

The first order of business was to understand the financial condition of the airline.

Imagine the reaction when reviewing the audited report as at 30 June 2007. Total assets, current and fixed, was $37 million and total liabilities, current and long term, was $90 million. It took a while to fully absorb the numbers. Net operating loss, including non-operating income (expenses), was $16 million. Staff costs at $29 million represented 39% of income.

There was one item that particularly caught our attention and that was accrued vacation totalled $3 million. It was also interesting that retroactive salary payments to union contract employees were made by our predecessor Board totalling over $3 million.

The Hon. Neko Grant held Bahamasair as a part of his ministerial portfolio. In August 2008 the Board and management presented to Minister Grant a comprehensive report on Bahamasair. At the conclusion of the meeting, there were a number of outcomes that were articulated, including the recognition that the government could not continue to fund Bahamasair to the extent it had in the past, and the Board's directive to management was to find a way to narrow the funding gap through increasing revenue and cutting costs.

In reviewing the budget for 2008-2009, Minister Grant said very forthrightly, "Ladies and gentlemen, I know that Board and management will work energetically to bring financial order to Bahamasair but today you are seeking an increase in subvention from government that is greater than last year. This will be a bitter pill to swallow."

He added in conclusion, "I recognize that you are facing an uphill battle and on behalf of the government I thank you for your commitment to get Bahamasair on the right track."

And so we had our marching orders. The task ahead was monumental but the Board members were not dismayed in any way.

Management would soon discover that the Board was not going to act passively but intended to be very active in offering direction without being overly aggressive.

In conjunction with the Managing Director, Henry Woods, we established some goals that exceeded historical performance.

The annual audit of 30 June would be completed and issued by mid-December. This to our knowledge had never been accomplished. Disa Harper's committee was quite forceful in pursuing this objective. Eloise Rolle, CFO, was somewhat taken aback but in the end responded well and enabled successful attainment of the goal.

The Annual Report to government and to the public generally was normally slow in getting to completion. The goal was to have it finished by 30 November. With pushing and pulling with Phyllis Johnson, Henry L. Woods, John Fowler and other senior managers, the job got done. The result was excellent and it was a pleasure to issue the report to Minister and government and other stake holders within the set deadline.

The reputation of Bahamasair was very poor indeed with the travelling public. Internally, staff morale was at an all-time low. For the Board and senior management, the approach for reversing the status of the airline was to work on many fronts but to do so systematically and strategically.

As a result of the concerted efforts of all team members, some victories were achieved.

For the year ending 30 June, 2010, on-time performance for domestic travel was 83 percent and 64 percent for international travel. Best results in our history and exceeded industry standards.

All C-checks on all Dash-8 aircraft were being undertaken by Bahamasair's technicians resulting in several hundred of thousands of dollars being saved. This change was a historical milestone for Bahamasair since aircraft previously were taken to Canada for such heavy maintenance checks.

Complaints by passengers were being attended to quickly and successfully. A rule put in place was that each complaint had to be dealt within forty-eight hours of receipt of complaint. The efforts of John Fowler and his team produced very satisfactory results.

Management at the urging of the Board introduced two initiatives—Revenue Improvements and Cost Reductions, which produced commendable results. Through these efforts millions of dollars flowed beneficially to the year-end financial results.

While positive operating results were relatively slow in coming, the traveling public acknowledged the steady improvement in Bahamasair's service.

While at Board level with executive management, the operations were producing better results. There were other major pieces of the puzzle that required our focused attention—privatization of Bahamasair, and/or significant restructuring of the fleet and major revamping of operational parameters.

With these two burning matters confronting the company, we engaged a highly reputable consulting firm, MBA (Morton, Bayer, Agnew) to evaluate the current operating model and to advise the Board on how to change the composition of the fleet of planes and provide financial models that could possibly change Bahamasair into an efficiently operated airline with better prospects for getting, at minimum, to a positive cash flow.

While these complex issues were swirling around in my head, I had to understand the reality of the situation. The Board comprised members without airline experience but what was available collectively was the experience and knowhow on running a big business with multifaceted elements. And this kind of knowledge was going to be put to good use.

I said to the Board, "It is absolutely essential that we radically change the operating structure of Bahamasair. If need be, nothing is to be considered sacred."

MBA had begun its evaluation of the airline.

While this was in progress, we heard about the progressive action of the Trinidadian government to eliminate its government-owned airline, British West Indian Airlines (BWIA) and to create a new airline—Caribbean Airlines.

In speaking with George Myers, I made mention of Caribbean Airlines and the demise of BWIA and he said that he knew the Chairman, Arthur Lok Jack.

"Rothnie," (I always called George by his second name) I went on, "It would be great if we could talk with the Chairman and obtain some insight on how such a change was accomplished."

"John," (George always called me by my first name) he said, "Arthur is coming to Nassau soon. Maybe I can arrange a meeting with him."

"If you could do that, it would be first prize for us."

A couple of weeks later, Arthur Lok Jack was staying at the Ocean Club and arrangements were made for a meeting.

On a Saturday morning, all members of our Board, including Henry Woods, met in the VIP Boardroom at the Ocean Club.

Arthur was pleased to meet with us and understood clearly that we were at the crossroads at Bahamasair.

He recounted in considerable detail the BWIA negotiations. The story was not dissimilar to Bahamasair. BWIA had been operating for sixty-five years, producing huge financial losses which had to be underwritten by government compounded by being substantially overstaffed.

The government of Trinidad sought international advice on restructuring.

Arthur emphasized that the changes contemplated were radical and very politically sensitive.

He added that in the final analysis there was little choice but to make the hard choice. BWIA was to be dissolved.

The cost of dismissals and benefits totalled approximately $59 million. A new airline was to be formed and to be owned by government.

Caribbean Airlines came into being. Outside management was initially engaged. Some of the 2,200 employees were directly affected through redundancies.

Caribbean Airlines hired about 1,200 of the 2,200 persons who were terminated and each person was given an individual contract of employment.

Wages and salaries were lower than those paid at BWIA, the reason being that the government always bowed to the pressure of the unions. Additionally, the government was investing substantial sums of money to acquire new jets, which would enable penetration of markets that were previously out of reach or could not be properly served.

Arthur got into other information to flesh out the story but the bottom line was that the change had to be made for the benefit of the country and to be consistent with good governance. An invitation was extended to us to see firsthand what Caribbean Airlines was all about.

At the next meeting of the Board, the content of the meeting with Arthur was fully expressed.

"Board members, we have an invitation to visit Trinidad to obtain a firsthand view of the operation of Caribbean Airlines," I stated.

It was agreed that at a convenient time in the near future, a delegation comprising Ken Kerr, Wendy Warren, Henry Woods and me would travel to Trinidad. Within a matter of weeks arrangements had been made and we were on our way.

Arthur had set up an intense itinerary for us, starting with a meeting with him and the Managing Director of Caribbean Airlines who had previously been engaged as a senior manager at British Airways.

Throughout the day we met with departmental managers of Caribbean Airlines. They took their time in answering our many questions. We visited their offices at the airport and looked at the reservation systems, flight scheduling, maintenance programmes and so on. This was a comprehensive exposure to Caribbean Airlines. And for us the fact that profitability was within grasp was most compelling.

The day before we left, Arthur took me to visit the Arthur Lok Jack School for Higher Education. It was an institution of which he was inordinately proud and for good reason. I spoke with a number of faculty members, which was enlightening in that there was a spirit of unity in what they were doing. Coincidentally, there was a presentation to Arthur by the principal and others who expressed their recognition of all that he had contributed to the learning institution. The message to me was that Arthur was using wealth for the betterment of Trinidad's youth.

What had happened in Trinidad with the airline industry was far beyond our immediate reach but we were heartened by what could be if there were the resources and political will to proceed in the direction of meaningful change.

We reported to our Board on our findings and impressions of our inspection of the Caribbean Airlines miracle.

In concluding my comments to the Board, I was obliged to convey the reality of our Bahamasair situation.

"Directors, our exposure to the great change in Trinidad in the creation of Caribbean Airlines was uplifting. However, we have to confront our own reality. We are definitely constrained by the lack of resources to duplicate the Caribbean Airlines model. However, we must continue with our determined quest to make Bahamasair a much better airline and wherever possible celebrate our successes."

I added, "We will continue with our plans to review the fleet and just maybe, there will be a good outcome. It won't be easy."

My contact with Arthur did not end with our visit to Trinidad. There was another opportunity presented by Arthur with respect to Bahamasair.

It all happened in a roundabout way. Air Jamaica was owned by the government of Jamaica and operated at annual losses that continued to expand. The state of Jamaica's economy was such that it was necessary to seek support from IMF in the form of a standby letter of credit for $500 million, Concurrent with this request, the Chairman of Air Jamaica announced that for the recent operating year the airline lost $150 million. This, of course, was a loss to be absorbed by the government.

The IMF agreed to a standby letter of credit provided the government rid itself of Air Jamaica. The reason for this was obvious.

Caribbean Air's Board led by Arthur saw this as an opportunity to acquire Air Jamaica under conditions similar to what had happened in Trinidad with the demise of BWIA and the creation of Caribbean Airlines. A deal was struck and Air Jamaica became a sister airline to Caribbean Airlines. Employees were made redundant and payments based upon length of service were made. Most of the dislocated employees were hired by the new company but at lower rates of pay and with individual contracts of employment.

It was obvious that the government had no choice.

At the conclusion of the acquisition of Air Jamaica, Arthur called me and advanced a very interesting proposition. Arthur said, "Barrie, while we have momentum in the Caribbean Airline industry, I am thinking that it could be opportune to absorb Bahamasair into the group and thus create a truly Caribbean Airline, serving the entire region."

"Arthur," I replied, "I find this proposition very exciting and if there is a way to reach a determination on how participating countries could be best served it could represent a huge unifying opportunity to help our economies."

Arthur added, "I am sure we can find a way to get the most appropriate structure affording maximum benefits to each participating country."

"I will speak with Prime Minister Ingraham to determine the degree of interest. And thanks for calling," I replied.

I was truly optimistic of having a positive response from the Prime Minister. However that was not to be. After reaching the Prime Minister and putting forward the idea enthusiastically, there was immediate skepticism as to the value of such a move on relatively short notice. He in effect said that he would want to see how well the expanded version of Caribbean Airlines worked before he would consider advancing such a concept to Cabinet colleagues.

I was tempted to elaborate the idea further but my intuition was that the Prime Minister was not prepared to fight that particular battle with the global economy as well as our own being under significant pressure. Further, the political pressure from the unions would have been immense.

I called Arthur the next day and had to say with regret that my government did not have an appetite to wade through issues that would have to be contended with once the government decided to go in such a direction.

Arthur said to me, "Barrie, it is too bad. An airline for the Caribbean region would have produced many economic benefits."

We would speak again but on a vastly different plane. Arthur was also Chairman of a conglomerate that operated in Trinidad and Barbados and in particular supermarkets. His company held an interest in Bahamas Supermarkets Ltd., the company that owned City Markets. I was Chairman of BSL and was to experience a business nightmare that has haunted me to this day. Arthur and I on occasion had to address some common interests which in the end became uncommon.

With Caribbean Airlines out of our picture, we had to refocus our energy on finding solutions for getting Bahamasair to an operating level that would allow us to escape the quagmire of total financial inadequacy.

MBA evaluated our business with a critical eye that relied upon their vast experience and knowledge of the airline industry.

Our management team—comprising Paulo Cartwright, Tracy Cooper, John Fowler and Henry Woods with the accounting support of Eloise Rolle—compiled an incredible amount of information that in conjunction with the information collected by MBA formed the basis of a comprehensive plan that could change Bahamasair's negative operating results over a six to eight-year period.

The fleet composition was to be changed completely. A new operating model would produce a far more nimble and efficient Bahamasair. There was consensus in the Board and executive management that given the deteriorating product there was not a single employee who did not accept that significant change in Bahamasair was absolutely necessary.

Once the fleet renewal plan had been accepted by Minister Grant we convened a general meeting with employees and spoke to change.

My opening remark: "We have developed a plan that will give us mobility, flexibility and will place us in a much stronger competitive position." I added, "Our plan is yet to get the final approval of Cabinet."

The basic elements of the plan were to replace the Dash 8s with thirty-four-seat SAAB 340 B aircraft. The reason being that the Dash 8 aircraft were nearing the end of their useful life, plus the cost of maintaining these planes was very high added to which fifty-seat aircraft for inter-island service was not economical.

Next, replace the two 737/200 jets with Bombardier Q 400 aircraft with seventy-four-seat capacity. These were turbo prop but with cruising speed of about 400 MPH. The cost of operating was so much less than the jets that we calculated that the payback based upon savings would be approximately eight years.

Henry Wood and I met with the President of SAAB who was based in Washington and negotiated a lease for eight planes for five-year periods. We also included a provision that allowed for the purchase of the SAABs at a time most convenient to Bahamasair.

On the matter of staffing, there were going to be changes that in some instances would require a decrease in compensation for some pilots.

Meanwhile we considered that without significant change in the way Bahamasair was structured and managed, there was little or no hope that the financial burden that was being perpetually placed on the backs of the taxpayers would even be alleviated.

We met with employees to explain the way forward. Our message of hope included the opportunity to control our destiny—to establish a foundation of stability that allowed expansion, no reduction in staffing (instead more staff were needed: twenty to twenty-three pilots and approximately twelve flight attendants), adjusted compensation for pilots, and the vision of being a significant player in tourism with the assured support of the Ministry of Tourism.

MBA had taken into account all factors related to changing the way Bahamasair was being operated. Board members recognized that there would be resistance to change, particularly from the pilots who in the future scheme of things would have adjustments made to their compensation packages. However we were facing the reality of potential closure without positive change.

In the Board meeting I remembered Archdeacon Cartwright saying, "We are faced with extraordinary challenges and will need the Lord to guide us through safely."

The Board and management were fully indoctrinated in the proposed model advanced by MBA. The compelling element of the presentation was the financial future of Bahamasair, anticipating that we could get all in place by 3 December 2012.

We estimated that by 2019 Bahamasair would have a positive cash flow. What did this mean to the country? Bahamasair would be independent of subventions from the Public Treasury.

We made arrangements for the entire Board to meet with Minister Grant. He had sight of the plan before we met and was thus familiar with its content.

When we finished presenting the Minister took a deep breath, sat back in his chair and looked at members with appreciation.

"Chairman and Board members, I have never seen such an all-encompassing business plan for Bahamasair. You are to be congratulated."

Of course we were ecstatic with his response.

He added, "I will submit to my colleagues and will make arrangements for you to present to Cabinet."

We experienced a couple of false starts with respect to the presentation to Cabinet but finally the day came.

The presentation went well but there was obvious negativity in the air. I suppose I could sense it more than others by the nature of the questions. At the end, we were directed to put our plan aside and to direct our attention to getting replacement jets as this was to be the way to the future.

My personal impression coupled with a dose of intuition was that the pilots were in a position to make a strong lobby against the plan and obviously succeeded.

It reminded me of the description of insanity: "You continue to do it all in the same way, over and over and still expect a different result."

The Board was undeterred and was determined to make Bahamasair a better airline despite the setback.

Acquiring replacement jets required substantial investigations as to availability and to get the best available craft at a price that made sense and could be funded by government. Henry Wood, Paulo Cartwright and Tracy Cooper were outstanding in their pursuit of replacement aircraft.

It was with relief that a deal was made with the Argentinean airline for Bahamasair to purchase two Boeings 500—of 1995 vintage. The plus factor was that at the expense of Argentinean Airline, C-checks were to be performed prior to delivery. With

C-checks being done every thirty to thirty-six months at a cost of approximately $1.5 million per plane it translated into a cost per plane to Bahamasair of about $2.5 million.

The planes were piloted from Argentina by Bahamasair pilots and after a couple of short delays caused by customs issues, delivery of the first plane was made within forty-eight hours.

A ceremony was held at the Bahamasair hangar to celebrate the introduction of a very modern jet plane.

Minister Grant was effusive in his comments in acknowledging the achievement of Bahamasair team with the purchase of a first-class jet aircraft, and said, "Ladies and gentlemen, it is with very considerable pride that I say that with the introduction of this newly acquired Boeing jet, we are elevating the operating capability of Bahamasair—a move that we believe will play a major step towards a better Bahamasair.'

It was a great day. The pilots loved it.

The second jet was soon to be delivered but the General Elections were held and the Free National Movement was defeated and the Board by protocol was required to resign forthwith.

For me it was a huge disappointment because in my mind with five more years at our disposal we would have converted Bahamasair to a status far above the one that was embedded in the minds of the travelling public.

Bahamians were now flying on Bahamasair with a confidence that had diminished under previous leadership.

Being a nation builder with enthusiastic application, I took it upon myself to call the new Chairman to discuss a few matters that I considered important as they involved the integrity of certain employees. The Chairman was accompanied by a fellow director who had served on the Board under the previous regime.

The information handed over to my successor was compelling and irrefutable. It involved the dismissal of two employees and the factual information on a number of others similarly affected. I thought it important for the new Board to deal with this matter.

Imagine my disappointment when the matters were not proceeded with and an even greater shock when I learned that the two dismissed employees were reinstated at the direction of the Board.

My thought to myself was: *How in heaven's name we can believe that we are able to hold employees accountable for wrongdoing when those in power are prepared to turn a blind eye for the sake of political gain?*

Atlantis Construction Site, 1997
Sol Kerzner, J. Barrie, and Prime Minister Hubert Ingraham

CHAPTER 42

THE KERZNER YEARS

In history there is imbedded the storybook belief that in all confrontations with formidable challenges, good fortune favours the strong of heart.

For Merv Griffin, he had a deep belief that his substantial investment in Resorts International would be happily successful. After all he was bringing his Hollywood star power into the equation and his successes in TV and the silver screen would be the foundation for the complete renaissance of Resorts International.

Alas the stars did not favour such an outcome but there was hope. I can remember Merv talking to George Myers and me on the morning that the new Paradise Island airport was to be officially opened.

"George, this could be vital to the promoting of the casino. Imagine flights day and night, coming in directly to Paradise Island from Miami and Fort Lauderdale. I believe that this is a platform for bringing new energy to Paradise Island."

It was a bright sunny day with a cool breeze gently blowing

from the northeast when Sir Lynden Pindling and Lady Marguerite arrived at the terminal. Merv was smartly dressed in a navy double-breasted jacket with white slacks. He was beaming as only Merv the entertainer and entrepreneur could do.

Mr. Pindling was most complimentary about Merv and the prospect of growth in tourism going forward.

"Mr. Griffin, your fame is such that we have great expectations that under your leadership and with your connections with Hollywood, the future of The Bahamas will be enriched."

Lady Pindling cut the traditional ribbon and thus another milestone within the history of Paradise Island was created.

But fate was not kind to Merv and despite the "brave heart" by mid-1993 the financial future was extremely bleak.

And so against this backdrop, Sol Kerzner, CEO of Sun International, advanced his interest in acquiring Paradise Island. In a later conversation with me Sol said that he came to Paradise Island in the mid-1980s and was immediately attracted to the beauty of the Island, the striking colours of the ocean and the magnificent beaches. He added that he knew that if the circumstances were good he would return to The Bahamas and Paradise Island as an investor without hesitation.

While Merv's ability to stay in the business was severely diminished, the way was cleared for Sol particularly in two ways—Apartheid in South Africa had come to an end and Nelson Mandela, who was friendly with Sol, gave him a full and absolute endorsement with the Ingraham government.

Here was the beginning of a tourism journey that was to produce huge rewards for the entire Bahamas and its citizens. Hubert Ingraham was the new Prime Minister possessing a depth of futuristic thinking that was incredible.

Sol Kerzner and Hubert Ingraham were similar in many ways—both goal-oriented, hard-working men who lived by the principle of always living up to the given word and at the same time to be straightforward in language.

An all-encompassing Heads of Agreement for the development of Paradise Island was crafted and signed. Prime Minister Ingraham broke new ground in that his intention was that any committed investor in pursuit of governmental approval for a development would only be required to undergo "one stop" in obtaining necessary approvals in principle. The prior governmental approach was for an investor to obtain approvals from each ministry agency or department, which generally was a time-consuming process and in any number of situations was most vexing.

The Agreement called for the effective transfer of ownership to take place on 1 January 1994 but given certain operational restraints it was agreed that Merv Griffin Resorts would operate for the benefit of Kerzner until 1 May 1994, at which time Kerzner would assume operational control.

While all the negotiations were in progress, there were any number of Sun's executives conducting visits to obtain an understanding of the entire operation. The due diligence was exhaustive because it was important that there were no unanticipated surprises once Sun took possession.

It was late December 1993 that Butch, Sol's son, came to visit and to obtain a firsthand look at the business. At thirty years of age, the son of a legend in tourism and casinos in South Africa was venturing into untested waters. He wanted to be immersed in what the country was all about in addition to getting to know the business.

Butch was most engaging and lacking any sense of self-importance. From the beginning he called me "JB."

"I want to learn as much as I can about the business and about The Bahamas and the people. This is a big step for me" he said to me.

"Butch, I will try to give you insights of the country that you will hopefully find useful. In fact, I will arrange for my children to show you life on the other side of the bridge."

He was agreeable and enjoyed the time with the young Farringtons.

During the time that Butch was familiarizing himself with Paradise Island, we took the opportunity to dine on our own at Café Martinique. I can recall our dinner in mid-November 1993.

It seemed appropriate to hear from me how I envisioned the development of Paradise Island.

"Butch, I am so excited with the idea of creating a destination that will be the envy of this hemisphere."

At this time of night we were the only two in the Napoleon Room. It was quiet, and the colourful lights on the far shore of the lagoon added to the atmosphere for describing a dream.

I do believe that it was on that night that a permanent bond between us was formed even though he was young enough to be my son, a very special relationship indeed.

At the time that Sol acquired the Paradise Island properties, I shared the office of the President with Michael Williams. We both recognized that in all likelihood the organization would be changed. I suppose being a Bahamian having experience in tourism as well as being politically connected, my future seemed secure. Michael was not so fortunate. Sol decided to bring in an outsider who had been a senior executive with Disney World – France.

The new person was Sanjay Varma, who quite surprisingly assumed an extremely aggressive management style that quickly alienated the management team.

At a Saturday morning meeting he was especially intrusive. I had little choice but to take exception, which made him angry with me.

Afterwards he summoned me to his office and said, "Barrie, I did not like the position you took in the meeting." He then added, "If you are not with me, you are against me."

"Sorry you feel that way Sanjay but I am obliged to express myself when something is wrong," I retorted.

It did not take long for Sol and Butch to recognize that their selection of a President was defective.

Sol did not hesitate to remedy the error in judgment. Sanjay by arrangement quietly made his exit from Sun International and The Bahamas.

On the other hand Sol was immersed in structurally and decoratively transforming the hotel complex—the Paradise Island Resort and Casino. There were parts of the hotel that required extensive work.

He admitted that he did not realize that the kitchens were in such bad condition. He had no choice but to tear out the innards and start over, a costly and time-consuming undertaking. It was extraordinarily hard trying to operate the resort while so much work was going on. The employee situation had to be delicately handled. Sol hired hotel employees to work on the construction site and the remainder of the workforce worked one or two days per week. Hard but that was the way it was.

Sol had made a commitment to the Prime Minister that he would not terminate any employees and would use them to the extent possible. The hotel union leadership was informed as well and once they had been made privy to the development plans, they accepted the position.

Tom Bastian, during an introductory meeting, was especially effusive. "Mr. Kerzner, this is good for the country. I am hopeful that we will be able to work together for the common good."

Originally, the name for our resort was going to be "Skull Mountain" with a pirate theme, and then the unexpected happened. Sol received an invitation for tea at Government House. This was during the time Sir Clifford Darling was Governor General. Lady Darling, who was quite perceptive, said to Sol, "Mr. Kerzner it is going to be extremely important for the name of the revitalized resort to be one that captures the spirit of what you are doing." Sol was intrigued and asked what specifically did she have in mind? Whereupon began the story of the lost continent of Atlantis and how it would arise from the mighty depth of the ocean.

Sol was captivated and yet non-committal. Over the next few days he absorbed the prospects of an Atlantis, discussed it with Butch and some of his marketing executives, and during these meetings there emerged a fairytale that could be made symbolically real. The decision was made and Atlantis was born.

Thanks to Lady Darling, Atlantis with the genius of Sol Kerzner has become the premiere resort in this hemisphere.

Sol was driven to complete Phase I of the reconstruction of the resort within seven months, which most of the experts said was impossible. But, on 13 December 1994, and $150 million later, Atlantis was launched with much celebration.

There were any number of meetings between Sol and Prime Minister Ingraham to iron out the issues that could not be avoided but since there was commonality of purpose there was mutual understanding.

One Saturday morning, Sol came to my office in quite a state. He said that there was a situation with several building permits that required the Prime Minister's intervention. He added, "I am reluctant to try to reach the Prime Minister but it is vital to our maintaining our schedule of work if we are to reopen in December." I took him at his word and rang the Prime Minister, who was reluctant at first but relented in the end.

Arrangements were made for Sol to see the Prime Minister at 2 p.m. at his Cable Beach office. On Monday when I saw Sol he said, "I explained my problem to the Prime Minister and he understood immediately. Barrie, Mr. Ingraham is a good leader and The Bahamas is lucky to have him at the head."

About ten days later, Sol, Butch and I met in the Boardroom. At this stage we were probably midway to completion of Phase I reconstruction.

Sol immediately without preamble said, "I want to begin the planning of Phase II of Atlantis. We should add 1,200 rooms and move the casino to the centre of the complex."

He could see the look in our faces of amazement but he went on.

"We must have a resort that is without equal and which will be in demand irrespective of what might happen with Cuba.

"We must write a letter to the Prime Minister giving our initial thinking on a 1,200-room expansion at a cost of about $250 million."

We talked about it for a while longer.

Obviously a new Heads of Agreement would have to be agreed because of tax consideration for the casino.

We prepared the letter to send and by that time Sol also wanted to create new convention space and multiple meeting rooms.

And then came the question of a new bridge.

In the original Heads of Agreement the reference to a bridge was to be a shared responsibility of government and Kerzner. In subsequent discussions, the question became debatable as to responsibility even though there was never any question about the critical need of a new bridge.

While this discussion was going on, the scope of the project was enlarged and the cost increase was commensurate.

The directors of the company were a bit dubious about moving ahead so rapidly but Sol was relentless.

After all was said and done, the scope included a new casino of 50,000 square feet, a night club off the floor of the casino, a gourmet restaurant with a celebrity chef, a coffee shop adjoining the casino floor, an all-purpose buffet restaurant, a high-end shopping area—Crystal Court, and a marina to accommodate yachts up to 200 feet in length.

With regard to the marina, the question arose as to how would vehicular traffic be handled particularly if there were a drawbridge, which would be very slow. Sol, the genius, had the answer albeit it would be expensive to build a tunnel under the sea to solve the problem of vehicular traffic and easy access of large yachts into the marina. Then came the idea of Marina Village, a place for specialty shops, gourmet and signature restaurants coupled with limited entertainment.

It was patently obvious that what was being created exceeded, by far, what Sol, Butch and I discussed in the Executive Boardroom. And, of course, negotiating with the government took on new proportions. Some of the crucial items included the number of new jobs to be created during construction with the clear declaration that of the work crew required, the ratio of Bahamian and non-Bahamian workers be set at 70/30.

Additionally, weekly reporting of the number of workers currently employed had to be submitted to the Minister of Labour.

Once open, Atlantis would require 125 work permits for non-Bahamians and the Bahamian workforce would total 8,000 or more. There were concessions on casino taxation for a period that corresponded with the life of the Heads of Agreement.

One important inclusion that became contentious was the right of Kerzner under a Most Favoured Nation provision, which meant that no other developers could be granted conditions under a similar development agreement that were better than those granted to Kerzner International. Baha Mar did present a problem in this regard but Sol and Prime Minister Ingraham worked it out amicably.

The bridge issue was resolved by the Paradise Island Bridge Co. Ltd., making a bond offering to the public, redeemable at different time intervals and at sufficiently attractive interest rates which were immediately taken up by the market. And, so the funding was raised without discomfort to Kerzner and the government.

The construction of the new bridge was coinciding with construction of Atlantis Phase II with the grand opening set for the 13 December 1998. What an extraordinary feat of perseverance, fortitude and foresight.

Believe it or not, the official opening of the new bridge happened on 12 December 1998.

In 1997, as President of the Bahamas Hotel Employers' Association I was under pressure to ensure that the industry remained stable during the period of anticipated growth. We were in the midst of negotiations of an industrial agreement that was to expire in January 1998. I knew that getting to the end game was going to be very complicated with stakes being extremely high.

Tom Bastian, President of the Hotel Union and a very crafty and knowledgeable negotiator, was determined to use this opportunity to exact as much as possible almost irrespective of the cost to hotel owners.

Our Employers' Association collected information on the history of Bahamian tourism as well as on all competitive destinations including the new and larger cruise ships. The comprehensive information, when pulled together into a single presentation, made it abundantly clear that tourism in The Bahamas was under fierce competitive pressure by other emerging destinations. Our industry with respect to capacity had shown little growth as compared to major destinations in the Caribbean such as the Dominican Republic, Jamaica, Puerto Rico and Mexico (Cancun), not to mention the cruise ship explosion in recent years.

We shared all of our information with the union leadership as in our opinion it was important that there was a full understanding what our industry's position was in relation to an ever-expanding competitive field.

Sometimes negotiations did not proceed smoothly. In fact there were occasions when public exchanges between the parties were most unpleasant. In the meantime, construction of Phase II was proceeding with great urgency. In consultation with the architects and contractors, Sol and Butch realized that the pace of construction needed to be accelerated. Otherwise we would not be able to have the grand opening mid-December 1998.

For me, this period of unbelievable positive and expanded change in our tourism product was more exciting than anything I had ever experienced. I worked every Saturday and Sol knew this, so it was not unusual for him to show up at my office and say, "Okay, Barrie, let's go and see where we are." Here I was walking though the construction with a visionary of gigantic proportions.

I remembered him saying to me, "Barrie, almost all visitors who experience the resorts I have constructed like and enjoy what is offered, but don't really know why."

I sensed that he was about to tell me.

"The fact is I pay attention to detail, which makes an impression without being clearly discernible by the beholder."

Sol went on, "Many attempts have been made to duplicate what I have constructed and to do that they would photograph what I have created and then try to draw plans for constructive copying. But no one has been able to do that yet."

I was always amazed with what extent Sol would go in order to get it right. He flew to Italy three times to select the right marble for the floor of the Royal Towers lobby. The hand railing on the stairways leading from Royal Towers lobby to the Aquarium and the entrance to The Dig was expressly made in Sheffield, England. The Dig was a simulated archaeological site containing a maze of underwater corridors and passageways among the ancient ruins of Atlantis. It is quite an attraction and once again amplifies the creative imagination of Sol and his team.

The tale of Atlantis arising from the depth of the ocean is murally painted on the ceiling of the Royal Towers lobby—a magnificent depiction in oil and the work of a Spanish artist who could not speak a word of English. Simply astounding creativity.

Sol was obviously happy with what he was creating; however information obtained otherwise indicated that the original capital budget would be significantly exceeded.

In parallel to this exposure with Sol, I was becoming more attached to his son, Butch, and he with me. There was a kind of common sensitivity as to what the project meant to The Bahamas and the way of life.

It is hard to describe the expanse of the project such as creating the aqua venture water park complete with a lazy river ride—with water warmed during the winter; an aquarium containing many thousands of marine-life species, and of course the marina and a tunnel for motor traffic under the waterway into the marina.

With negotiations with the union going on longer than anticipated, Butch expressed his anxiety about the prospect of becoming polarized on any issues with the union. He then came up with the brilliant idea—the union leadership needed to have a better understanding of the competition confronting The Bahamas, in particular from Orlando/Universal and Las Vegas. He suggested a special trip for Tom and his colleagues to see firsthand what we were up against in the world of tourism.

When I discussed it with Tom, he was most receptive to the idea. Arrangements were made—a Learjet was chartered to fly us to Orlando—Tom Bastian, Pat, Leo, Michael and me.

Plans were put in place for us to stay at the Disney Hotel. Because we were flying in a private jet, we were required to land in West Palm Beach to clear U.S. Customs and Immigration and then fly on to Orlando where the arrival was impressive—alongside the Learjet appeared a white limousine, which we entered upon exiting the plane. As we sat in the limousine, Tom excitedly said to our small group "this is damned good." We laughed. We stayed two nights and were given tours of the property and surrounds.

A short insight into the Disney operation was sufficient to give us an understanding of the vastness of the operation and the extent to which all activities were efficiently coordinated.

From Orlando we took a commercial jet, Delta, to Las Vegas where we were greeted by Drew Goldman, who was to be our coordinator for the next three days. We stayed at Caesars Palace, which was a delight and impressive, so Drew arranged for us to tour all parts of the hotel and casino including the back of the house. We met executives of the Las Vegas Chamber of Commerce which was a most eye-opening experience. At that time Las Vegas boasted a room capacity of about 100,000 rooms and growing. The Venetian and the Bellagio were under construction.

We were all quite impressed with Las Vegas. One night I spent a few hours with Dave Hanlon, who was the former President of Merv Griffin Resorts and a friend. He was then President of Del Rio. I remember going up to the Jazz Club on the nineteenth floor and looking across the city at the magnificent array of magically multicoloured lights and buildings—a land of wonderful imagination.

Dave also took me to see the hotel's wine cellar. With unabashed pride he said, "Barrie, it was our intent to create a facility like no other. We have a vast array of wines with a value of about $7 million. As an added attraction, our guests can venture into the cellar and go through a wine tasting session at the end of which they can order their wine for dinner that evening."

This was indeed impressive.

For me there was an unexpected turn of events involving Pat Bain. As it happened, Pat and I were sitting by ourselves at breakfast on the second day and our talk turned to what we had experienced so far and how we could possibly transfer this kind of action to The Bahamas. Pat said that he was not content with the union and its leadership. As you can imagine, this came as a complete surprise but I listened intently as he went on to say that he wanted to be involved in the industry and asked if I knew of any opportunity for which he could be considered. I did not have any ideas, mainly because Pat was viewed as an agitator and thus hotel management would see him in that light. The question about his loyalty to the ownership/management of a resort at all times would be raised.

I had high regard for Pat and felt that he could be a good manager but that kind of conversation could not be pursued.

Drew Goldman paved the way for various tours throughout our visit which contributed greatly to its success.

We left from Las Vegas with questions of the unknown and returned to Nassau brimming with enthusiasm.

We agreed for the need to capitalize upon this breathtaking exposure. After discussing the value of the trip, we decided that a larger group of workers—line staff and managers—should have the same experience.

Following our arrival in Nassau, we commenced consultations with our colleagues—union and employers—on how to achieve the next phase. Butch was truly engaged and pressed for our return to Las Vegas before the Atlantis grand opening.

It was agreed that a group of about thirty persons would go to Las Vegas comprising twenty-two line staff and eight managers with Michael Reckley, Sandy Sands, Vice President of the Bahamas Hotel Employers' Association and Leo Douglas of the union accompanying the group. The itinerary called for Tom Bastian and me to fly to Las Vegas three days later to be a part of the wrap-up.

All went well as anticipated. Tom and I spoke with our group at Caesars Palace and the response was happily overwhelming.

One of the attendees during the final meeting said, "Never in my life have I had such an experience. We gotta make it happen in our country."

Once back in Nassau, we went one step further.

Atlantis Phase II was close to completion. Butch and Sol wanted the union and managers to have a tour of the facilities, which would give them a perspective of Atlantis as compared to Las Vegas. This was arranged in short order. At the end of the tour and a special presentation, there was full accord on the quality and scope of the Atlantis. Tom expressed it best when he said, "Colleagues, this proves that we are as good as Las Vegas."

As a final gesture of goodwill, I arranged for Tom, Pat, Leo to have a short meeting with Sol and Butch.

Time was running short before the planned spectacular launch extravaganza which was set to occur 12 to 15 December 1998. The stars were aligned even in the face of enormous logistical challenges.

It was a night to remember—Michael Jackson, Leonardo DiCaprio, Quincy Jones, Michael Jordan, Stevie Wonder, Monica Seles, Natalie Cole and Julia Roberts all attending, just to name a few. And there was Grace Jones descending from the sixth floor to the pool deck amidst a spectacularly designed fireworks display portraying the mythical Atlantis rising from the depths of the ocean—just sheer magnificence. Amidst it all was the new and modern 50,000-square-foot casino.

When all was said and done, to have taken part in the creation of Atlantis was to have it indelibly etched in my memory bank. Afterwards, in the days that followed, it was back to the daily routine work.

Negotiations with Tom and the union leadership were proceeding with some difficulty but there was a better understanding of what we were doing in tourism and the roles of everyone associated with the industry.

We completed negotiations and ended with a five-year agreement.

While all this was going forward, Sol and Butch were faced with making certain that there was a strong senior management team in place. After all, Atlantis was catapulted into the realm of global tourism as the resort that had it all. They sensed that with strong marketing underpinned with superior customer service, Atlantis would achieve iconic status. And so it turned out they were right.

The euphoria from the opening was contagious. The employees possessed a new enthusiasm in the providing of service, which was reflected in the abundance of glowing praise expressed by guests. Being number one was very nice indeed.

The demands of moving forward with Phase II, compounded by the relentless pressure of negotiating with the Bahamas Hotel Catering and Allied Workers Union for a new industrial agreement, was electrifying but wearisome at the same time. Then of course due to the size of the project and the importance to the Bahamian economy, there were many exchanges with government, ministries, corporations and agencies, resulting in time for family and relaxation being very limited.

In 1994, the Prime Minister asked that I serve as Chairman of the Board of the Bahamas Electricity Corporation. I willingly accepted and as we all know with Hubert Ingraham there was no choice but to agree. BEC was most challenging but I was determined to do my best at all costs.

Time for me was at a premium, and partitioning the day into manageable slots was crucial. Thank goodness my dear wife,

Susan, gave me support and understanding without which my life would have been pure hell.

Then came a most wonderful surprise. Through the days and months, my relationship with Butch became so extraordinarily special. Obviously there was a defined business relationship but in other important ways we shared a positive outlook on life generally. The mutual respect and warmth of working together caused me to think of Butch as if he were my son.

Unknown initially to me, Butch arranged for Susan and me to travel to South Africa for a ten-day odyssey to which was added a twelve-day cruise in the Mediterranean aboard the Crystal Symphony.

He stopped by my office and without sitting (he never sat because his mind was so active, he paced back and forth) said, "Commander, I want to do something special for you and Susan." My mouth dropped open with a question forming. "Oh my, what can that be?"

Butch called me Commander because of the honour bestowed upon me in 1997 by Her Majesty, Queen Elizabeth II—CBE—Commander of the British Empire. And because Butch reminded me of a young Winston Churchill, I called him "Young Winston."

He wrote me in March 1999.

> Commander,
>
> I have been meaning to put down in writing certain thoughts that are perhaps on the sentimental side but which I nevertheless wish to express. I have written this note because all too often important sentiments are left unspoken. I now find myself on AA 908 winging my way to Colorado and find it opportune to put these thoughts down on paper (the virtual kind).
>
> Most of what we do at work is often trivial (in the grand scheme of things) and usually boring. We are not working on any of the profound questions of life, no great discoveries taking place, no enduring works of art being created. But then, it is, by and large, a pleasant diversion and every now and then something fulfilling happens. Working with you is one of the aspects that I have found fulfilling.

When I first started working in The Bahamas I found it incredibly frustrating. I found that the path to success is often circuitous. There is little instant gratification. This was unlike the environments that I had previously been accustomed to and I was also less mature at the time. I had only just joined the company and had begun, for my first time, to be involved in management as opposed to deal-making on Wall Street. I believe that I was very fortunate to encounter you at this time.

I have learned a lot working with you. I have learned about fairness and treating people with respect. I have come to appreciate that this is not only the correct way to behave but it is also good business practice. One should endeavour to establish a reputation for fairness; a person that people like to do business with. This does not exclude one from being "firm." Working from the premise of fairness is not only good for business but it also helps one maintain a more positive "karma," more peacefulness. Many people pay lip service to this but I have seen you practice it. Further, at times I have watched you display great patience and I have similarly tried to learn to maintain a calmness in the face of obtuse behavior (although I cannot pretend to have made huge progress in this area and continue to lose my temper too often). Clearly I still have a long way to go; improving management and negotiating skills is a never-ending task.

Working with you has been fun. We have laughed a lot. Even during some very tense moments with our good friend "the Doctor" we have often been able to see the lighter side of things. I think that we have worked together well as a team. Our disagreements are few, and yet, it is important, that when we do hold different points of view, they are easily expressed in a straightforward manner. This is healthy and is the sign of a comfortable relationship.

Commander, in conclusion, and without question, most importantly, I think that I have found a good friend in you. Thanks.

Young Winston

And so in September Susan and I flew to Johannesburg and stayed at the Sandton Sun Hotel. During our few days there, we went down into the depths of a gold mine and at the same time a group of school children with an adult leader were also exploring the underground. We were on the way up from thousands of feet below the earth's surface when in a nearby shaft the children began to sing an African lullaby. The experience was beautifully emotional and spiritual. It was like being touched by God. Oh my goodness! I put my arm around Susan and just felt the depth of the moment.

We had another memorable moment.

Our driver, a delightfully engaging man, would converse with us on a variety of subjects. One day he talked about his children with enthusiastic pride. "My son is a lawyer, my daughter is in her final year of school and will be an educator and my third offspring is studying to be a CPA."

Susan and I almost in one voice said, "You have every reason to be extraordinarily proud. This is wonderful for you."

He was from the township of Soweto which is one of the poorest and disease-ridden places in South Africa. He told us, "In every week there are at least forty funerals for those who had died of AIDS." And then on a less somber note he asked, "At what stage of your life do your children stand on their own?"

As a voice of long-standing experience I replied, "Sorry to tell you this but such independence never comes."

We laughed pretty loudly together in acknowledgement of that truth. What a story! A man with purpose living in the most substandard conditions was able to lift himself above it and attain the kind of success that was an expression of the strength of him and his family.

We took the company's plane to the township where Sun City and the Lost City—Sol's two mega resorts—were located beyond the jurisdiction of the Central Government. Upon experiencing these magnificent and creative operations, we then realized the basis for Sol's fertile mind in designing Atlantis. We wanted to do everything while visiting.

The next morning we went on a hot air balloon flight over the Pilanesberg National Park, which was adjacent to the Lost City.

We were driven back to Johannesburg across country sparsely inhabited except for randomly situated settlements in which far too many people had to live. Such places reminded me of the Haitian-created "Shanty Towns" in The Bahamas.

Next came Cape Town and then it was on to the Sol Kerzner's estate at Hout Bay. From that base we went to Victoria Falls, and stayed at the Sun Hotel, located in Zimbabwe. The bronze stature of Dr. David Livingstone at the Victoria Falls was commemorated by King Edward at an official ceremony in 1936. It was a strange sensation looking at the statue of Livingstone as there is an identical one located in the Versailles Gardens at the Ocean Club, Paradise Island.

Our first Safari experience was to be at Mala Mala, recognized as the best vacation experience in the entire world. After a week at Sol's estate, Leeukoppie, we travelled to Italy to join the cruise ship for a twelve-day cruise that could only be found in Alice's Wonderland.

And then, we were ready to return to Nassau and so we took our seats in the aircraft. I looked at Susan and said, "Good fortune has embraced us and has given us the most unforgettable life-sustaining experience."

And one other event contributed to the completeness of our journey. While at Sol's estate, we watched on TV our Bahamian sprinters win the gold medal in the 4 x 100-meter Relay at the 2000 Olympics in Sydney, Australia. Oh my! What an exciting few minutes for us and many thousands of Bahamians.

Phase II of Atlantis is so elaborate and spellbinding that the inadequacy of using mere words to offer a description is beyond reality. But Sol was unrelenting in his ambition to create a world-class mega resort of proportions that stretched the imagination of the most optimistic and futuristic Bahamian thinker.

Unfortunately there were some landmark casualties as the Atlantis dream was being created. In 1999, the Paradise Island airport was closed as it occupied acreage that was to be blended into the plan to create a residential development in and around the golf course. The progression of development was mind-boggling, as Sol and Butch were singled minded about reaching the goal of the world's most complete and exciting resort experience.

I was intimately involved with every aspect of the Paradise Island Development and as such was made a director and assistant secretary of all the Bahamian-formed companies, including those that were relevant to developments and associations with other investors in other parts of the world. The Kerzner enterprises were spreading their business tentacles globally.

But then events far beyond the control of the U.S. Government and in effect the entire world occurred when terrorists on the 11 September 2001 attacked the World Trade Centre in New York and the Pentagon in Washington D.C., a tragedy that had a disastrous affect on tourism in The Bahamas and travel globally.

With so much at stake, hard decisions had to be made, one of which was how to deal with staffing given the decline in business. In discussing this with Butch and Sol, the decision was to lay off a fairly substantial number staff but not terminate them.

While addressing this bad situation, Butch and Sol offered a view point that was encouraging.

"Even though disaster is parked on our doorstep, we will not panic. We must intensify our TV advertising and marketing—in fact spend more dollars."

Sol added, "We are not going to follow any of the hotel chains that are reducing room rates. In fact we will maintain our rate structure as this crisis will pass in due course and we do not want to begin a new initiative from a lower rate."

Sol was right as there was a return to near normalcy within the industry within a relatively short period of time.

And there came political change—unexpected but nonetheless very real. In May 2002, the Progressive Liberal Party under Perry G. Christie became the new government. In keeping with protocol I offered my resignation to the Prime Minister as Chairman of Bahamas Electricity Corporation. This in no way diminished my position with Kerzner International, nor with the Bahamas Hotel Employers' Association. For me it merely meant a recalibration of my life's activities.

Relations with the hotel union changed as Tom Bastian was voted out of office and Pat Bain became the new President. On looking back at this change of leadership, there were signs as the elections got closer that Tom had lost the will to fight and had in fact surrendered.

He and I would meet on a wide variety of matters affecting Atlantis, and to facilitate the ongoing and frequent meetings I set up a banquet table in my office.

Finally, one day I said to Tom, "Mr. President the election battle for the presidency of the union is being waged at an ever-increasing pace. Shouldn't you be out there engaging the members on the worthiness of you being re-elected?"

"Don't worry JB, I have everything under control," he replied. I thought it odd but I misinterpreted the message.

Sol Kerzner was again looking to the future and felt driven to expand the Atlantis kingdom further. My direct contact with the government hierarchy had been blunted by the reversal of fortune for the Free National Movement in 2002 but I nonetheless was still integral to all aspects of the business.

Sol and Butch in 2003 communicated with Prime Minister Christie that the company wanted to increase its room capacity with an additional 1,500 rooms within the resort, which would include new restaurants and entertainment facilities as well as a substantial expansion of aquaventure, the magic land of water activities and integration with marine animals.

The government was ecstatic with the prospect of such an expansion under its watch.

Butch, as to be expected, took the lead in working with government and as such developed a close and mutually respectful relationship with the Hon. Allyson Maynard Gibson. He was very comfortable working with this Minister.

My relationship with Butch gained in dimension in that not only did the business aspect of the company bind us together more closely but at a personal level, a closeness emerged that was so special.

On a Sunday at my home, Susan and I were looking at the array of books in our library. Susan, who is always observant, stood thoughtfully with brow furrowed, and said, "Barrie, do you think we could ever read all of these books?" The answer was obviously in the negative. She went on, "What can we do that will have a positive impact upon others?"

"Maybe if we donate to a school we should get the best outcome," I replied.

"Which school?' she asked. We decided to look at the library at the St. Anne's School in Fox Hill which was a part of the Church. Next day we visited the school and were given the opportunity to have a look at the library.

Quite frankly we were horrified with the conditions. We needed to put the premises in shape before we started placing books in there.

I went back to the office to speak with Butch. I explained what needed to be done and suggested that the two of us as a private project carry out repairs and refurbishing. Butch was immediately enthused. Without hesitation, he called our development division and spoke with Richard Watkins, who coordinated much of Atlantis' development.

We ended up with a very nice library completed with a computer lab. Susan and I gave in excess of 100 books from our library.

Father Walkine at a small gathering blessed the library. And this was just the beginning. The kindness of Butch was to shine brightly like a beam in the night.

Cynthia Wells, the principal, asked me to invite Butch to come to St. Anne's to speak with the student body and faculty about the Kerzner investment and what it meant to be a part of The Bahamas.

This was arranged. Butch and I arrived at the school and were greeted warmly by Mrs. Wells and other staff. Butch was touched by the reception and as he spoke of his time in The Bahamas, he made it clear that he had developed a strong attachment to The Bahamas.

He paused near the end of his talk and then said, "I love The Bahamas and I want my children to be a part of your country." This was such a strong and emotional statement and one that he meant.

It just so happened that the Anglican churches at that time were in the midst of their annual Synod and an element of the week was a swimming competition between members.

While explaining this to Butch and me, Cynthia proudly

told us that St. Anne's had finished second in the swimming competition and this was accomplished without a swimming pool in which to practice. Very laudable. She did say that they had been developing plans for a pool for several years but had not brought the project to fruition mainly due to a lack of funds. We left St. Anne's feeling quite buoyed by the experience.

Butch was silent for a minute then said to me, "I want to help with the building of a pool for them. What do you think we should contribute?"

How should I respond? "I think that if we gave them $100,000.00 they will be overjoyed."

Butch said, "That sounds good, but let's think about it?"

When we got back to Paradise Island, we parked and started toward our offices. When we got to the point when we would separate, he said, "JB, come to my office for a moment."

We went up the stairs and into his office.

"I want our company to give a donation but it should be $250,000.00," Butch advanced.

I could hardly believe this.

"Young Winston, we have to go back to the school tomorrow to tell them. This is too hard to absorb at once."

He said, "Okay, let's do it."

I called Mrs. Wells and told her that we wanted to return to make a special announcement next day. She replied, "Of course, shall we say at 10:30 a.m.?"

And so it was set.

The next day was going to be a day that could never be forgotten.

We arrived and were escorted to the auditorium. As we entered the entire student body broke into song. The chills up and down my back are still vividly remembered.

When Butch announced the $250,000.00 donation from Kerzner International there was a spontaneous eruption of cheers of joy. Mrs. Wells actually jumped up off the floor.

I felt so proud of Butch. He was obviously an extraordinarily sensitive, thoughtful and kind person.

* * *

While construction was moving forward on the additional rooms and amenities, the Board of Directors decided to privatize Kerzner International as it was a publicly traded corporation and it was felt that the SEC reporting requirements were too onerous and impeded the decision-making ability of the company. For a while the process moved along pretty smoothly but then quite suddenly a new enterprise which involved former employees of Kerzner entered the bidding process to gain control of Kerzner. In fact it became quite hostile.

I didn't understand the rules of engagement but one piece of the process was that any declared and recognized bidding entity had the right to conduct "due diligence," which included a right to interview all senior personnel of Kerzner. My interview was incisive and relatively dispassionate on their part but for me my loyalty was with Butch and Sol, so they probably recognized that I was not embracing their approach. However, when we reached the bottom line as to my disposition toward a change in ownership that did not include the Kerzners, I told them that should ownership exclude the Kerzners I would resign. It was brave statement from me but one that I would execute.

After a relatively short but mutually aggressive encounter by competing bidders, the Kerzners' position prevailed but at a price that exceeded the anticipated cost to purchase all shares from all shareholders of record.

Initially, with respect to the Atlantis room expansion, the intent was to add 1,500 rooms to inventory. However, in re-examining the mix of accommodations, Howard Karawan, head of Sales and Marketing, convinced Sol and Butch to alter that position. Instead what was agreed was the construction of a 700-room luxury hotel that would be limited to adults, the idea being to develop a different brand within Atlantis, called the Cove. The additional 500 units would be a part of a condominium hotel to be labeled "The Reef," which would be developed in conjunction with a company that specialized in developing resorts of this kind.

The Cove, comprising 600 luxury suites and rooms and which was completed in mid-2006, was officially opened with great excitement by Prime Minister Christie. The work on the Reef continued. For tourism generally in The Bahamas, the

Reef represented a departure from the normal concept of hotel accommodations. The introduction of a condo-hotel comprising almost 500 rooms added variety in travel options for vacationers seeking a Bahamian experience.

* * *

Following the unpleasant episode regarding the hostile takeover bid by the un-welcomed corporate raiders, life took on some semblance of normalcy. Sol was on the prowl and with Singapore declaring its intention to introduce casino gambling coupled with high-end resorts, he decided to make a strong bid to be awarded one of the five licences to be approved by that government.

Sol and Butch were forever on the lookout for business opportunities within the four corners of the world, which included growing the One and Only Brand.

The government of Singapore in 2005 announced a policy statement that was to dramatically change the economic landscape of that country. Casino gambling was to be introduced, which was to include Las Vegas-type resorts. Four licences were to be awarded on the basis of designs that would be beyond spectacular. Butch had been charged with preparing the Kerzner application and for this he engaged the foremost creative architects and designers that could be found with the intent of constructing the most authentic and spectacular all-encompassing resort in the world.

All proceeded extremely well—the design content had been approved by Butch and Sol—and a model of the finished resort was constructed. The stakes were very high—the preparatory work necessary for a presentation to the Singapore officials cost about $30 million, including creative elements.

It was estimated that if Kerzner was successful in obtaining a licence, the cost of getting to the finished resort would be about $5 billion.

If there was ever a time in the company's history that all the stars of the universe were perfectly aligned, it was now. And then tragedy that could not have been imagined struck a mortal blow to our existence.

I was traveling from Stowe, Vermont, after spending two weeks enjoying the season of foliage and was about to leave the terminal at Nassau International Airport when I received a call from Gladys Darville. She was hysterical. After a few moments of a disjointed conversation, I gathered the impact of what she was saying. Butch was missing in the Dominican Republic and there was no concrete news. It was about 5:30 p.m. on 11 October 2006. An overwhelming fear gripped me that caused me to be virtually paralyzed.

I made my way to Paradise Island in a daze. Our people in the executive office were putting hope against hope that the initial news was too sketchy to draw a conclusion. The story was that Butch had travelled to the Dominican Republic with the President of our One and Only company, Paul Jones, and a potential investor from Florida, to look at several sites to consider for constructing One and Only Resorts.

When all the pieces were finally put together, it would seem that they had the use of two helicopters, one used by Butch and Paul and the other by the investor. On the morning that they were making final preparation to fly back to the airport to catch a commercial flight back to the U.S., the weather was slightly unsettled but not prohibitively so.

In a matter of minutes Butch, at the suggestion of the investor, changed his mind about flying with Paul and instead flew in the other helicopter. It seemed that following lift off there was a squall line that had to be flown through which apparently caused more turbulence than expected.

The helicopter never made it through the turbulence and crashed. Butch was killed along with the investor and two pilots.

My sorrow was and still is so deep that the absence of Young Winston lingers in a way that I am perpetually enveloped with his presence and his sense of doing what is good and right. The tears flowed as if the reservoir of sadness could not be contained. At forty-two years of age, he was on the brink of doing some great things for The Bahamas and for Israel, a country for which he held great feeling because of his heritage.

Life without Butch was going to be so hard. He was like a son—a son who will never be forgotten.

With Butch not being present, I had little choice but to understand the limits of certainty and to grapple with the uncertain future.

The burning question for me was: What is life likely to be without Young Winston?

I was to find out over the weeks, months and years ahead that so many things would be different. Intuitively, I realized that destiny would be the indiscriminate master of our future.

* * *

The year 2007 with its twists and turns was a defining year for the country. In May of 2002, the Free National Movement had lost the government to the Progressive Liberal Party, which catapulted the Rt. Hon. Perry Christie to the office of the Prime Minister. And as it turned out the Atlantis III expansion was constructed under the appreciative watch of the PLP government.

And then the unexpected happened. The FNM was returned to power in May 2007 and the Rt. Hon. Hubert Ingraham was instated as the Prime Minister.

On the 19th December 2007, the Reef was officially opened by Prime Minister Ingraham. When he started speaking, he graciously acknowledged the presence of the former Prime Minister. Fully understanding the irony of the moment the Prime Minister gently quipped, "The intervention of Fate has deprived Mr. Christie of the privilege of leading this official opening" to which he added "but that is just the way life is sometimes."

The opening of the Reef was bittersweet because Butch was absent from that which in many ways he created. The Prime Minister who had high regard for Butch Kerzner said, "It is impossible to speak of the Phase III expansion of Kerzner International without recalling the very important role of Howard 'Butch' Kerzner in its planning, development, and construction." He concluded by saying, "This phase in particular is a fitting homage to his memory."

As I sat there in the midst of it all, so many memories of Butch came flooding into my mind. To my inner self I said to Butch, "Well, Young Winston, we have traveled far together and not in vain." In keeping with our normal exchanges he responded, "Yes. Commander, we have."

* * *

Vanessa, Butch's wife, and I had a few quiet talks some months later and it was obvious that her heart was aching intensely.

There was little option but for Sol to reassume complete command of the company. Trying to refocus the corporate contributors was to require all of his energy and purpose. I knew that Sol was at the stage where he wanted to reduce his day-to-day involvement with the company and for Butch to virtually assume the mantle of CEO of all aspects of the organization.

With Butch no longer there to drive the process, it rested with Sol to carry the weight of putting all the pieces together and to make a strong and effective presentation to the government of Singapore.

The preparation was meticulous and Sol was confident that the company's position could make a significant impression on the decision makers.

Our company in the final stages was not selected. This was very disappointing to Sol. I was not directly involved yet I could not help but think that without Butch a certain forceful spirit was lacking. And this was understandable because of the tragic and fatal accident.

* * *

We look for meaning in virtually everything in life that escapes the ordinary. I do not consider myself as being very religious but by the same token I cannot help but interpret special experiences that occur in a dream.

One night in the midst of a dream taking place in South Africa and The Bahamas at the same time, Butch appeared on the perimeter of a small group of people sitting around a fire on a beach. Butch, upon seeing me there sitting on the ground, walked around to my place, knelt on the sand, reached over and kissed me on the cheek.

Awaking immediately, I was enveloped with a wonderful sense of peace. Intuitively, I believe that he was telling me to complete the story I was writing and to never forget the good work that was done to make our country a better place.

Like everyone else I know, I am unable to ignore events that may foretell a future occurrence that may be in some way associated with a past incident.

Sol and Butch were determined to proceed with the construction of Atlantis Phase III. The government had changed in 2002 and development of Phase III excluded Hubert Ingraham.

Prior to Butch's passing, it was the day of the official launch of construction in mid-2005, with Prime Minister Christie, other parliamentarians and other dignitaries in attendance when a special event with spiritual overtones went wrong. Sol and Butch wanted to designate Phase III as a powerful and sustainable addition to tourism, in a way signaling a new beginning.

To mark the importance of such a launch, Butch had organized the release of twelve white doves. Doves represent spirituality and symbolize the purity of purpose. Unfortunately, when Butch opened the cage containing the doves, there was a flutter of many white wings emerging except for two which remained unmoving inside. Butch tried to look unfazed but it was easy to see that he was disturbed.

With the company now privatized and with substantial debt, it was crucial for the company to reach budgeted profit margins and to produce sufficient cash flow to meet debt obligations.

There is no way to predict with any certainty future events. This is particularly true with politics as the pendulum of political future is unpredictable. In May 2007, the Free National Movement won the General Elections and Hubert Ingraham, now Prime Minister once more and who shared Sol Kerzner's vision for tourism growth, was quick off the mark to push Phase III along.

At the same time, Ingraham was faced with a deal crafted by Prime Minister Christie with the Izmirlian family to create Baha Mar, a mega resort which was being financed by the Chinese government through its development arm.

Atlantis Phase III was completed during the third quarter

of 2007 and it fell to Prime Minister Ingraham to officially acknowledge the opening of The Cove and The Reef—adding 1,200 units to Atlantis and to the overall Bahamian tourism product.

The company was undergoing senior management changes, which in different ways impacted the performance of the company. Paul O'Neil, former CEO of Caesars Palace, Las Vegas, who possessed vast experience at a most senior level, had been recruited to be CEO of Kerzner Bahamas and in this capacity exerted a steadying and progressive influence. Paul had the full confidence of Butch and Sol and from this position made it a priority to train and promote Bahamians. His efforts produced results recognized by all.

During the same period, Alan Leibman a long-serving senior member of management within Paradise Island was made President of Kerzner Bahamas. Alan was a no-nonsense hotel operator who demanded perfection from operations personnel.

During the intervening years, Sol and Butch had developed a relationship with the leadership responsible for development in Dubai, Emirates. With Butch leading the negotiations, an agreement was reached for the construction of an Atlantis in Dubai with Kerzner Inc., holding a 50 percent equity position in addition to having a management contract. The Dubai Atlantis was virtually a duplicate of Atlantis Paradise Island except that there was no casino operation.

Alan Leibman, at his request, was transferred to Dubai as President representing ownership as well as leader of the Kerzner Management Company. The scope of his authority expanded to include two One and Only resorts, the brand being developed for boutique and luxury resorts with a presence on both sides of the Atlantic and Indian oceans. For us, the best known One and Only resort is the Ocean Club on Paradise Island.

A new president was named for Kerzner Bahamas. George Markantonis arrived in 2005 as a relative unknown except that he was a hotelier out of Las Vegas with substantial marketing and casino management experience. He, from the very beginning, brought high energy and creativity. He possessed an outgoing personality with a sense of humour that immediately disarmed anyone who might be looking to engage him aggressively. He was destined to make his mark upon the company's operations and its premier position within the tourism industry, nationally and internationally.

From the outset, George made it clear that he believed in transparent communication and team building. Not long after he assumed his position we met briefly and right away he said, "JB, it is my intention to make Atlantis a mega resort of unparalleled distinction." And with a smile he added, "I want it to hum and I am not talking about music."

Atlantis, with its 3,500 rooms available for tourism supported by a sparkling casino plus an expanded capacity to handle groups and conventions in an integrated Convention Centre, which coupled with a water park with entertainment features, surpassed every other resort in the world.

And so the future looked brighter. We had survived the 9/11 terrorist attack in New York City which had the entire hotel industry in the U.S. resort to panic-stricken marketing. Atlantis held its ground and survived with better results than others.

Little did we know that a bigger change was lurking in the days ahead. In September 2008, world financial markets crashed and panic swept through every country. Hotel occupancies plummeted. Retrenchment was the order of the day. At Atlantis and the Ocean Club it was necessary to reduce the workforce by more than 800 staff plus the rescheduling of short weeks, a crisis day for sure.

Downsizing created a big problem with the hotel union. In an attempt to minimize the serious downward impact upon workers, the Board of Trustees of the Bahamas Hotel and Allied Industries Pension Fund—Health and Welfare Fund was able to craft an extraordinary plan to provide financial assistance to distressed workers. Roy Colebrook, President of the BHCAWU and board member, said at the press conference, "We know that our members are hurting. What we are doing today is intended to soften the financial blow that has been inflicted upon our members. It may not be perfect and we are prepared to review again at a later date. May the good Lord hold you in His care."

Industry recovery was slow and painful.

Negotiations with the hotel union were fragmented and

getting to a new industrial agreement required producing a variety of untried options for accommodation.

And then another crisis emerged that was to affect the financial stability of the company.

Managing Kerzner International as a pubic corporation was becoming increasingly difficult because of the substantial reporting requirements being imposed by government regulatory agencies. The controlling shareholders decided that privatization of the company would enable the company to continue unimpeded with the plan to expand Kerzner globally.

In order to move forward with new development, Kerzner International arranged to borrow a substantial sum of money to complete privatization and to proceed with expansion globally. The loan, totaling $2.6 billion dollars, was negotiated with a consortium of eighteen lenders, with Brookfield Asset Management being the lead lender. The terms made provision for the payments of interest and principal predicated on anticipated profits and cash flow. The agreement incorporated dates on which debt payments were to be made. The company unfortunately could not meet all of its obligations and after exhausting all avenues for meeting obligations, the company was facing the prospect of going into default.

The seriousness of the situation was of such a magnitude that it was necessary for Sol to engage the government in straightforward talks on ways to avoid what was seen as a disastrous outcome for Kerzner Bahamas and as a further consequence the unacceptable impact upon tourism generally. Atlantis by sheer industry prominence, nationally and internationally, in many ways was the cornerstone of the Bahamian economy.

Prime Minister Ingraham understood completely the urgency of resolution. But fate was not inclined to be kind to Sol and shareholders.

The inevitability of Kerzner being in default of its obligations under the loan agreement seemed like an unchartered hurricane looming ever so menacingly on the horizon.

The consortium of lenders with the Brookfield Hedge Fund leading the charge made it clear that the intent was to remove Kerzner International from the scene.

Needless to say, many options were being examined by Kerzner and Brookfield because the stakes were very, very high.

The end game was to be excruciatingly dramatic.

In my position with the company, it was my obligation to attempt to bring balance with the negotiations with government. The stakes were painfully convoluted and thus difficult to define.

Prime Minister Ingraham wanted a resolution without compromising government's position on behalf of the Bahamian people whom he served.

Finally, with Sol, company's directors, senior management and high-powered and extraordinarily skilled legal and financial advisors, a position was established for a crucial discussion with government.

Since I had been a participant in the preparation of a position paper with specific talking points, I was appointed intermediary for approaching the Prime Minister.

This was for me a huge responsibility. I had to figure out how to best approach such a complicated matter. In my possession was a document which in large measure would determine the future of Kerzner International.

I called the Prime Minister's office and was able to get a meeting for 3:30 p.m. It was at this moment I recognized that to meet with the Prime Minister and to walk through the "talking points" without the Prime Minister being prepared would be hellishly difficult.

"What to do?" was probably the most important question I could have posed to myself.

The document I held was fairly explicit and in the main could be followed but not without some elaboration. Also, I knew that the Prime Minister would not be happy if any part could not be explained satisfactorily. I decided to call the Prime Minister's senior advisor, Teresa Butler. I told her of the arranged meeting with him and knowing that he was in Cabinet, asked her if she could send him a copy of my talking points. She agreed to do so.

About thirty minutes later, the Prime Minister called me and sounded a bit put out. He said, "J. Barrie, I do not intend to meet with you until Kerzner knows exactly what they want to do in order to get this matter resolved."

"Prime Minister," I responded, "it is really important for me to see you."

When he remained negative on the meeting, I had little choice but to remain insistent without being disrespectful.

In my last appeal I said, "Let me come to see you and if after five minutes you want me to leave I will do so."

To my total relief he relented and at the appointed time I was at his office.

The Prime Minister's office and the executive office for the Ministry were now located in the building previously occupied by SG Hambros Bahamas.

I did not know what to expect but was pleasantly surprised that his welcome was quite congenial.

My five minutes passed and the Prime Minister then referred to the paper that I had sent to him via Teresa Butler—much to my relief.

At the conclusion the Prime Minister said, "J. Barrie, I believe that there are some areas on which the government may agree but I am obliged to speak with my Cabinet colleagues." I fully understood and was pleased that I had not been thrown out of his office.

I reported to Sol and his advisory group of what the potential was for getting to the goal line. There were still a lot of details to be worked out and which required Brookfield's involvement.

In the end, after laboring through a number of iterations of the agreements for the transfer of ownership to Brookfield, there was an unforgettable shift in the most important period in our tourism history and, in fact, in our country.

The vision of Sol Kerzner and Butch would now be relegated to history. For me I was saddened by the outcome, but with maturity comes the understanding and acceptance of reality.

From my perspective the question was "where do I go from here?"

At that moment I was Chairman of the Board for Bahamasair with almost five years having passed. However, a General Election was to take place in May, the year being 2012.

The election campaigning was vigourous and regrettably,

much too brutal. Surprisingly, the Progressive Liberal Party won by a substantial margin.

I knew within myself that I would retire from my job at Kerzner International when through some spiritual realization the time for retirement was drawing nigh. I was also battling with a disease known as hairy cell leukemia—a cancer that is now completely under control, thank goodness.

As my mother had a profound and lasting impact on my life, I decided that I would officially retire from the company on 12 January 2012, the 95th anniversary of her coming into the world in 1906.

George Markantonis, with the assistance of many associates, arranged for me a most memorable series of farewell events—the first was being escorted by a group of Junkanoo performers from my office to my waiting car at the front entrance. I danced my way through visitors and fellow staff members enthusiastically but with a heavy heart. I was truly surprised by the outpouring of sentiments along the dancing route.

And then there was a celebratory party attended by my fellow associates and my family, some of whom were flown in from Florida and North Carolina. Much to my delight, Andrea Belkan, head of Brookfield, also attended. To top it all off, the Prime Minister Perry Christie, former Prime Minister Hubert Ingraham together with Sol Kerzner, the visionary, were also in attendance. The comments by Prime Minister Christie and Hubert Ingraham were extraordinarily complimentary. Sol reminded us all of the close relationship of his son Butch and me.

When I spoke, the memories of the forty-one years spent with Paradise Island came flooding through. I ended with my favourite saying, which was the mantra of Dr. David Livingstone, the most famous explorer: "If success attend me, grant me humility; if failure, resignation to Thy will."

And then Sol and I were standing alone on the deck in thought. At the same time we turned our backs to the crowd and looked to the magnificent and beautiful Atlantis wonderfully enshrouded in numerous emphatic lights. I said, "Sol, the journey in creating Atlantis was like a fairy tale. Thank you for allowing me to be a part of your creation."

He just smiled and stuck his hands in his pants pockets as he was wont to do when in thought.

Forty-one years of service and no regrets.

My final act was to resign from some twenty-odd Kerzner companies of which I was a director and assistant secretary.

Attending a special event at the height of the Kerzner years, 1997

Enjoying a few moments with Prince Philip before he personally presented the prizes to outstanding young participants in the Bahamian chapter of The Duke of Edinburgh Awards

L to R: Alan Leibman, J. Barrie, Susan, and Prince Philip, Duke of Edinburgh

CHAPTER 43

IMPORTANT HELPERS ALONG THE WAY

Leaving the Montague Beach Hotel and the Pilot House in late 1971 was painfully difficult. It represented a rupturing of an important part of my working life that began in June 1954 at the Nassau Yacht Haven and Pilot House Club. And leaving my good friend, partner, and brother by good fortune, Bernard Perron, to piece together a bankrupt business covered me with a hard-to-define sadness and worry.

Once at Paradise Island and on the job, reality had to be confronted dispassionately. About eighteen months went by before Steve recognized that for me to be fully engaged with management, it was essential for me to have a full-time executive secretary.

George Mackey, Director Human Resources, once given the green light, diligently searched for the right person for me. The list of applicants was short but it was Cleomi Parker who possessed all the skills. Imagine taking dictation in shorthand, translating without hesitation, with English and punctuation being exact—most impressive credentials.

Cleomi had an excellent grasp of grammar and a broad vocabulary. There was no hesitation in giving Human Resources the okay to engage her.

Prior to Cleomi becoming a part of my office, Judith Burrows, who was included in the Executive Secretarial Pool attending to Duncan Rapier, President of Paradise Island, Fred Schock who preceded Duncan as well as Peter Krollpfeiffer, General Manager, was transferred to my office due to the rearrangement of the Executive Office. Judith was most knowledgeable of all the players in the executive suite as well as in offices of the operational officers of the Britannia Beach Hotel. Her guidance and willingness to undertake any task was invaluable. Seldom do you find someone who is so highly motivated, professional and engaged.

And so it was throughout my years as part of the executive team. I am very gratified that Tanya Nuñez brought organizational skills and sunshine to my office; Valarie Smith, with unassuming grace made the days of hectic activity easier to contend with; Sundae Ferguson, with a quiet determination and unerring attention to detail ensured that I kept pace with business demands of everyday; Alice Rodgers, although possessing entrenched habits of administration, proved to be dedicated and loyal to the success of the company. My last assistant, Secoya Bain, was quite enterprising and possessed an enthusiastic willingness to expand her administrative horizons.

When I came to a personal understanding of my future years with the company, I decided that my new assistant should be someone who had an interest in broadening their experience in preparation for assuming more administrative responsibility. With the assistance of Human Resources, I conducted a number of interviews with persons who showed potential to advance.

And this is where Secoya appeared. She really wanted to work with me because as she put it, "I want to expand my learning far beyond the ordinary."

I asked, "Why do you think you want to work with me?"

Her reply surprised me. "I googled you and gained an understanding of the expanse of your involvement in tourism and generally in the development of the Bahamas."

That was a deal closer.

But it was Cleomi who, after being promoted to Director of Risk Management, was an ally, confidant, and advisor who made my business existence a more confident one. The friendship that evolved is one that I continue to cherish.

There were so many who became close associates on account of having encountered innumerable business obstacles which we overcame through sheer determination and an unspoken belief in each other.

Even though some names are not recalled in this story, I am able to say without reservation that their contribution to our people and country was and continues to be vital to the economic success in tourism. They are indeed "unsung heroes."

CHAPTER 44

STOWE, VERMONT

When I married Lee Rose at twenty-one years of age, I had little experience in travelling abroad. And with John and Bruce being born during the first two years of our marriage, there was no discretionary money available for going out of the country nor did I develop an interest in venturing overseas. Circumstances in the following years changed my attitude. Lee Rose moved to Mexico taking Scott with her by mutual agreement. Somewhere in my inner self there resided the prospect of reconciliation. John and Bruce were in school in Toronto, Canada, and for me being alone was like a festering sore—an affliction for which I had no immediate cure. I made a trip to Mexico City and although without incident it was upon reflection, ill advised.

With Jo, my interest in travel was awakened. Even though Robyn was very young, we decided to take an early fall holiday into New England. In a station wagon borrowed from Jo's brother, Steve, who lived in New Jersey, we drove into New England without a special destination except Adeline, Jo's mom, said that we should visit Stowe, Vermont.

We did travel to Stowe and purely by chance stayed at a small resort called Topnotch. The timing could not have been better—it was foliage season when the leaves change colour—brilliant red, yellow, orange with a mixture of green—enhanced by the cool of autumn in preparation for winter. In so many ways it was magical. The impression was penetrating and as it turned out, a lasting one.

In the autumn of each year following, we spent two weeks in Stowe. Our attachment was so deep seated that in 1986 we purchased a ten-acre parcel in Hidden Valley. Even though I was a Bahamian, I was able to obtain bank financing. Of course we were living in a time when security was non-intrusive.

As a fate would have it, Jo and I separated and divorced in 1990.

Susan entered my life and thus began a fairy tale of great happiness.

While standing in the middle of the meadow at Hidden Valley, Susan said, "Barrie, why don't we build a vacation home here?"

Although I was slow to answer, it was an appealing idea.

"I think we should, Susan."

We engaged an architect, Roger Jones, and the planning began. Roger has been a close friend ever since. And our lawyer, Rebecca Olson, was most attentive and she too is now a very dear friend. Amazingly, Northfield Bank in Waterbury was willing to give a mortgage. Being so easy was another indicator of the trust that was so much a part of daily life generally.

Although only partially furnished, we moved in with a song in our heart. It was September 1995.

It is hard to describe how different it is from living on an island. Years ago, I purchased a Charles Dickens antique desk made in 1860s and put it into a studio used by Susan for her watercolour painting. At this desk I spent time writing and viewing the landscape with my iPod playing a Bach concerto for cello. The setting is so magnificent that I feel transported to a place of spiritual and emotional peace.

The house is in the middle of a forest with a variety of beautiful trees that tower over the land.

The separation from the hectic world in which we usually live affords us the chance to reaffirm the centre of our universe and to acknowledge the goodness of the Almighty.

In this remote area, even with wildlife in the forest, we felt secure and thus could move about with absolute freedom. Once while shaving I looked out of the window and there were more than thirty wild turkeys crossing the lawn. What a sight.

On the other hand, there are animals of which you should be careful.

One day, I was sitting in a wicker rocking chair near the driveway enjoying the day. I dozed off. Susan opened the front door and stood there gesturing. I didn't know what was happening so I stood up and then realized that a black bear was about six feet away. My heart skipped several beats but thank goodness the bear was startled as well and ran into the nearby forest. What a relief.

Stowe, Hidden Valley, is a special hideaway that affords us a most uplifting experience and place to give thanks for our good fortune.

*Pearl Melinda Farrington at twenty-five,
relaxing near the seaside*

CHAPTER 45

PEARL MELINDA FARRINGTON

Recently I came across a most interesting and heartwarming birthday card from my mom to me with the following introduction: "For a Son who means so much" and on the inside, and in her own handwriting—"Dear Barrie, God Bless. You have been loved from the day of your birth. From mom, who knows."

In later years, after Earle had come home from his medical studies in Scotland and with Ramon visiting from Canada, the family would gather just to reconnect. With mom in attendance, I would teasingly ask the question, "Who is mom's favourite son?"

There would be plenty looks of shock in the face of such a question. After bantering back and forth, they had to admit gleefully that "Barrie was the favourite son." In a way, I believe that I was embraced that way because I stayed at home to take care of her and our dad. I can never tire of recalling the special things she did that added so much to the meaning of love of a mother for the last born.

For some reason known only to mom, she decided to start each working day of mine by making contact by telephone. As it developed, she would call my private number at exactly 8:00 a.m. each day. This ritual was eventually well-known among associates with whom I had frequent interactions.

I remember on one occasion I was in midst of an early morning meeting with an associate, when my private telephone rang. Before I could answer the person sitting opposite to me said, "Okay, Barrie, that is your mother calling. I will come back later to finish."

And so this early morning bonding with my mother was established and remained in place for years. It was important to her and was equally as important to me. A memory that I cherish.

Pearl Melinda at her ninetieth birthday party with her children

L to R: Earle, Fay, Mom, Ramon, and J. Barrie

Susan and Barrie at a special event at Atlantis

CHAPTER 46

SUSAN

A life without sharing a deep and abiding love built on a foundation of mutual respect, concern, and a joy for living life to the fullest is a life that is constantly enveloped with almost total darkness.

There is no formula for attaining such a happy state because we learn from the lessons of life, which, for me, were harsh and life-altering. Is it faith that sustains us in the "dark" days or is it a matter of walking through each day doing, as my mother told me, "Barrie, you can only do the best you can."

For me, the lessons associated with existence tested my resolve to doing the best I could do. And yes, there were times when the agony and frustration pushed me to the very edge of surrender.

And so it was in my personal life. My first marriage began when I was too young and it was the same for my wife. Children came quickly. Coping was hard without a family model to follow. A near-death illness of my wife was devastating. And then came the realization that our road to maturity had placed us on separate paths—the result was an unhappy ending with emotional scarring.

My second foray into matrimony seemed to have all the right ingredients. But with the passage of time, emotional distortions entered the union until the damage to our beings became irreparable.

It was during the period of a deteriorating relationship that through serendipity I met Susan Jane Sargent.

When we met there was an instant skip of my heartbeat and I do believe she felt the same thing.

The way events unfolded could be poetically penned by someone like Sir James Barrie who wrote the fairy tale of Peter Pan. For sure the dark clouds of emotional uncertainty were pushed away.

We were alike in many ways. She grew up in a small New England township, Sunapee in New Hampshire. The family residence was a farmhouse built in the mid-1700s, which included some 150 acres. Life on the farm was very simple and modest. Tending to a fair-size herd of Scottish Highland cattle and numerous horses, as well as pigs, goats, chickens, ducks and geese, plus harvesting the summer hay to feed them all during the winter meant that chores were distributed amongst all family members.

While attending high school, Susan worked in her grandparents' restaurant, Woodbine Cottage, which was a favourite of residents and visitors who came to Sunapee during the spring, summer and autumn to enjoy the enduring beauty and peacefulness of this unspoiled area.

Susan had a strong interest in watercolor painting and in the early days, with little instruction, developed this natural talent. Over the years she continued on this path and acquired a mastery of the medium, painting a variety of natural subjects. She has held several solo shows and her work has been accepted into art shows in The Bahamas and across the USA.

Destiny meant that we should be together for infinity.

We both left unhappy marriages and discovered that we could commit to being together without reservation. It was not simple but Susan displayed a kind of courage far beyond a level that I possibly could have developed.

She decided that she had to find out for sure if I was the man she wanted to be with for the rest of her life. She had spent a year on the west coast of Florida but had moved back to New Hampshire, and for her this distance that separated us was too great.

During a telephone conversation she said, "Barrie, I want to be with you and I need to find out if our relationship is paramount. I have decided to move to Nassau." And so she did arriving in November 1990.

And so the love story continued.

We spent all our time together and after years of devoted sharing, we married on September 9, 2011.

There was complete harmony and happiness, which continues.

CHAPTER 47

NEW YEAR'S EVE

Traditions and history have special meaning to me and for reasons that are fully clear to me I try to give meaning to this thinking.

The history I venture to speak about has broad and impersonal interpretations and yet is purely personal.

Celebrating the beginning of a new year has assumed an unexpected and essential importance to me. It is a time in space to mark the point at which a section of life has passed and upon which we reflect—a short examination of what we have done or should have done to make a difference for others. It is also a time when I try to set realistic goals for the next twelve months—goals that may be physical, emotional, spiritual, and family-based as well as how to contribute to the broader community, in a positive way.

About thirty-five years ago, I added something special that made my passage to a new year much more memorable.

Following every New Year's celebration with family members or on occasion with a circle of friends, I return to my home and go for a swim in my pool. The time could be anywhere between 1:00 a.m. and 2:30 a.m. Since the pool is not heated, the temperature of the water is cold.

During the first few years, I found that I was the only one who would brave the weather and the cool water for a swim. And then one year, my daughter-in-law, Mariellen Farrington, Bruce's wife, upon being requested agreed to swim with me.

My open question to all was "is anyone willing to swim with me to celebrate the New Year's dawning?"

Mariellen responded at once, "Dad, I would love to swim with you!" I was absolutely delighted.

And so we swam joyfully but cold.

We managed to repeat our swim together for a few years. She remembers to this day our first New Year's morning swim.

The tradition continues with Susan, my constant companion, getting into the pool sometimes with mild protestations.

With lights on, in and around the pool and the stars twinkling merrily in the dark heavens, we know that God is watching over us and also over all people.

We have soft melodic music playing, which is a catalyst for us to acknowledge our good fortune even with so much social disorder in the country. These moments in the Farrington pool is an expression of thanks for life.

CHAPTER 48

HEALTH, FITNESS AND QUALITY OF LIFE

Is there a time in my life that I can point to when I realized that my body was a "temple" that had to be honoured? At this stage I can say emphatically "no." However, I can recall with clarity an exchange with a teammate of the Burn's House Baseball team that made me think inwardly.

It was a Saturday afternoon on the baseball diamond on the Western Fort and our team was having an intense practice session. Our second baseman, Nelson De La Rocha, a citizen of the Dominican Republic and a very talented player who made it on to a triple-A professional team, one step away from the major league.

Nelson was a perfect example of a training ethic that superstars subscribed to. We were standing side by side trying to cool down from our practice when he said to me in his Spanish accentuated English, "If you take care of your body when you are young, it will take care of you when you are old." I agreed with him but at that moment I did not realize how profound and prophetic his statement was, a simple truth that made life different for me.

I am now in my late seventies and I cannot recall precisely how often I have used Nelson's life-sustaining statement—suffice it to say many times. More importantly I have lived my life in recognition of this mantra.

My brother Ramon was quite athletic and although somewhat slight of build wanted to develop his body so that he could improve his performance on the rugby field, a sport for which he held a passion. And so it was in his years while reaching for manhood he discovered Charles Atlas—a man who suffered physical inferiority when young, and embarked upon developing a fitness and physique-building programme that captured the minds of many young men. Ramon was such a young man and became an avid subscriber.

I was impressed with Ramon's dedication to his exercise schedule. I can still see him using two dining room chairs between which he would lower his body and then with great exertion raise his body, until arms were fully extended—a method for building chest and shoulder muscles. After all his exercises were done he would stand sideways to the mirror and give his best Charles Atlas pose.

"Barrie, are you impressed?" He was directing the question to me but he really wanted our brother Earle to take note.

And so at an early age I was exposed to care of the body and then as I grew older I followed in Ramon's footsteps but with less fervour. During my rugby days, being in superb physical condition was essential. Even when my teammates had left the practice field I would continue to do wind sprints and push-ups. It was usually quite dark when I left the pitch and walked to the family home on Hawkins Hill.

After Lee and I were married and moved to our new home, I acquired a set of barbells which I placed on the patio. I worked out regularly and sometimes Roger Ludwig joined me.

Roger was an overzealous rugby player who was a fellow team member. He gained the nickname "Killer Ludwig." Quite frankly his workout ethic was inspirational.

As my financial condition improved, I was able to build an exercise room in the back garden with the assistance of Neville "Butch" Carey and Lorne Jenkinson, who both worked for the Paradise Utility Company. I would not have been able to get it done without them. When it was finished, painted white with blue trim, I moved my exercise equipment into the space. I just knew that I would spend many hours exercising in preparation for rugby and baseball. Not long after the room's completion, Lee and I were standing on the patio looking at what was to be my "special" room.

I was not sure that Lee approved of this addition but she stood next to me and with her blue eyes mischievously sparkling said, "Well, Barrie, you now have a room for making your body beautiful."

"Well Lee, there is nothing that prevents you from joining me in such an endeavour," I said.

It was a warm and gentle exchange.

In the years that followed I slowly understood the significance of being in good physical condition and the importance of regular exercise accompanied with a healthy and nutritional eating regime.

In later years, unfortunately, the spiritual and emotional element of my total being was virtually absent. With Lee out of my life through divorce, I found myself working longer and longer hours at the Nassau Yacht Haven and Pilot House Club.

When Josephine joined me in the continuation of the journey through life, there came a renewal of determination to relight the inner fire to achieve maximum physical condition and to sustain the quest through healthy eating and drinking.

When Jo and I sold the house on Prince Charles Avenue, we purchased a larger house in San Souci from Captain Johnny Gates with sufficient space to accommodate our family, comfortably. And after carrying out essential repairs and some upgrading of certain areas, I turned my attention to my continuing fitness programme.

Jo was not surprised when I declared my intention to create an exercise room. We did not have much excess money but she was very supportive.

"Barrie, I know how much you enjoy exercising and maintaining your fitness so we should make this little project a priority."

We used the area that was previously used for parking of cars by Mr. and Mrs. Ernest Callendar, who built the house many years previously. Upon completion I put my exercise equipment into my special space and thus began another stage of maintaining a healthy body and mind.

Jo and I also understood the need of having proper nutrition. As we were both working full time, we took a huge step toward living a healthy lifestyle.

"Barrie, there isn't time for me to do the necessary meal preparations if we expect to improve our health lifestyle."

"So, Jo, what are you proposing to correct this deficit?"

"I have found a qualified and experienced cook and I think that we should employ her on a part-time basis," Jo answered.

This we did and were able to complete our healthy way of life.

When my wife, Susan, later became a loving part of my life, our healthy ways became a permanent part of our existence. In fact, it was enhanced in a number of ways. Susan with significant experience in cooking made sure that our diet was supremely healthy. I developed a routine for myself health care that I follow to this day.

Sunday
- 1-2 hours on tennis court in the morning.
- 3:00 p.m. – an experienced therapist gives me a two-hour massage.

Monday
- care free

Tuesday
- 4:00-6:00 p.m. – workout in the exercise room. For about fifteen years I had a trainer, Mark Sterling, who took me through a rigorous routine.
- 6:00-7:00 p.m. – a physiotherapist ensures that my surgeries (both knees, rotator cuff and Achilles tendon) remain supple so that my tennis is played at maximum efficiency.

Wednesday
- 7:30-8:30 a.m. – full body stretching by trainer Larry Nairn at the Ocean Club on Paradise Island.

Thursday
- 7:00-9:00 a.m. – tennis at the Ocean Club with Leo Rolle. Prior to this current arrangement, I played with Peter Isaacs and later on with Gaby Sastre.

Friday
- 4:00-6:00 p.m. – a full workout with Mark pushing me to the limit.
- 6:00-7:00 p.m. – physiotherapy for my entire body.

Saturday
- 7:30 a.m. – 1½ hours of tennis

From time to time, the words of Nelson Da La Rocha reverberate in my brain: "Take care of your body when you are young, it will take care of you when you are old."

I have come to understand as well that peace of mind and heart is crucial to good health.

Most mornings I arise early and prepare a pot of green tea—one cup worth. It is usually still dark with evidence of a new dawn in the east. With tea, honey sweetened, and my iPhone and Bose speaker, I find my way to my rocking chair. With soft music touching my heart and mind I give thanks.

And it is here that I seek tranquility—with a gentle reminder that this state of mind is to be reserved for every waking hour of my life. Through determined practice I have begun to make each day a spiritually fulfilling one. When anger finds its way into my day, I am able to remind myself that such behaviour is destructive.

I discovered that the quality of life can be as good as you might really want it. When I was young, my spontaneous anger was my enemy. Unfortunately I did not realize it then.

I always remind my Susan that "good fortune has smiled on us in abundance."

J. Barrie hitting a backhand during Ocean Club tournament

CHAPTER 49

MY LIFE IN TENNIS

Rugby was a game I loved to play with complete abandon and it was this kind of recklessness on the pitch which imposed physical injury.

At thirty-three years of age, the pain caused by a pulled hamstring muscle was reason enough to seriously ponder my future in rugby. I had suffered through too many injuries and recovery was getting harder and slower. And then something quite unexpected happened which changed my life in sports. Following the 1967 sale of the Nassau Yacht Haven and Pilot House Club, I remained as an officer and director of Condotel Bahamas Ltd., which was headed by Bernard Perron, who always looked to the future for new opportunities.

In 1969, Bernard with British American Insurance purchased the Montague Beach Hotel, which required my moving office to the new acquisition.

The Montague was constructed in the late 1920s with the structure being an expression of a past overflowing with old-world charm. It was here at the Montague Beach Hotel that I discovered tennis on the four clay courts picturesquely situated near to Waterloo Lake, which was owned by the hotel.

We wanted to have the complete resort, and since tennis was gaining in popularity we hired Bill Tym, a former touring tennis player, to be our resident professional. He was soon to be joined by his wife, Alice, who had just left the women's professional circuit. She possessed the happiest outgoing personality that you could ever imagine. She was however of very strong character and it was obvious that she ruled the roost.

I decided that I would venture onto the tennis court as a kind of test for weaning myself away from rugby. Bill became my daily instructor. At noon every day I made my way to the courts.

Since we had staff housing behind the main building, I requisitioned one for my use, the reason being that after being on court for an hour or more I needed to shower before returning to my office.

After a month or so of daily instruction, I discovered that I was fairly rapidly becoming proficient in playing tennis. Of course, Bill made it fun as well as challenging. And thus began my love affair with the game of tennis.

The question then remained what to do about rugby? Quite frankly it was a fairly easy decision. The prospect of being virtually injury free was quite compelling. I never played another game of rugby and, in fact, never went to watch rugby being played. As my game improved, my reason for playing tennis soared with unbelievable speed.

In addition to being afflicted with playing, I simultaneously turned my attention to involvement with the expansion of the game throughout The Bahamas with particular emphasis on youth development.

Because of my own intense interest in the game, my children had little choice but to go along with my direction. John, Bruce, and Scott spent much time on the tennis courts.

The Farringtons became known as a tennis-playing family. And then came an involvement with the administration of tennis in The Bahamas, but mainly in Nassau.

During my first term as president, a youth development programme was introduced. Our team of association officers and supporters generated quite a lot of interest in tennis. Throughout the work with the youngsters, Vickie Knowles was a pillar of strength.

The Bahamas Lawn Tennis Association (BLTA) gained prominence in the Bahamian community as a result of local financial support. One very significant accomplishment was the re-establishing of annual national championships—senior and junior.

With rugby days behind me, I competed locally and internationally in the various age groups—35 and over, 45 and over, 55 and over and achieved satisfactory results.

I ventured overseas as well. Peter Isaacs was my doubles partner and shared the passion for the game. Our first tournament was in Orlando in November 1974. In singles we lost in the main draw in the first round but in the consolation competition we ended up in the finals. We could not extend our time in Orlando as we had to drive back to Fort Lauderdale to catch our flight to Nassau. The tournament director gave us permission to play the final in Nassau with the requirement for the result to be communicated back to him.

And so Peter and I played our singles final on court #1 at the Ocean Club. It was all very official. At that time Tex Schwab, a frequent visitor and president of a men's professional organization in the U.S.A. was with a group at the Ocean Club. I asked him to umpire the match. He agreed. In fact I can recall him saying, "I am delighted to officiate your match, which will allow me to lay claim to having refereed a championship tennis match at the Ocean Club on Paradise Island." Tex was a tall man who hailed from Texas and always wore a ten-gallon cowboy hat.

Oh yes! I managed to win the match in two sets.

Peter and I travelled to Costa Rica, Caracas, Venezuela, São Paulo, Brazil, and Mexico to play in the Stephen's Cup, which was created for the Americas. Eventually, as we became better known within this circuit I was requested to host the event at the Ocean Club. Leslie Fitzgibbon, a veteran tennis player and officer of United State's Lawn Tennis Association, encouraged the change of venue and gave his substantial support to making the event successful. I recall, while in Costa Rica participating, being approached by Otto Hauser of Argentina to take on the responsibility of organizing the Stephen's Cup. Otto was a big man, with a dark moustache and he possessed a very intimidating demeanour. Additionally, his movements were slow and deliberate—he was never in a hurry to go anywhere.

We were sitting on the bleachers in San Jose, Costa Rica, when he posed the question about transferring the event to The Bahamas. How could I refuse?

The highlight of my presidency was when the International Tennis Federation gave The Bahamas full membership. This meant that The Bahamas could participate in Davis Cup as well as Federation Cup under our own flag. Previously, we participated under the flag of the Commonwealth Caribbean Lawn Tennis Association.

Our first Davis Cup competition was against Venezuela in February 1989 on the courts of the old Sonesta Beach Hotel. Our first success was exhilarating. John Antonas was our captain. The requirements of the ITF for hosting the Davis Cup were quite extensive and required an extraordinary effort by many persons who supported The Bahamas Lawn Tennis Association.

In the next year, the BLTA participated in its first Federation cup—the competition for the top female players of member ITF countries—in Atlanta, Georgia. Vicky Knowles was captain.

I was honoured to serve as president of the BLTA on two separate occasions. Through the years so many persons contributed to the success of the BLTA but in particular I pay tribute to Kit Spencer who, as president and by sheer dint of effort, successfully obtained sufficient financial donations and created the National Tennis Centre, a facility that for many years was badly needed.

One perk that accrued to me by virtue of my BLTA presidencies was the right to obtain accreditation from the All England Lawn Tennis Club to attend Wimbledon. The thrill of Wimbledon is so enticing that I have attended Wimbledon championships for more than thirty years.

*J. Barrie and Peter Isaacs competing in Stevens Cup
Costa Rica, 1992*

With Eugene Lytton Scott, who inspired me to have incredible tennis experiences. Our friendship was one that was marked for eternity. He possessed an incredible mind that continually explored the boundaries of existence and did so fearlessly.

CHAPTER 50

SPECIAL PEOPLE

Whenever I drive over Hawkins Hill, I always slow down in order to recall the days of my young life in the hood.

Although the appearance of buildings has changed dramatically mostly for the worse and there are empty places with only remnants of concrete walls, the question I pose quietly is "where did my neighbours go and what happened to them?"

I slow down even more as I am about to pass the corner of Fairwind Street, my street. So many memories come flooding back and at the same time I acknowledge that my life's journey has taken me very far from Hawkins Hill but the memory of humble days spent there lingers indelibly.

It is funny that as I think of yesteryears I have no recollection of wanting to meet people who occupied a station far above what I occupied. And yet despite my unvarnished youth, I had no fear of those who lived in an elevated society.

I remember once when I was about twelve years of age or so, I had been given some raffle tickets to sell for a bazaar to be held in St. Matthew's schoolroom. As it happened on a Sunday at

St. Matthew's, a special religious service was being celebrated with Bishop Spence Burton leading the service.

When the service was over, his Lordship was being escorted to his chauffeur-driven car that was waiting just outside of the south entrance on Shirley Street. As he was about to enter this big car, I approached him.

"Your Grace, will you please buy some raffle tickets for our bazaar?" He looked at me and smiled, probably taken aback by such an approach. He spoke to me kindly and asked, "How much are the tickets?" I replied, "One shilling each." He smiled again and said, "I will take four."

I was overjoyed with making this big sale. Later on it dawned on me that he was wearing a white, full-length cassock with no visible pockets and yet he produced a four-shilling note.

This memorable encounter was my first occasion of coming eye to eye, so to speak, with a very important person. As I grew older I began to understand the importance of my own being and my value to society.

Before starting at the Nassau Yacht Haven in 1954, I worked at Hobby Horse Hall in the parimutuel. Along with Charles "Junior" Lunn, I shared the responsibility of controlling the betting machines, which were manufactured by the American Totalisator Company. And then one day at Yacht Haven, I met Mr. Richard Weingart, owner of the yacht Serendipity, which was docked there. He was a small man with grey, bushy eyebrows and yet exuded confidence in contrast to his size. While speaking with him one day quite unexpectedly, he said to me, "Barrie, I am associated with The Bahamas through business."

I am sure he wanted to go on and I enquired, "And in what way, Mr. Weingart?"

"I own the American Totalisatar Company and my machines are used at the race track—Hobby Horse Hall."

This revelation made me look at him differently but not with undue deference. For me it was like a dawning of my own worth. I cannot explain why it happened at that moment. Maybe it was because I had mastered the use of his invention at Hobby Horse Hall.

In times subsequent I would make confirming statements to myself. "No one is smarter than me. If there is a difference it has to do with the lack of opportunity."

My level of sophistication was elementary but this did not deter me from moving forward.

My first trip to Miami was to play soccer. To get there the team travelled on the yacht Alpha, an 80-foot steel-hulled ketch owned by Captain Lou Kennedy. At eighteen years of age, this was my first big adventure. This trip opened my eyes to the much bigger world beyond our country's border.

With my confidence growing, I was becoming better equipped to meet what life had to offer on more equal terms.

I recall at the Nassau Yacht Haven when the yacht Vagabondia III—an 85-foot luxury yacht—arrived at the Nassau Yacht Haven with two very special guests on board: world-famous movie actress Elizabeth Taylor and her husband, Mike Todd. One day she was standing just on the south side of the Nassau Yacht Haven building with a head scarf on, tight-fitting pants, a sleeveless blouse and no makeup on. She was most beautiful. Our verbal exchange was very brief.

Mike Todd came out of the dockmaster's office after checking for mail. He was not very tall but with the boat captain's cap jauntily on his head he looked impressive. Here before me was the man who masterminded and produced *Around the World in 80 Days,* a movie that captured the imagination of millions of people.

In 1967 while in the Senate, Queen Elizabeth and Prince Philip came to The Bahamas in the Royal Yacht Britannia. All parliamentary members were extended an invitation to have cocktails aboard the Britannia. I still have the invitation. Needless to say this was going to be the biggest day in my life. And so we all trooped aboard the Britannia and were introduced to her Royal Highness Queen Elizabeth and His Royal Highness, Duke of Edinburgh.

And so the boy from Hawkins Hill had his touch from the Queen who held incredible influence over all Commonwealth countries which, although self-governing, were once British territories.

While Merv Griffin owned Paradise Island and still held sway in the world of Hollywood, television and the silver screen, he would entertain many famous persons and in every instance Jo and I would be invited to such gatherings. One evening we went to his house and there standing on the patio was President Ronald Reagan and his wife, Nancy. He was the man who during his presidency put the United States on a strong economic foundation and skillfully gained the support of virtually all elected members of Congress, Republicans and Democrats. He was a great man and his greatness is still recounted by those who seek election to the highest office in the U.S.A.

President Reagan was most congenial with a wonderful sense of humour. He regaled us with many stories that kept us laughing constantly. He was President and a movie star who was referred to as "The Great Communicator."

The evening at Merv's residence was simply unbelievably amazing. As you can imagine, Jo and I were still glowing from the experience during our drive home. As we turned East after crossing the Paradise Island Bridge, I said to Jo with an unexpected depth of feeling, "This evening was so extraordinary that we could not have possibly asked for a better way to end our day." Jo was quick to say, "You are so right, Barrie." We both knew that it would be a story we would repeat to our family and friends for years to come.

J. Barrie and Vanessa Kerzner at the dedication of the swimming pool at St. Anne's School in memory of Butch Kerzner, 2007

Barrie walking with the elephants on safari at Camp Abu, Okavango Delta, Botswana

CHAPTER 51

TRAVEL

My father, Ira, did not travel beyond the shores of The Bahamas before he was seventy years of age. Why so late? He was afflicted with a cancer that started on his lower lip due to long exposure to the sun on too many occasions. My brother Earle, now a prominent surgeon at the Princess Margaret Hospital, decided that advanced treatment could only be obtained in the U.S.A.

And so my father's first trip to Miami was due to an unkind fate. On the other hand, and at a very young age I did not feel intimidated by the thought of going beyond Nassau.

At about ten years of age when I climbed onto the roof of our home on the top of Hawkins Hill, and looked to the horizon, my imagination carried me to a far off place like Long Island (Maurice's mom was from there) and the Current in Eleuthera, where my friend Sidney Kelly's parents were born and lived during their youth.

Of course, I did not have any idea of how big the world was, and besides nobody in the neighbourhood had television. So it was all in the geography books that we used in school. However, this kind of exposure failed to excite me.

Living in very modest circumstances, there was no hope in hell of travelling to some far off and exotic place even if my imagination had been stimulated.

My mom, before she married dad, for a while had lived with relatives in Jacksonville, Florida. Every once in a while, she would tell us about her life in Florida. It was during these moments that she would stop speaking briefly and into her eyes would come a "wistful, faraway look." She was happy there but after marrying dad and having children, her way of life changed significantly.

Throughout my marriage to Lee Rose, because we did not have any extra money beyond living expenses, any thoughts of Lee and me travelling were out of the question. But in the end, Lee did not let this stand in our way. Even at a young age she demonstrated grit.

Our very first trip for fun was to Miami. We were so excited. Scott was about three years of age with John and Bruce five years older. Staying aboard the yacht Vagabondia III caused us to be deliriously happy, plus visiting many tourist attractions brought us so close together as a family.

This first family travel was most important because just four-and-a-half years earlier Lee had almost died. It was a miracle for sure.

For me, my travels abroad started in 1966 when I captained and played on the Bahamas softball team in the 1966 World Softball Championship in Mexico City. Playing at 7,500 feet above sea level was such a weird experience. At that elevation, the ball travelled a lot faster and for greater distances than at sea level.

We had a great team with Foster Bethel's outstanding pitching enabling us to finish in a very respectable fourth position out of ten participating countries. And then in 1968, we played in Oklahoma City. There again the result was acceptable.

When Lee and I divorced in 1969 and with John and Bruce at school in Canada and Scott with Lee in Mexico, I was left to my own rather lonely devices.

In 1972, I met Josephine Elizabeth awkwardly but love was in the air. After marrying Jo in 1973 our horizons for travel changed. Jo was American and her parents, Bob and Adeline (Adi), lived in Hallandale, Florida, and were absolutely devoted to Robyn after she was born. Robyn had become the focal point of their lives.

Jo's brother Steve, who was a veterinarian, lived in New Jersey. Because we could leave Robyn with Bob and Adi, it allowed us to go on vacation through New Jersey, borrow a car from Steve and then drive into New England.

I remember the journey as if it were just a short time ago.

Before we left Hallandale Adi had said to us, "Once you are in the northeast, you simply must go to Stowe, Vermont." And off we went. Jo had no fixed itinerary but agreed that Stowe would be nice particularly because it was late September and foliage season would be peaking.

We luckily ended up at a small resort, Topnotch, in Stowe with just twenty rooms and four tennis courts. With the leaves changing colours, it was such a wonderful experience. We fell in love with Stowe much like the Von Trapps who settled here and are famous from *The Sound of Music,* the musical story created about how they had to abandon their beloved Austria during the German occupation of World War II and found that Stowe was a beautiful reminder of their homeland. I have visited Stowe every year since 1974 and ever since 1995 have been visiting three or four times a year.

I am now married to Susan and as we share so much together, the times in Stowe and Sunapee, New Hampshire, her home, are made all the more wonderful and memorable.

On account of my newfound love for tennis and having previously served as President of the Bahamas Lawn Tennis Association, which held membership in the International Tennis Federation, I was entitled to accreditation which allowed access to The Championships at Wimbledon. This was a perk that I certainly did not expect however it was like a dream come true. With each year at Wimbledon, our eyes turned to expanding the scope of ventures into unknown territory.

Annually and prior to the start of Wimbledon, a visit was made to my sister, Fay, and her husband, Phillip, who resided in Goosnargh, a small country village in Lancashire with a population of about 1,200 persons. We made the trek to Goosnargh even after my sister and husband had passed away to visit with my niece, Lindy, and family who remained there.

Our travel expeditions carried us into Southwest England to Cornwall and Devon, including a short excursion on to the Moors, which reminded us of the Sherlock Holmes mystery *Murder on the Moors*.

Another year found us motoring into West England and into Wales, where we stayed in a converted roadside inn located in Cardiff, which was in fashion during the days when inter-county travel was by horse and carriage. The room we occupied did not have a telephone and the quaintness of our room was made funny by the large sign painted in red which read: "In the event of fire, open door and shout fire." After thirty-six hours there, we decided it was time to return to London.

For a couple of years we travelled to Scotland following our visit with Lindy. The Scottish highlands were magnificently glorious. Exploring old castles was so impressive given the mysterious history of each one.

After travelling in Great Britain for a few years, we decided to look farther afield.

My friend Gene Scott, a former semi-finalist in U.S. Open Championship at Forest Hill in 1968, was consumed with the adventure of crossing different boundaries as well as geographical and territories within the realm of tennis. In a way he was like Christopher Columbus in search of a new tennis order. He was instrumental in organizing the Kremlin Cup in Moscow. Since we had established the Bahamas Open at the Ocean Club some twenty years previously and shared a passion for tennis, I was not surprised when he extended an invitation for Susan and me to be his guests at the tournament in Moscow. While in my office in the Britannia Beach Hotel, my private line rang. It was Eugene Lytton Scott on the other end.

"Bear," he used the phonetically shortened version of my name, "the Kremlin Cup is in late November. I want you and Susan to be my guests in Moscow." My response was immediate: "Yes, Gene, absolutely." How could I say no?

In 1995 we stayed at The President Hotel, formerly the Red

October Hotel, as we wanted to have the Russian experience. We had the most amazing time mainly because everything was so different from the West. Boris Yeltsin, President of Russia, attended most matches. He was a dedicated tennis player but of limited talent. We returned to Moscow in 1996 and had an even more enjoyable and memorable time. The tournament was complete with the inclusion of a Swiss caterer who provided superb meals, including beluga caviar and champagne.

For Susan and me, the time spent in Russia was extraordinary in so many ways that we continue to relive those exotic days and nights.

Once we began the process of preparing for our Russian adventure, first and foremost, we had to contend with complying with certain visa requirements to enter the country. Gene was familiar with this situation, which oddly enough required obtaining them through the Swiss Embassy in New York. Then we were told that since we had to transit through Germany I would also need a German visa. Fortunately there was a German consul in Nassau who willingly accommodated our request. However because my passport had only a few blank pages remaining, instead of allowing me to have pages added, the consul insisted that I acquire a new passport to meet their entry requirements.

Our arrival in Moscow was intimidating. We entered down a set of stairs to a dark immigration hall filled with officers in military uniforms. I handed my documents to the Russian official who, upon examining the same, became rather agitated. The officer placed the passport on his desk, sat back in his chair, looked directly at me and said, "We have a problem."

The reason quickly became clear: my new passport number did not match the passport number printed on the Russian visa. Fortunately I'd had the foresight to make a copy of my original passport which, of course, had the correct information. He then picked up my passport and copy and announced that he had to refer the matter to a senior officer. He returned quickly, indicated that all was in order, and commenced the final act of stamping and signing the relevant passport. He then asked me, "Do you have a pen?" I handed him my new and expensive Waterman ballpoint pen. He signed the appropriate place in my new passport and handed it back to me. To my surprise he said, "I keep pen, yes?" My reply was, "Of course, by all means." And thus began our Russian experience.

Reflecting on the journey, there were several occasions when the differences between the Western and Russian character were crystal clear. And, of course, there was a recognition of the richness of the country's history.

We were thrilled that the tournament committee appointed Natasha to be our personal guide. Coincidentally she was, in her other life, a physicist dealing with experimental matters in outer space.

On our first day, we were given an official tour of the interior of The Kremlin Palace. We visited the personal residence of the imperial family with its fine woodwork and malachite fireplace mantle. The apartment ran like a hallway down one side of the palace. Each door that led into the next room opened with a huge doorknob of tigereye, lapis lazuli or some other semiprecious stone. The final chamber was the bedroom of Grigori Rasputin, the self-proclaimed holy man who was attached to Czar Nicholas and who gained considerable influence politically.

We were then shepherded through the massive and opulent ballroom. We were instructed to walk on the carpet that ran the circumference of the room and not on the highly polished and unscarred parquet floor and were chastised for cutting the corner to catch up with our group. The next stop was the ornately decorated gathering room.

The following morning we were given a tour of the Armory, which was adjacent to Red Square. We were amazed to view the vast accumulation of jewels and crowns. There were collections of enormous bibles encrusted with emeralds, rubies and diamonds and valuable antique statues of gold. In addition to this were hordes of diamonds and other precious gems. It was overwhelming to say the least.

We were later guided to one corner of Red Square towards an unassuming enclosure, Lenin's Tomb. Imagine our great surprise to be shown the embalmed body of Lenin, the man who led the national communist uprising, in a clear glass-encased coffin.

We were disappointed with the condition of Gorky Park,

where much of the Cold War spying occurred. It was tiny and overused, with a small collection of children's amusement rides being the most notable feature. The reality was vastly different from the suspenseful spy movie *Gorky Park*.

We finished our sightseeing of the day with a visit to the country hunting lodge of Peter The Great, who ruled Russia from 1682 until 1725. It was an unimpressive building, which now sat in a suburban area outside of the main city.

And then something amazingly wonderful happened. The next night, by special invitation, we attended a performance at the Bolshoi Theater. The theater had been built long before the communists took over and was breathtaking. And imagine our delight to see Tchaikovsky's *Nutcracker*, performed in Russia by the Bolshoi Ballet company, just before the start of the Christmas season. Sheer good fortune!

Our Russian experiences were all so wonderful and will be long remembered. Our friendship with Natasha had grown to such a level that we arranged for her to visit us in Nassau. Her experiences with us in the Bahamas, so different from her Russian way of life, caused her to say, "it has been pure magic for me."

The crowning experience for us in our world travels was going on Safari in South Africa. Butch Kerzner arranged our first venture into this unknown. We stayed at Mala Mala, rated as the best of Safari camps in Africa. Our appetite was whetted. In succeeding years, we went to Abu in Botswana. Imagine riding elephants across the plains and into the bush. Susan fell in love with these intriguing leviathans. Being an artist, she has had several elephant-themed art shows. Our first visit with the elephants was not enough. We returned the following year when the Okevango Delta was flooded. This was the result of the accumulation of rain in Angola that flowed south into the Delta. Riding the elephants through seven-foot-deep water while seated on specially made "saddles" was simply euphoric. At camp at night we talked endlessly of our day's adventure.

"Susan, it is because of you and your love that I gained the absolute confidence to see the world. I enjoy so much witnessing 'the Alice in Wonderland' affect upon you."

Her response was simple, "Barrie, I am so happy and content."

And so it has been throughout our travels—tennis in São Paulo, Brazil, as well as Caracas, Venezuela—experiencing the bright lights and entertainment of Las Vegas, which included a helicopter tour of the Grand Canyon. And then to cruise to Alaska and to fly into the Fijords where no man had settled and then to be on board a helicopter which landed on a glacier. We had a short guided tour on the glacier with the ice crunching under the sole of the specially designed "overshoes."

Standing on the afterdeck of the cruise ship Silver Sea Symphony at 6:00 a.m. to witness and hear massive pieces of glacier falling into the ocean filled us with awe.

Susan turned to me, "Barrie, this experience makes me feel that we are so insignificant on this planet. I wish I understood more about the spirituality of our existence."

"Susan!" I replied, "We have such good fortune which I believe is not accidental. We can make a difference with many lives by reaching out our hands to help."

Believing in the greater good must be imbedded in our very being which affords us a selflessness that benefits others. And besides there is an inner voice that guides us to do what is right.

Our travels abroad have been gloriously uplifting. While we are sitting in our balcony at our Nassau home, I paused and conjured up the image of me standing on the roof of our family's Hawkins Hill home, oh so many years ago, and thinking about going to the Current Eleuthera.

Amazing!

Amazing!

"How Great Thou Art."

*Susan and Barrie in Cape Town, South Africa, at Chapman's Peak
August 1996*

Leaving the job with four decades of wonderful memories

CHAPTER 52

FINAL DAY ON THE JOB

When I reached my sixty-fifth birthday in 2001, I knew without reservation that I was not ready for retirement. However, to go beyond this threshold would require the support of Sol and Butch Kerzner which I felt would be given unhesitatingly. Butch for sure always wanted me nearby.

On the other hand, I had to acknowledge that the day would come when I would have to "hang up my spurs."

When Butch tragically died in 2006, I felt as if I had been kicked viciously in the "gut." There was also my own stark acknowledgement of the acceptance of my own mortality. Life does not go on forever and as temporary inhabitants of this earth we have difficulty with the reconciliation of this fact.

It was in this reflective mood that I concluded from what I have always deemed as a higher consciousness: "I just knew that when my time had come to officially leave Paradise Island, I would know."

The global financial collapse of 2008 was a watershed event for Kerzner International. The burden of the debt taken in order to achieve privatization of the company in 2006 became unbearable. With the company in default of its obligations for repayment under various loan agreements, the dreaded day arrived unceremoniously. In later 2011, Brookfield of Canada, a hedge fund company that was one of the key lenders, by exercising certain rights under the loan agreements placed the Kerzner company into default and thus became the owner of Atlantis on Paradise Island as well as other associated assets.

For me, it made me accept without any remorse that my time officially of being an integral part of Paradise Island was drawing nigh. And so I decided that I should retire. This was not an easy decision.

I met with George Markantonis, President and CEO of Atlantis, to discuss my retirement. George and I had developed a warm and understanding relationship that is not easy to describe—total trust, freedom of exchange, and a common belief in what we were doing for the company and country. There were no hidden agendas and never a cross word passed between us.

But it was with a slightly heavy heart that I said, "George, the time has come for me to say 'au revoir'. The time spent has been unbelievably great."

George said, "JB, I would like to convince you to do otherwise but you know what is in your heart."

I told him that I wanted my final day to be the 12th January—my mom's birthday. And so the die was cast.

With my confidant and personal assistant, Secoya Bain, we began the process of sifting through many files that had accumulated through the decades.

With each file review, the memories of times past came flooding back like the water cascading over Niagara Falls.

How many times did I pause and say to Secoya, "Do you remember this occasion when we panicked over completing a project for Sol Kerzner?"

When she replied she did so with a playful smile on her lips and with a wistful look in her eyes.

I remember pushing back in my chair and with my feet upon the credenza—feeling overcome with nostalgic thoughts—accompanied by emotions that were in many ways uplifting—

a journey that was ending after fifty-eight years of working. Imagine starting as a junior clerk in 1954 at the Nassau Yacht Haven and ending in high office in the most important tourism development in the history of the country.

And then a satisfying thought took control of my mind. My physical being may be departing the resort but my spirit will always hover over this familiar terrain. In fact the next day George made a pronouncement that was totally unexpected but joyfully received.

"JB, I know how attached you are to our company so I am keeping your office empty and whenever you wish, you can come in and use it.

So I knew that the complete physical separation from Atlantis was to be happily, slow.

At Government House, the receipt of the CBE Queen's medal with sponsors Sir Durward Knowles and Sir Geoffrey Johnstone

CHAPTER 53

I ALWAYS DID MY BEST

There are times when I, for reasons unclear, am overcome with the strongest of urges to look both inwardly and outwardly to fully understand the purpose of my life's journey.

Today is such a time.

My mother gave me a birthday card many years ago in which she wrote:

> *I have loved you very much*
> *from the day of your birth.*
> *Love mom who knows.*

I ponder this declaration periodically wanting to fully understand the depth of her feelings for me. "Mom who knows" seems to go beyond what a mother may ordinarily say to an offspring on any special day. Maybe it is just me wanting the message to be extra special.

In my mind's eye, I picture being held by my mother shortly after delivering me from her womb—maybe she sensed that the future was to be one of emotional and spiritual uncertainties and because of that knew that she would find a way to guide and protect me.

Now in my twilight years, I better understand that it was her complete love that provided me with strength and purpose in the face of adversity which was best expressed to me at every opportunity—"Barrie, you can only do your best."

CHAPTER 54

CONCLUDING THOUGHTS

Looking through life dispassionately is not possible unless there is an indifference to truth. Crossroads are exactly what they imply: a point at which those elements of life that comprise your being represent potential conflict and need to be addressed rationally or irrationally. There is no resting place with indefinite time to reach a peaceful place or station.

There are too many times when I pause to think about the past and wonder if there were certain points which, had I been capable of holding a different attitude and intent, could have produced a much better outcome.

My thinking had become tortured when the dark days of unhappiness and sadness came too sharply into focus. With supreme effort those memories, like the windows that are shuttered during a storm, are opened so that sunshine and calm are regained.

Oh yes! I wish I would have done some things differently. Even now I murmur quietly my regrets to those to whom I caused pain.

In my much younger days, I was too quick off the mark when angry. On the other hand with the passage of time I gained maturity and with it the ability and desire to be a positive and enduring member of my country and my people.

For me, it was like an epiphany to understand the new purpose of my life. I discovered the truth of a saying I read many years ago: "Good people do good things and good things happen to good people."

There are too many occasions when I have reached out and helped someone in great need, only to discover that in some way I am rewarded. I am not speaking about monetary repayment, but more about the spiritual joy bestowed upon me.

So many times I have been told that what I did was "selfless." I always disagree because the happiness that I gain from each such event makes me feel happy and as such in a way is "selfish."

From a time that is as far back as I can remember, I wanted to serve my Bahamaland in positive and meaningful ways—love of country was essential.

Today I frequently walk through the Versaille Garden at the Ocean Club on my way to the tennis courts. Towering over the lowest terrace with the water lily pool is the bronze statue of Dr. David Livingstone and emblazoned on the pedestal is his personal mantra and one that I have adopted.

"If success attend me, grant me humility; if failure, resignation to Thy will."

SPECIAL MEMORIES

The photographs in this section and all through the book bring back special memories of persons who, in different ways, created heart-warming times throughout my life and live on as cherished reminders of a ten-year-old Barrie standing on the roof of the family home on Hawkins Hill imagining adventures beyond the horizon. These images depict a life in which experiences of love, happiness, human endeavors, family unity, a mother's unfettered devotion, and enduring friendships contributed so much to a supreme quality of life. Good fortune has been a most faithful companion.

*Grandfather Clarence Thorpe with sons
Ira Willis [Barrie's dad] immediately on his right*

Susan and Barrie meeting Queen Elizabeth at Government House

Brothers Ramon and Barrie at residence in Nassau

Cousins in Nassau

L to R: Michael, Douglas, Scott, Bruce, Robyn, John, and Craig

Farrington Clan Winter Vacation, Stowe, Vt.

Top row [L to R]: Scott, Margo, Barrie, Robyn, Javier, Melanie, Susan
Bottom row [L to R]: Chase, Triston, Elizabeth, Taylor, Nicholas, and Christopher

Kremlin Cup in Moscow, Russia, 1994

L to R: Eugene Lytton Scott, editor publisher of Tennis Week, *J. Barrie, Susan Sargent Farrington and Frank Hammond, the most famous umpire at The U.S. Open*

Boyhood friends John Knowles and Paul Aranha

*Sharing a moment with Anna and Phyl
Mayfair Hotel, London*

Royal Towers, Atlantis

Susan and Barrie on Meade Glacier near Skagway, Alaska

EPILOGUE

My passage through life covering decades has been anything but ordinary in many ways. First and foremost, I honor the profound and infinite impact of my mother, Pearl Melinda, in molding my character and being from the morning of coming into this world. With the strong spiritual foundation created while I reached for adulthood, I recognized and embraced life's ever-changing nature without passively settling for easily defined principles for everyday living.

Unquestionably through full participation in life's adventures, I have been able to gather and absorb pathways to actively shaping fundamental tenets of our everyday human existence. And so I now share the ways that helped me over time to reach a better place in life.

- Spend as much time with your family as you can and build happy memories, because our loved ones are not going to be around forever.

- Love your family unconditionally and express your love whenever you can. Saying "I love you" at the end of each conversation adds so much to all moments shared. This is not limited to family, but applies in friendships as well.

- Offer a helping hand or a kind word to those who have suffered due to harsh circumstances outside of their control.

- Tell your partner-in-life that you love them—this will continue to enrich your togetherness.

- Never let anger be the cause of harsh words with another person. Remember that kind words are the soothing ointment for all emotional hurt.

- Give guidance and a helping hand to young persons who are striving to climb the ladder of success. This is your investment in a better future for many.

- Be generous with your hugs to friends, associates and those in your employ. Such acts reinforce your recognition and acceptance of them as worthy human beings.

- Don't be afraid to help someone who has been opposed to you through the years. It will be a way to show that you are committed to a peaceful coexistence.

- Be prepared to look foolish as you reach for knowledge and progress. Too often failure falls upon those who are unwilling to take a chance.

- Through selflessness, reach out to assist others and it will make you feel good. Remember: "Good people do good things and good things happen to good people."

- In your quest for success and recognition, do not neglect your loved ones. There can never be justifiable reasons for such neglect. Although it may be difficult share every step of the way, keeping love whole is vital.

- Don't be afraid of your mortality—it exists. All the time you have can be used for great purpose if you are emotionally and physically committed.

- Develop every relationship with respect and dignity, irrespective of someone's station in life.

- Through deep conversation, share the joy and love of life.

- Constantly strive for a life of tranquility. In this way, you avoid the anxieties of discord that invade society.

- Get up early and venture to a place where you can give witness to the dawn of a new day.

  ... and you will glorify that which God has created.

www.ingramcontent.com/pod-product-compliance
Lightning Source LLC
Chambersburg PA
CBHW020136130526
44591CB00030B/65